Anti-Racism, Feminism, and Critical Approaches to Education

Critical Studies in Education and Culture Series

The Problem of Freedom in Postmodern Education
Tomasz Szkudlarek

Education Still under Siege: Second Edition
Stanley Aronowitz and Henry A. Giroux

Media Education and the (Re)Production of Culture
David Sholle and Stan Denski

Critical Pedagogy: An Introduction
Barry Kanpol

Coming Out in College: The Struggle for a Queer Identity
Robert A. Rhoads

Education and the Postmodern Condition
Michael Peters, editor

Critical Multiculturalism: Uncommon Voices in a Common Struggle
Barry Kanpol and Peter McLaren, editors

Beyond Liberation and Excellence: Reconstructing the Public
Discourse on Education
David E. Purpel and Svi Shapiro

Schooling in a "Total Institution": Critical Perspectives on
Prison Education
Howard S. Davidson, editor

Simulation, Spectacle, and the Ironies of Education Reform
Guy Senese with Ralph Page

Repositioning Feminism and Education: Perspectives on Educating
for Social Change
*Janice Jipson, Petra Munro, Susan Victor, Karen Froude Jones, and
Gretchen Freed-Rowland*

Culture, Politics, and Irish School Dropouts: Constructing
Political Identities
G. Honor Fagan

ANTI-RACISM, FEMINISM, AND CRITICAL APPROACHES TO EDUCATION

Edited by
Roxana Ng, Pat Staton, and Joyce Scane

Critical Studies in Education and Culture Series
Edited by Henry A. Giroux and Paulo Freire

BERGIN & GARVEY
Westport, Connecticut • London

Library of Congress Cataloging-in-Publication Data

Anti-racism, feminism, and critical approaches to education / edited
    by Roxana Ng, Pat Staton, and Joyce Scane.
        p. cm.—(Critical studies in education and culture series,
    ISSN 1064–8615)
      Includes bibliographical references and index.
        ISBN 0–89789–327–1 (alk. paper).—ISBN 0–89789–328–X (pbk. :
    alk. paper)
        1. Critical pedagogy—Canada. 2. Feminism and education—Canada.
    3. Multicultural education—Canada. 4. Discrimination in education—
    Canada. I. Ng, Roxana. II. Staton, P. A. (Patricia
    Anne). III. Scane, Joyce. IV. Series.
    LC196.5.C2A58 1995
    370.11′5′0971—dc20   95–5160

British Library Cataloguing in Publication Data is available.

Library of Congress Catalog Card Number: 95–5160
ISBN: 0–89789–327–1
      0–89789–328–X (pbk.)
ISSN: 1064–8615

First published in 1995

Bergin & Garvey, 88 Post Road West, Westport, CT 06881
An imprint of Greenwood Publishing Group, Inc.

Printed in the United States of America

The paper used in this book complies with the
Permanent Paper Standard issued by the National
Information Standards Organization (Z39.48–1984).

10 9 8 7 6 5 4 3 2 1

Contents

Series Foreword

Within the last decade, the debate over the meaning and purpose of education has occupied the center of political and social life in the United States. Dominated largely by an aggressive and ongoing attempt by various sectors of the Right, including "fundamentalists," nationalists, and political conservatives, the debate over educational policy has been organized around a set of values and practices that take as their paradigmatic model the laws and ideology of the marketplace and the imperatives of a newly emerging cultural traditionalism. In the first instance, schooling is being redefined through a corporate ideology that stresses the primacy of choice over community, competition over cooperation, and excellence over equity. At stake here is the imperative to organize public schooling around the related practices of competition, reprivatization, standardization, and individualism.

In the second instance, the New Right has waged a cultural war against schools as part of a wider attempt to contest the emergence of new public cultures and social movements that have begun to demand that schools take seriously the imperatives of living in a multiracial and multicultural democracy. The contours of this cultural offensive are evident in the call by the Right for standardized testing, the rejection of multiculturalism, and the development of curricula around what is euphemistically called a "common culture." In this perspective, the notion of a common culture serves as a referent to denounce any attempt by subordinate groups to challenge the narrow ideological and political parameters by which such a culture both defines and expresses itself. It is not too surprising that the theoretical and political distance between defining schools around a common culture and denouncing cultural difference as the enemy of democratic life is relatively short indeed.

This debate is important not simply because it makes visible the role that schools play as sites of political and cultural contestation, but because it is within this debate that the notion of the United States as an open and democratic society is being questioned and redefined. Moreover, this debate provides a challenge to progressive educators both in and outside of the United States to address a number of conditions central to a postmodern world. First, public schools cannot be seen as either objective or neutral. As institutions actively involved in constructing political subjects and presupposing a vision of the future, they must be dealt with in terms that are simultaneously historical, critical, and transformative. Second, the relationship between knowledge and power in schools places undue emphasis on disciplinary structures and on individual achievement as the primary unit of value. Critical educators need a language that emphasizes how social identities are constructed within unequal relations of power in the schools and how schooling can be organized through interdisciplinary approaches to learning and cultural differences that address the dialectical and multifaceted experiences of everyday life. Third, the existing cultural transformation of American society into a multiracial and multicultural society structured in multiple relations of domination demands that we address how schooling can become sites for cultural democracy rather than channeling colonies reproducing new forms of nativism and racism. Finally, critical educators need a new language that takes seriously the relationship between democracy and the establishment of those teaching and learning conditions that enable forms of self and social determination in students and teachers. This not only suggests new forms of self-definition for human agency, but also points to redistributing power within the school and between the school and the larger society.

The Critical Studies in Education and Culture series is intended as both a critique and as a positive response to these concerns and the debates from which they emerge. Each volume is intended to address the meaning of schooling as a form of cultural politics, and cultural work as a pedagogical practice that serves to deepen and extend the possibilities of democratic public life. Broadly conceived, some central considerations present themselves as defining concerns of the series. Within the last decade, a number of new theoretical discourses and vocabularies have emerged that challenge the narrow disciplinary boundaries and theoretical parameters that construct the traditional relationship among knowledge, power, and schooling. The emerging discourses of feminism, postcolonialism, literary studies, cultural studies, and postmodernism have broadened our understanding of how schools work as sites of containment and possibility. No longer content to view schools as objective institutions engaged in the transmission of an unproblematic cultural heritage, the new discourses illuminate how schools function as cultural sites actively engaged in the production of not only knowledge but social identities. Critical Studies in Education and Culture will attempt to encourage this type of analysis by emphasizing how schools might be addressed as border institutions or sites of crossing actively involved in exploring, reworking, and translating the ways in which culture is produced, negotiated, and rewritten.

Emphasizing the centrality of politics, culture, and power, Critical Studies in Education and Culture will deal with pedagogical issues that contribute in novel ways to our understanding of how critical knowledge, democratic values, and social practices can provide a basis for teachers, students, and other cultural workers to redefine their role as engaged and public intellectuals.

As part of a broader attempt to rewrite and refigure the relationship between education and culture, Critical Studies in Education and Culture is interested in work that is interdisciplinary and critical, work that addresses the emergent discourses on gender, race, sexual preference, class, ethnicity, and technology. In this respect, the series is dedicated to opening up new discursive and public spaces for critical interventions into schools and other pedagogical sites. To accomplish this, each volume will attempt to rethink the relationship between language and experience, pedagogy and human agency, and ethics and social responsibility as part of a larger project for engaging and deepening the prospects of democratic schooling in a multiracial and multicultural society. Concerns central to this series include addressing the political economy and deconstruction of visual, aural, and printed texts; issues of difference and multiculturalism; relationships between language and power; pedagogy as a form of cultural politics; and historical memory and the construction of identity and subjectivity.

Critical Studies in Education and Culture is dedicated to publishing studies that move beyond the boundaries of traditional and existing critical discourses. It is concerned with making public schooling a central expression of democratic culture. In doing so, it emphasizes works that combine cultural politics, pedagogical criticism, and social analyses with self-reflective tactics that challenge and transform those configurations of power that characterize the existing system of education and other public cultures.

Henry A. Giroux

Acknowledgments

The production of a book always involves more people than the names that finally appear. Many people have contributed to this book. Without the financial support of the Ontario Ministry of Colleges and Universities (MCU), this project would never have begun. Many individuals at the Ontario Institute for Studies in Education (OISE) have played critical and supportive roles throughout the project: Gail Guttentag (former equity officer) drew our attention to the special MCU funding and brought us together; Walter Pitman (former Director of OISE) and Angela Hildyard (then Assistant Director of Research and Field Development) provided much needed administrative and moral support; Roger Simon and Jim Cummins gave us valuable suggestions and encouragement; Carole Ann Reed assisted in the writing symposium. Manuscript production was made possible by a Small-Scale Research Grant from the Department of Sociology at OISE, and this onerous task would not have been possible without the expert assistance of B. J. Cook. To all of them, we extend our heartfelt gratitude. We are grateful to the authors for their contribution, as well as their patience, hard work, and good humor through this protracted process. Finally, we thank our publishers, especially Sophie Craze and Lynn Flint at Bergin and Garvey and Ann Nicholson at OISE Press, who saw the project to its completion.

Roxana Ng
Joyce Scane
Pat Staton

Introduction

Roxana Ng
with Joyce Scane and Pat Staton

BACKGROUND AND PROCESS OF THE PROJECT

In North America, multiculturalism and multicultural education has a longer history in Canada than in the United States. With the promulgation of multiculturalism as state policy in Canada in the 1970s and its subsequent enshrinement as law in 1988, multicultural education has been an integral part of the educational agenda since the mid-1970s, in rhetoric if not in reality. Meanwhile, escalating racial tensions in urban centers and political struggles between the dominant power (represented by the federal and provincial governments) and the aboriginal peoples have led many progressive educators to question the viability of multicultural education to accommodate and appease Canada's diverse population. In the past, multicultural education has tended to focus narrowly on the celebration of visible "ethnic" and "cultural" differences, with the implicit goal of promoting cross-cultural understanding and tolerance. It did not examine how these differences are produced historically and ideologically or their social and economic consequences for minority groups. Since the 1980s, therefore, there have been numerous attempts to reformulate multicultural education from various critical perspectives. It is within this climate of critical education that the present collection was conceived.

This book came into being as a result of a research project, funded by the then provincial Ministry of Colleges and Universities (Ontario, Canada), to explore the relationship and forge links between the discourses on multicultural and anti-racist education and critical pedagogy. We, the editors, wanted to develop a collection of readings on recent advances in these areas for students and teachers who were looking for new ways of addressing issues of race, class, and gender that went beyond the superficial celebration of difference. As feminists working within predominantly white, patriarchal, and hierarchical structures, we have experienced different forms of institutional marginalization, be it based on gender, race, class, or other axes of inequality.

When we began this project in 1990, writings that attempted to integrate multicultural education and critical pedagogy were practically nonexistent.[1] Alternate forms of educational practices, including anti-racist education, critical pedagogy, and feminist pedagogy, have developed along different paths. Thus, it was an interesting and worthwhile challenge for us to identify writers developing links between and among these areas. In compiling the writings in this emerging field, we also wanted to develop a collaborative and inclusive way of working with writers.

To develop a set of criteria for identifying writers for the project, we began by noting the gaps in the literature. Two glaring omissions were women's and aboriginal experiences. Thus, we felt strongly that these experiences and perspectives must be incorporated into a project of rethinking multiculturalism, anti-racism, and critical pedagogy. Furthermore, we wanted to work with writers as they developed their writings. We also wanted to include, as much as possible, scholars from marginalized groups who were forging links between their experiences and critical educational theories.

We wanted this to be a primarily Canadian contribution; thus except for Cameron McCarthy (whose work in critical multicultural education is exemplary),[2] all the contributors were writing within the Canadian context. In addition to the writers' cultural and racial positioning, we wanted to include regional and gender perspectives. To do this, we screened major journals of education and consulted prominent Canadian scholars about possible contributors in drawing up our initial list of people to be contacted. This was not an easy exercise, since at the time we began the project there were only a few scholars who fitted these criteria. As well, funding and time constraints determined how hard and far we looked for potential contributors, and the absolute number of people who could be included in the project.

After identifying a group of potential contributors, we asked those interested in the project to submit abstracts of their proposed papers. We then asked them to submit completed papers and designed a weekend writing symposium. The symposium brought together these writers to critique each other's papers (the first drafts of which were circulated before the symposium), to identify gaps in the proposed collection, and to work on a common theme for the collection. Individual papers were then revised according to the feedback received at the symposium. Thus, what appears here is very much a collective project of the group of people who came together in October 1991 to share with and learn from each other.

In spite of our effort to represent a range of diverse perspectives, there are obvious omissions and oversights. For example, there is no francophone perspective represented here. We were severely criticized for having "white male" writing about aboriginal anti-racist education. The regional perspectives are not as present in the papers as we had hoped.

Furthermore, as contributors met and debated with each other and revised their papers, the final product as represented here is somewhat different from our original (and we must confess somewhat simplistic) conception of making the connection between multicultural and anti-racist education with critical pedagogy. The result is a more complex and diverse collection than our original conception. However, we think that ultimately this has become a better collection as a result.

Our purpose is not to define a new critical educational approach, but to open up dialogues among scholars and educators about how minority perspectives can challenge and inform existing educational practices. Although the experiences and examples reported in this book are mainly Canadian, the issues addressed here are relevant to all multicultural societies. Apart from providing much needed information on multicultural education, the critical approaches documented here can be adapted to and improvised for different settings and according to the different needs of learners and teachers.

ORGANIZATION OF THE COLLECTION

The collection is organized into two parts. Part I examines the variety of policies and approaches grouped under the ubiquitous rubric of multicultural and anti-racist education. With the rise of multicultural education, the mainstream curriculum has been criticized for being Eurocentric and assimilationist by ethnic communities and progressive educators. Boards and ministries of education have been attempting to remedy this pitfall by introducing minority perspectives into the curriculum and policy formulation. However, there has been little consensus as to what constitutes a multicultural or anti-racist policy or curriculum. The chapters in this part of the book share a major commonality: they analyze and criticize the myriad policies, programs, and curricula that have been named multicultural in order to bring clarification to the ongoing debate surrounding multicultural and anti-racist education. They all end with a vision of what education for change in a pluralist society may look like.

Writing from the perspective of a practitioner, Goli Rezai-Rashti examines the report of the Advisory Committee on Race Relations for the province of Ontario (1987) and responses to the report by school personnel, and discovers that while the language of anti-racism was used in the report, its assumptions were based on the liberal ideal of multiculturalism. To address the problems confronting a multiracial and multiethnic society, she proposes a marriage between critical pedagogical theories and anti-racist education and suggests that teachers and theorists should play the role of "organic intellectuals" formulated by Antonio Gramsci, one of the forefathers of critical pedagogy.

While Cameron McCarthy's chapter focuses on different approaches to multicultural education in the United States, his analysis is relevant to U.S. and Canadian education alike because he points out the two core assumptions of existing multicultural programs despite their differences. First, they treat racial categories as stable and unchanging phenomena; in fact, racial categories shift across time and space. The present configuration of race relations and multiculturalism is itself a product of historical struggles (see also McCarthy & Crichlow, 1993). Second, the preoccupation with race in existing multicultural programs eclipses other dimensions of power operative in contemporary North American societies, notably gender and class. Instead, McCarthy proposes a "critical emancipatory multiculturalism," combining anti-racism, anti-sexism, and critical pedagogy, which insists on the inherently political and relational nature of knowledge production and promotes a program of "common learning."

In Chapter 3, Jon Young shifts our attention from policy making and curriculum to an examination of teacher education in Britain and Canada, to see whether teacher training prepares students for a multiracial classroom. The result of his survey is predictably disappointing. While the historical escalation of racial tensions in Britain means that there have been more initiatives to address racial, ethnic, and cultural issues, neither country has made major attempts to revamp teacher training. What has developed, in the British context, is a clearer articulation of anti-racist versus multicultural discourses (see also Gill et al., 1992; Braham, Rattansi, & Skellington, 1992), which is useful to educators concerned with progressive teaching generally.

In accordance with the spirit of various forms of critical pedagogical practices, Part II of the book is engaged with a reflection of the actor in the educational process. The chapter by Robert Regnier provides a much-needed discussion of the Meech Lake Accord and Oka crisis in Canada, a subject neglected by most educators. By examining two major protests of the aboriginal communities (Chief Harper's negative vote during the Meech Lake negotiations for a Canadian constitution and the struggles between the aboriginal people and the Quebec government in the summer of 1990), Regnier makes politics the central feature of critical education. He argues that these two examples represent aboriginal anti-racist educative moments. By capturing media attention, aboriginal leaders brought into public view the historical oppression and suppression of aboriginal cultures and the demands of aboriginal peoples for self-determination and self-government. He suggests that educators have much to learn from these strategies for the development of a critical anti-racist education.

Writing from the perspective of a practitioner working within a board of education, in Chapter 5 Goli Rezai-Rashti describes and analyzes existing school practices in dealing with high school girls from different ethno-cultural, racial, and religious communities. She found that Eurocentric assumptions, held by school personnel, of nonwhite and non-Christian groups as backward and inferior (i.e., racist attitudes) make it impossible for them to grapple with the complex, intertwining dynamics of racism and sexism. As a result, both multicultural and anti-racist education have failed to adequately address the experiences and needs of minority female students. She recommends a more complex and nuanced understanding of racism and sexism in empowering these students.

Using his own experience teaching a SUNTEP course, Rich Hesch actually attempted to combine anti-racist education with a critical pedagogy approach. In his chapter, he reflects on the trials and tribulations of a white, middle-class male teacher teaching an exclusively aboriginal female student body, and the contradictions inherent in this process. Hesch's account addresses the tension of race, class, and gender in the educational experiences of students and teacher. In addition to giving a sensitive account of this process, this chapter contains practical suggestions that can be applied to other educational settings.

In the final chapter, using her own teaching experience as a starting point, Roxana Ng explores the contradictions minority teachers find themselves in when they attempt to instill critical consciousness among the students. She integrates dynamics of gender and race in understanding power and authority in the classroom and shows how sexism and racism operate at different levels: between professors and students, and among students themselves. She draws attention to the pervasiveness of sexism and racism both in the classroom and in the larger university environment, and asserts that altering existing power dynamics in the classroom must be a collective, rather than an individualistic, responsibility.

In summary, the pieces in this collection represent a collective effort on the part of educators to analyze, understand, challenge, and envision educational changes as we move from Anglo conformity and assimilation to postmodernity. By examining and challenging dominant forms of knowledge and educational policies and by engaging with critical educational practices, the authors share with each other and with the readers their own uncertainty, dilemmas, and struggle as they work for change. In so doing, they expose the political and contested nature of education itself. Education is not stable or fixed; it is open to challenge and reformulation. The writings in this collection are themselves part and parcel of the political process of educational change. If there is a common theme in this collection, it is that critical education is not to achieve consensus but to open up the educational process for interrogation and debate.

NOTES

1. This is no longer the case. The 1990s has seen a burgeoning of writings, notably in critical pedagogy, which begin to explore the connection and interconnection of previously disparate and different areas of education. See, for example, Giroux (1991), Arnowitz & Giroux (1985), Henley & Young (1991), Luke & Gore (1992), Moodley (1992), Giroux (1993). However, there is still no volume that links anti-racism, feminism, and critical pedagogy.

2. See McCarthy (1988 & 1990).

I

Multicultural and Anti-Racist Education: Comparative and Critical Perspectives

1

Multicultural Education, Anti-Racist Education, and Critical Pedagogy: Reflections on Everyday Practice

Goli Rezai-Rashti

The introduction of a national policy on multiculturalism in 1971 generated great debate, controversy, and confusion. The Canadian Prime Minister, Pierre Trudeau, in introducing the legislation, criticized the then dominant assimilationist ideology and called for a Canadian society that was proud of its multicultural diversity. As he stated, in unambiguous terms,

> There cannot be one cultural policy for Canadians of British and French origins and one for aboriginal people and yet a third for all the others. For although there are two official languages there is no official culture, nor does any ethnic group take precedence over any other. No citizen or group of citizens is other than Canadian, and all should be treated fairly. (Trudeau, 191:1)

The Liberal government's initiative provided the impetus to introduce multiculturalism into selected aspects of Canadian society. This was in accordance with liberal ideas about egalitarianism and social justice. Accordingly, the educational system was targeted as the site from where multicultural ideas, views, and principles could be diffused among young Canadians. Students were perceived as the individuals most likely to be receptive to the new programs of educational pluralism and exposure to other, non-Western, cultures. They, therefore, could easily adapt and respond to the needs of a rapidly changing Canadian cultural mosaic.

This chapter is based on reflections of my work as a practitioner in different capacities for several boards of education in Metropolitan Toronto for the past ten years. I would like to thank Patrick Solomon, the members of the symposium, and particularly Roxana Ng for their useful comments on earlier versions of this chapter.

The acknowledgment of the significant role played by schools in pluralistic societies has translated into an abundant literature on multicultural education, especially in countries such as the United States, England, and Canada. In this literature, one can see two main theoretical approaches developing; the first one we will refer to as multicultural education, the other we will call anti-racist education.

MULTICULTURAL AND ANTI-RACIST EDUCATION

So far, a universally acceptable definition of what multiculturalism is has been hard to come by. The same is true for a conceptualization of what constitutes multicultural education. At the present time, a number of school-related activities can be said to be multicultural in nature, depending mostly on which approach to multicultural education is used. Among them, we can list some of the following:

1. *Education of culturally different groups*: This is designed to sensitize and prepare teachers to meet the needs of minority or culturally atypical students. Here we find programs such as English as a Second Language and Transitional Programs.
2. *Education promoting the understanding of cultural differences*: Programs of this sort advocate educational institutions' responsibility to understand the positive contributions made by culturally diverse groups.
3. *Education stressing cultural pluralism*: The emphasis here is on advocating the recognition of ethnic and cultural diversity and the acceptance that citizens have a right to retain their cultural identity. Well-known programs such as the Heritage Languages Programs figure prominently here.
4. *Bicultural education*: These programs are designed to prepare students who can become competent in at least two cultures.[1]
5. *Cultural/intercultural education*: This approach highlights every aspect of multicultural education, namely, the concerns for cultural and linguistic continuity, issues related to ethnic and race relations, aboriginal peoples' rights, integration of immigrants, bilingualism, and human rights (McLeod, 1990).

Liberal supporters of multicultural education during the 1970s and 1980s favored programs such as Heritage Language Programs and enhanced English as a Second Language programs. They stressed the need to have anglophone teachers and students become more sensitive to minority students so that equality of educational opportunity could be attained by everyone regardless of race, gender, religion, or ethnicity. They also called for reforms in school curricula and celebrated cultural diversity through mainly government-sponsored events, in order to break the ethnocentric bias of the educational system and of Canadian society at large.[2]

This liberal approach to multiculturalism has been subject to considerable criticism in recent years. Educators have called attention to the fact that multicultural education appears to be more concerned with social control than real social change. This is exemplified by the following remarks made by Michael Olneck:

Like intercultural education, dominant versions of multicultural education delimit a sanitized cultural sphere divorced from sociopolitical interests, in which culture is reified, fragmented, and homogenized, and they depict ethnic conflict as predominantly the consequence of negative attitudes and ignorance about manifestations of difference, which they seek to remedy by cultivating empathy, appreciation, and understanding. (Olneck, 1990:166)

These critical views of liberal-dominated education emerged mainly within the field of sociology of education. Known nowadays as the radical views on education, they comprise, in turn, the so-called reproductionist and transformative or radical pedagogy approaches. The former is mainly associated with the work of Samuel Bowles and Herbert Gintis (Bowles and Gintis, 1976) and their correspondence principle. According to them, there is a very close connection between the social relations present in schools and those in the workplace. What schools do, and do well, is to reproduce social and cultural inequalities upon which a class-divided society is premised. Accordingly, if that society is to be transformed into a more egalitarian one, changes are to originate at the level of the social relations of production and not necessarily at the superstructural level.

Rightly criticized for its economic determinism and its emphasis on schooling as a totally dependent institution, reproductionist views have been, more recently, superseded by some significant contributions that attempt to demonstrate that schools are sites where culture is produced rather than merely reproduced. The transformative theorists, for example, Stanley Aronowitz and Henry Giroux (1985), Michael Apple (1982), Roger Simon (1983), and Paulo Freire (1985), view schools as social institutions where critical thinking and radical ideas can be developed. The struggles that women, minorities, and other oppressed peoples are engaged in within schools open a "project of possibility" that could have positive repercussions in societal change. Real democracy is seen as the outcome of a critical pedagogy that is essentially political. Developing this critical thinking demands a radical transformation of teaching as presently conceived. In the best of Gramscian tradition, critical pedagogues advance the notion of the teacher as an intellectual committed to create an alternative collective will. This involves heeding the voices of those minority students that have been silenced for so long. In legitimizing those voices and empowering those students, a new voice for liberation and democracy will be produced.

More recently, Paulo Freire highlighted the political aspects involved in educational activities:

The educational proposals that I have been making for years basically derive from two rather obvious, non-simplistic ideas: First, education is a political act, whether at the university, high school, primary school, or adult literacy classrooms. Why? Because the very nature of education has the inherent qualities to be political, as indeed politics has educational aspects. In other words, an educational act has a political nature. . . . Second, education is a series of theories put into practice. . . . Once we are involved in this educational practice, we are also engaged in a practice of knowing. We may be trying to create a knowledge, or we may be trying to create a knowledge that does not exist yet, like research. All these educational practices involve the act of knowing throughout the world. (Freire, 1985:188–89)

Following in Freire's footsteps, Henry Giroux has called attention to the role of teachers in educating students in the language of critique and possibility; this, in turn, would involve furnishing teachers with the proper conceptual framework. The latter would allow them not only to critically analyze the schools' shortcomings in developing a true democratic ideal. More important, it would help to create new knowledge, to emphasize classroom social practices, and to generate a new curriculum aimed at cultivating a deeper respect for a more democratic, egalitarian, and just society (Giroux, 1986).

It is toward this theoretical framework that anti-racist educators incline in their discussion of the type of education minority students are receiving today. In embracing it, they highlight some glaring differences with the more traditional and liberal approaches associated with multicultural education. From the vantage point of the sociology of education, they argue that a true anti-racist education should concentrate on raising awareness as to the fact that, as presently conceived, the educational system is not necessarily functioning in the best interest of racially dominated groups. In criticizing current educational theory, they have come to join those who have been arguing that the consolidation of a state system of mass education cannot be seen as having brought benefits of much significance to working class students.

Acceptance of critical pedagogy has meant that a cleavage has begun to clearly differentiate a multicultural education from an anti-racist education. The two do not share the same origins, philosophy, assumptions, and end goals. According to Barry Troyna, there are irreconcilable differences between the two perspectives (Troyna, 1987). In Canada, anti-racist educators such as Barbara Thomas (1984, 1987) and Alok Mukherjee (1988) also discuss the differences between multicultural and anti-racist education. They argue that multicultural education originated from a liberal-reformist understanding of racism, while anti-racist education emerged from the struggles of racial minorities against imperial, colonial, and neocolonial experiences. Moreover, while the central assumption of multicultural education is that sensitization and celebration of difference can counteract biased and prejudiced attitudes among Canadians, anti-racist education concentrates on examining the histories and the practices that prejudice supports. Anti-racist education insists on closely studying and revealing the sites, institutions, and ways in which racism originates. In multicultural education, racism is understood primarily as the product of ignorance, which, in turn, is perpetuated by individual prejudice and negative attitudes. Anti-racist education argues that the persistence of stereotypes and prejudices must be met with a comprehensive analysis of their origins by way of questioning existing social and political structures. While the supporters of multiculturalism look at culture as if it were a static institution, anti-racist educators see it as a dynamic institution influenced by elements of social class and gender. While multicultural education assumes that minority students' educational failure can only partly be blamed on the system, since home and cultural factors are more important, anti-racist education claims that although social, economic, and home factors cannot be ignored, much of the blame for minority students' failure can be traced to the existence of institutionalized racism within the classroom.

In short, an anti-racist education approach is developing that is radically different from the liberal-influenced multicultural model. Anti-racist education aims at truly achieving equality, justice, and emancipation for minority students. Anti-racist education, in the words of Godfrey Brandt,

must be, by definition, oppositional. By oppositional, one is referring to an acknowledged intention to oppose in the education system whatever operates to oppress, repress or disenfranchise one set of pupils on the totally unjustifiable grounds of perceived "difference" within which there is an assumption of inherent inferiority. (Brandt, 1986:125)

POLICIES AND PRACTICES: ARE THEY MULTICULTURAL? ARE THEY ANTI-RACIST?

In 1979, the Toronto Board of Education became the first school board in Canada to set in place an official policy on race relations. Today, within the province of Ontario, there are more than forty boards of education that have followed that example and have approved race and ethnic relations policies. Some twenty-five other boards are in the process of formalizing similar policies. This situation contrasts somewhat negatively with the realization that more than half of the boards of education in Ontario still do not have a formal policy on race and ethnic relations.

More recently, in 1985, the Ontario government, through its Ministry of Education, moved to establish an Advisory Committee on Race Relations. The mandate of this committee included, among others, the following duties:

1. to promote the development of a Race and Ethno-cultural Equity Policy by all school boards in the province.

2. to assist and advise the Ministry of Education in the creation of guidelines for equity policy development and to recommend priority areas for policy development.

3. to identify strategies that will assist boards in developing and implementing racial and ethno-cultural equity policies.

4. to place concepts such as multiculturalism, race, and ethno-cultural relations and anti-racist education in their historical context as an aid to their proper use in equity policy development, and to identify the threads that link them. (Ministry of Education of Ontario, 1987:2)

In 1987, the Advisory Committee on Race Relations published its much awaited report, However, the report did not clearly differentiate between multicultural and anti-racist education. This occurred in spite of the fact that for a number of practitioners and academics in the field, the report was perceived to be biased towards anti-racist education. This perception was motivated by the fact that a number of proponents of anti-racist education were members of the Advisory Committee.

A detailed review of the report in order to understand its pro-multicultural or anti-racist education approach shows that even though the word anti-racist is repeatedly used, at no time does the report furnish an adequate definition or explanation of what is to be understood as anti-racist education and what the essential premises of anti-racist education might be. Nor does the report clearly spell out the differences between multicultural and anti-racist approaches to education. Anti-racist education was presented as a distorted, incomplete, vague concept which, in practice, had no significant differences from the more liberal-oriented multicultural education. Accordingly, the report states that anti-racist education is truly multicultural in a truly equitable society.

In the report it is stated, for example, that "the goal of anti-racist education is to change institutional policies and practices which are discriminatory, and individual behaviours and attitudes that reinforce racism" (Ministry of Education of Ontario, 1987:39). Having stated that, the report fails to explicitly indicate what kind of institutional policies and practices members of the committee had in mind when drafting the document.

Equally significant is the report's contention that the "premise [of anti-racist education] is that cultural diversity is not the cause of the denial of equal educational opportunity to students from certain racial and ethno-cultural groups" (Ministry of Education of Ontario, 1987:39). This begs the question that if cultural diversity is not the problem, then, what are the problems that anti-racist educators are to be concerned with?

Likewise, the report states that "anti-racist education does not negate the value of multicultural education . . . rather it is education that is truly multicultural, in a truly equitable multicultural society. . . . [I]t acknowledges the existence of racism and forthrightly seeks its eradication within schools and society at large" (Ministry of Education of Ontario, 1987:39). If this is so, then, what is it that makes anti-racist education different from multicultural education? If supporters of multiculturalism are similarly and equally concerned with racism, is anti-racist education needed at all? The report fails to realize that the two approaches are qualitatively different.

In my view, the report is most concerned with multicultural education and its shortcomings rather than with anti-racist education. The following paragraphs are quite telling in this regard:

However, multicultural education, as interpreted and practised over the last three decades, has demonstrated its limitations. Changes have often been fragmented in content and clarity, continuity and coordination. Initiatives have often relied upon untested assumptions about culture and the process of cultural transmission. Content often focuses on such material and exotic dimensions of culture as food, dress, and holidays, instead of linking these to the values and belief systems which undergird cultural diversity.

Too often well-intentioned educators have sought to ignore colour differences. Pretending to be colour blind in the face of the hardships encountered by young Asian, native and black youngsters, and professing not to perceive any differences in treatment, is still tantamount to side-stepping the problem.

Gradually, the question has been raised about the merits of the multicultural approach. Many believe that multicultural initiatives have not adequately addressed racial discrimination and inequalities that are systemic within the policies and practices of educational institutions. (Ministry of Education of Ontario, 1987:39)

Failure of the report to clearly set anti-racist education apart from multicultural education can be attributed to the fact that, for the most part, those members of the committee who advocated anti-racist education were practitioners and/or employees of the various boards of education. The overwhelming weight of institutionalized bureaucratic practices restrained them from openly criticizing their own organizations for the slow progress attained so far. These practices also restricted them from pushing for more radical changes of the current multicultural policies, which they could only afford to criticize in a lukewarm manner. To this can be added the unwillingness to dissociate from traditional liberal ideas, which continue to diffuse the myth of multicultural education as the main vehicle to deal with the obstacles that racial and ethnic minority students confront in their quest for a true equality of educational opportunity. The tensions and contradictions of the committee members are evident in the final report, which reflects their need to find a compromise solution amenable to supporters of both multicultural education and anti-racist education. In the end, the committee produced a report which, though well intentioned, opened itself to harsh criticisms from all sides.

Among those who felt that the report was influenced by anti-racist educators is University of Toronto Professor Keith McLeod (1990). He wrote that the report's authors, after "having established that multicultural educators were simple minded and misguided," went on to point out that "true multicultural education is anti-racist education" (p. 4). In rejecting this view, McLeod argued that multicultural education suffices to attain all the goals of a liberal democratic society. For him, anti-racist education is mainly advocated by Canadian left-wing militants. The latter have borrowed the anti-racist discourse from their British cousins. In Britain, anti-racist education originated mainly as the result of the failure of multiculturalism, which could not break the hold of a traditionally class-divided and unpluralistic society. Those who had supported multiculturalism and failed had no choice but to become even more radical by moving towards anti-racist education. The same situation was not applicable to a country such as Canada, where, according to McLeod, a more democratic society has developed and where support for multiculturalism is widespread among politicians and the citizenry (McLeod, 1990:4). Moreover, according to McLeod, Canadians have a Charter of Rights and Freedoms which gives explicit support to concepts such as social, economic, and cultural equality. McLeod's support for liberal multicultural policies cannot hide the fact, however, that racism in society and in the school system has become so prevalent nowadays that the mere existence of progressive legislation and other principles enshrined in the charter are in dire need of updating, if not a total overhaul. The existence of multicultural legislation and the power to enforce it is in itself a sorry indication that without the legislation, a large sector of the Canadian citizenry might not voluntarily abide by the principles of egalitarianism that Canadians hold so dearly. Calling for anti-racist legislation might have a great deal to do with being leftist, yet it also has much to do with the fact that multiculturalism has failed (or it may in the not-so-distant future) to maintain societal equilibrium. The support for the Reform Party's assimilationist view in the 1993 federal election is a case in point.

The failure of the report to clearly adopt an anti-racist position did not stop criticisms. After its publication, the report was sent to principals, teachers, and community organizations for critical evaluation. The Ontario Ministry of Education collected their responses in September 1988 and published *Synopsis of Public Responses to the Report of the Provincial Advisory Committee on Race Relations* (1988). Among the respondents, it was found that 15 percent viewed the report's emphasis on anti-racism and visible minorities as counterproductive. It was suggested that more positive strategies emphasizing the contributions of multiculturalism and ethno-cultural groups be adopted (p. 5).

The report was also criticized for being too complex, occasionally vague, and laden with jargon and terms that needed to be defined in order to make them easier to comprehend, especially for lay people (p. 6). Finally, although the report and the feedback were brought together in 1987 and 1988, it is remarkable that the Ministry of Education has not yet been able to legislate a specific policy on race relations. The latter remains exclusively a matter for school boards to decide. Recent political developments in Ontario, however, might generate some changes in the area of multicultural and anti-racist education. The September 1990 election brought the New Democratic Party (NDP) into power, along with its more progressive views on racial, ethnic, and minority issues. Prior to the election, the NDP, in its discussion of multicultural and anti-racist education, raised some key questions that demonstrated the party's more enlightened understanding of multicultural and anti-racist education (New Democrats, 1990, #2).

FROM POLICY FORMULATION TO PRACTICE

Following the Toronto Board of Education's lead, the other boards of education in the Metropolitan Toronto region have attempted policies on race relations.

In practical terms, this can be seen in the fact that at the administrative level, the boards have hired personnel to work as consultants or advisors on race relations. This person is usually in charge of implementing the boards' official policies. In some boards, this person may be assisted by members of the staff, who are expected to help in the implementation of the policy on race relations. Moreover, in most cases in which I have had personal experience, the work by race relations advisors has become an addendum if not a marginal aspect of the overall educational functions of the various boards. Schooling was not reorganized in order to facilitate the changes that a policy on race relations has implied; it has remained fundamentally the same. It is important to mention that the introduction of a policy on race and ethnic relations was not necessarily initiated by the boards of education or by the Ministry of Education. Rather, in most cases, the policy was introduced as a result of pressure from parents and community groups. It can be surmised that the development of race relations policies is a political response that is not aimed at changing teaching practices.

However, the development of a policy is not enough. While it is true that formulating a policy on race relations is an initial and significant step towards educating all members of society in the realization that racism is not to be tolerated, the acknowledgment that such a policy is indeed needed will not in itself suffice to attain the defined goal. The gap between the principles stated in any policy and the policy's actual implementation cannot be bridged if the human resources allocated to such an important activity are as meagre as I have indicated that they presently are.

The difficulties in implementing a race relations policy should have been expected by its advocates. Since programs of this sort are being introduced into what is mainly an ethnocentric culture, open or subtle opposition to it should have been anticipated. After all, as Cummins writes, given society's commitment to maintain dominant/dominated power relationships, it is predictable that educational changes threatening this power structure will be fiercely resisted (Cummins, 1986:33).

Two issues deserve special attention. They have to do with the work performed by the race and ethnic relations services provided by the various boards and are concerned with staff development and in-service training for teachers and raising awareness among the student population. These are elaborated in following sections.

Staff Development Programs for Teachers

Most teachers enter their profession with little or no training in race relations. Faculties of education do not offer the courses needed to train teachers critically about the role that schools play in the reproduction of inequalities based on aspects such as race, gender, and class.[3] The furthest some teacher training institutions might go is to offer courses on cross-cultural communications. However, in most cases, this is done to provide extra qualification to those teachers who are interested in teaching English as a Second Language courses.

In the absence of learning opportunities to develop critical thinking in race and ethnic relations, graduates who enter the teaching profession fail to realize how important these relations are in their everyday classroom experiences. It is commonplace for practitioners to listen to teachers who argue that they do not need race and ethnic relations training because "they treat every child fairly." According to Carol Tator, Enid Lee, a practitioner in the field of anti-racist education, has pointed out that one of the most serious problems confronting teachers is that they cannot recognize their own biases. There is an attachment to color-blindness among educators, who forcefully contend that they operate on the principle that all children are the same and should be treated the same. By denying racial differences, teachers are refusing to recognize children's full range of social experiences and histories, including membership in a racial or cultural group as well as the possibility of painful episodes of discrimination (Tator, 1987/1988:11).

A similar situation in the United States is discussed by Christine Sleeter, who points out how difficult it is to get white teachers to move significantly beyond "color-blind" thinking, as well as to have them stop treating all children alike. She writes:

For example, the concept of ethnic or racial identity is crucial to understanding the development and achievement of children of colour. Whites tend to take their racial identities for granted, as fish take water for granted, and they have difficulty understanding what it means to develop a positive racial identity. Most whites think of race and ethnicity as equivalent. And because they do not particularly value ethnic identity, they tend to reduce matters of ethnic identity to folk costumes or family customs. (Sleeter, 1990:38)

When it comes to implementing staff development programs for teachers in order to raise their awareness of racial and ethnic issues in the classroom, the present situation is, to say the least, abysmal. Systematic training on an ongoing basis in order to sensitize teachers about these important issues is almost nonexistent. There are two interrelated reasons for this situation: as we have already indicated, the whole approach to race relations within boards of education is a marginal one. It will continue to be marginal because the alternative is deemed quite expensive by educational administrators. To have an effective race and ethnic relations program in place, it would be necessary for the staff to attend in-service programs on a regular basis. The cost of a program such as this is considered to be prohibitive, since those attending seminars or working sessions would have to be replaced by substitute teachers. Sound financial management is often given as justification to delay the much needed changes.

Currently, staff development programs for teachers take the form of one-shot sessions, and participation in them is voluntary. This kind of staff development training is referred to by some North American consultants as "hit and run" or "flash and dash," which highlights the marginal nature of these programs within the school. Not surprisingly, many consultants in the United States are now refusing to participate in such staff development programs (Sleeter, 1990).

My own experience as a practitioner shows that when these one-shot staff development programs take place, they are mostly concerned with creating some measure of sensitivity among teachers as well as teaching them about different cultures. Often these efforts are followed by the organization of a variety of ethnic fairs in the schools. Not surprisingly, in time some of the teachers who had participated in these staff development programs simply turn themselves off by believing that they had learned everything that is to be learned about multiculturalism, and that the field has little more to offer to them. They distance themselves from ethnic and race relations activities, completely oblivious to the fact that they have failed to grasp the pervasiveness of institutionalized racism, both within the educational system and in society at large.

Recently, one of the boards of education within Metropolitan Toronto conducted a needs assessment survey among its teachers by focusing on sections of the race and ethnic relations policy. The survey intended to find out what the teachers' main concerns were when dealing with minority students in the classroom. The responses to this survey clearly underscore some of the serious difficulties that practitioners confront daily in our contacts with teachers. As some of the teachers' responses show, many of them are still opposed not only to anti-racist education, but also to the milder policies of multiculturalism. Most of them still support the outdated ideology of cultural assimilation, fashionable at the turn of the century and now explicitly rejected by Canadian legislation. Many believe in ethnic adjustment, that is, making ethnic minorities aware of what it is like to be a North American; some urge for a merging of ethnic minorities into mainstream Canadian culture; others state how important it is to explain to newly arrived students the expectations of Canadians and how to meet those Canadian standards. Still others, perhaps encouraged by the anonymous nature of the survey, felt compelled to express their true feelings: "I have been multicultural to death...ever heard of assimilation?"; "Teach the ethnic group to learn to fit in with the people who are living and working here already"; "This topic [race and ethnic relations] is bashed to death...soon scholastic buildings will be known as 'racism identification centres.' "[4]

From these statements it becomes apparent that these one-shot or hit-and-run staff development programs are not the answer to preparing teachers to deal with racial and ethnic issues in the classroom. If anything, they are counterproductive. Teachers need to be seriously reprogrammed; they need to learn to look at the world from a different perspective in order to comprehend why some minorities in our society are being oppressed and why their children are not doing well in school. Teachers ought to be educated so that they can critically recognize the dominant ideology that proclaims that we live in an open social system and that individual progress depends mainly on one's own education efforts. Teachers should be educated to relate to their students' life experiences and to learn from them firsthand about the structural and institutionalized barriers minority students and their families face in their everyday lives. The present flash-and-dash in-service training programs are in need of serious overhaul.

Raising Students' Awareness of Ethnic and Racial Issues

Within Metropolitan Toronto, the most common type of work in which the boards of education engage students involves what are called Multicultural Leadership Camps. These camps are usually provided for secondary school students, although several boards of education have in recent years started to provide this training for grade seven and grade eight students. These camps involve eight to ten students and one teacher from each school, four or five schools in total, in a retreat setting to raise students' awareness of racial issues. The camps are organized three to four times during the regular academic year. These camps are held from one single day up to four and a half days. Usually they are held outside the city and include outdoor educational activities that promote self-esteem and cooperative learning.

The central focus of these camps is on sensitivity training of students, although those organized by the Toronto Board of Education have adopted a more anti-racist approach. The activities include, for example, providing students with a broader perspective as to how racism was historically constructed, and discussing issues such as institutionalized racism. The leadership taken by the Toronto Board of Education in anti-racist education is reflected in the hiring of staff, not only to develop meaningful camp programs, but also to develop follow-up procedures after the camps. The latter aspect is particularly important since students are expected to develop and implement an action plan in race relations and multiculturalism upon return to their schools.

My recent experience working with students in these camps shows that, unlike teachers, the students have no difficulty in acknowledging the existence of racism in their own schools and communities. My perception is confirmed by a survey of twenty-eight secondary schools undertaken by the Toronto Board of Education to discover students' responses to issues of racism, sexism, and pop culture. The purpose of this survey was to provide board employees with a greater understanding of current issues as they are perceived through students' eyes.

The report of this survey stated that a great deal of overt racism is observed by secondary school students on a day-to-day basis. Most students answered that they believe racism to be a problem in Toronto and that blacks, Chinese, and Natives are the main targets of racist behavior. Students stated that jokes, comments, wall graffiti, and some gang violence are linked to the existence of racism in Toronto schools. The remarks made by one student are quite telling:

Some people don't think it [racism] exists. I'd like to know what planet they're living on. Probably they're living in a place where there's one kind of people so there's nobody to discriminate against anyway. I think people are threatened by anything that's different. It's human nature to be a little scared. I suppose if you are never given a chance to understand it, if it's different its wrong and kill it. (Vosko, 1989:30)

Likewise, in a recent meeting of the Metro Youth Task Force, young students and parents openly voiced their opinions on a variety of issues, including education and racism. Their perceptions of the problems are reflected in the minutes of that meeting. They stated, for example, the following observations.

- The current school system forces students to fit into a rigid system rather than developing a flexible system that could meet students' individual needs.
- Teachers should not stereotype students.
- Teachers should be more understanding, especially with regard to diverse cultures.
- Teachers should respect students as people.

- Teachers and the school system need to be more active in relating with immigrant parents.
- Teachers brand visible minorities and immigrants as troublemakers.
- The media have exaggerated the so-called "gang problem" in Metropolitan Toronto and what racism has to do with it; they indicated, for example, that a group of white youngsters hanging out is "just a group if kids," while a group of black teens is perceived to be "up to something."
- A number of those participating in the meeting had a racist experience to report.
- The suggestion was made that people need to understand more about each other's culture in order to effectively combat racism. They specially noted that people aren't born racist, that racism is learned. (Metro Youth Task Force, 1990)

Remarkable as these candid observations on the part of students are, the fact remains that students, in spite of witnessing or experiencing prejudice on a daily basis, cannot yet articulate and critically assess what the real causes of racist and ethnic prejudices and discrimination are. Nor can they, at this stage, come to terms with the remedies to current injustices. Again, this is not the students' fault; if anything, it is the responsibility of school administrators, teachers, and practitioners alike.

TOWARDS A CRITICAL PEDAGOGY IN ANTI-RACIST EDUCATION

I have indicated throughout that very little progress has been achieved in recent years in the field of anti-racist education, in spite of the rhetoric. Neither the Ministry of Education nor the various boards of education have come through with a meaningful, comprehensive, and practical policy on race and ethnic relations. Implementation of what already exists in this area leaves a lot to be desired. Much of it has to do with the fact that newer formulations have failed to transform the overall functions of schooling, the basic structure of which remains intact today. There is as yet no clear vision, not to mention theoretical clarity, as to what anti-racist education is supposed to be. As Cummins has correctly asserted, the definitions of the role of educators and of the school have remained largely unchanged despite new and improved programs and policies. The programs and policies, despite their cost, have simply added a new veneer to the outward facade of the structure that continues to disable minority students (Cummins, 1986:33). As we stated above, to a large extent, this is because the work performed by race relations staff in the various boards remains marginalized.

Anti-racist educators need to look for some positive direction. It is at this juncture that administrators, teachers, parents, students, and practitioners should begin to look at the contributions that critical pedagogy may make. Critical pedagogy can contribute in the two most important aspects of anti-racist education. We have already indicated that it can teach us how to relate to students' experiences and how to take their needs and problems as the starting point; it can also instruct us in how to re-educate teachers so that in their classroom practices they may, in turn, educate their own students in the language of possibility and critique, and empower those students so that with their own efforts they might help to bring about a more democratic and just society for everyone. Critical pedagogy can reveal the ideology underlying a hegemonic curriculum, its hierarchically organized bodies of knowledge, and the way this curriculum marginalizes or disqualifies working-class knowledge as well as knowledge about women and minorities. It calls attention to the need to unravel the ideological interests embedded in the various messages, especially those ingrained in the curriculum, systems of instruction, and the modes of evaluation (Giroux, 193:292). The attainment of this goal remains the order of the day. It is a critical goal that cannot be attained under the present conditions of sporadic encounters between practitioners, students, and teachers. Faculties of education should play a more active role by training new teachers as intellectuals rather than technicians in charge of pushing down students' throats a prepackaged curriculum. The curriculum itself should be re-formed by allowing teacher input; after all, in spite of their weaknesses, nobody knows students better than the teacher.

However, if critical pedagogy is going to make a real contribution to anti-racism, we need to seriously consider some of its shortcomings. As a practitioner, I have come to the realization that although critical pedagogy promises a language of possibility, it does not discuss how actual classroom practices can lead to students' empowerment. As presently elaborated, critical pedagogy remains a highly abstract set of theoretical principles. Its language, conceptualization, and scope are different for lay people (i.e., teachers, students, and practitioners) to comprehend and grasp. In a summer course in a teachers' training program, I was struck by the teachers' inability to grasp the most basic premises of critical pedagogy in some of the course's required readings. Although teachers' lack of understanding of what critical pedagogy stands for does not invalidate critical pedagogical theory, theorists should make these concepts more accessible to the front-line workers whom we expect to implement a new anti-racist curriculum.

On this last point I am not alone. Ellsworth has called attention to the abstractness and complexity of the language of critical pedagogy. She has stated that this language is more appropriate (yet hardly more useful) for philosophical debates and the highly problematic concepts of freedom, justice, democracy, and universal values than for thinking through and planning classroom practices to supports its political agenda (Ellsworth, 1989:300).

While the importance of critical pedagogy should not be dismissed, my experience as a practitioner is that it can be easily misunderstood and misused. In one case, Paulo Freire's methodology was used in an adult literacy program and an English as a Second Language program by one of the boards of education. To put Freire's idea that teacher should be based on the student's needs and experiences to practical use, the students were taken to a grocery store so they could learn the English names of the items available there. If the next day the student went shopping alone in the same store, the instructor or facilitator claimed that the student had become "empowered."[5]

Obviously this kind of "student empowerment" falls short of the political empowerment critical pedagogy is concerned with. As was the case with Freire's method, critical pedagogy can be misused if taken out of its political context. Yet, this type of misunderstanding may repeat itself due to the complexity of critical pedagogy language. It is up to critical theorists to furnish us with a more simplified, yet not simplistic, vocabulary.

I believe this can be accomplished by a more active interaction between academics and practitioners. Since both academics and practitioners fall within Gramsci's conceptualization of "organic intellectuals,"[6] they can help avoid such misunderstanding by working together. More important, they can help support front-line workers such as those progressive practitioners who sometimes feel helpless in the face of the structural limitations that operate to thwart their honest efforts and enthusiasm to create a more just and democratic society. Critical pedagogy theorists and practitioners should work closely to put forth an effective, useful, and liberating anti-racist educational platform. To paraphrase Antonio Gramsci: "The practitioner feels, but does not know or understand; the theorist knows and understands but he rarely feels."[7] True organic intellectuals ought to bring feeling, knowledge, and understanding together. Let us hope so.

NOTES

1. For a good review, see J. Young (1979), "Education in a Multicultural Society: What Sort of Education? What Sort of Society?" *Canadian Journal of Education*, 4(3), pp. 5–21. See also R. Magsino (1985), "The Right to Multicultural Education: A Descriptive and Normative Analysis," *Multiculturalism*, 9(1), pp. 4–9.

2. For a good discussion, see J. Mallea (1989), *Schooling in a Plural Canada*, Clevedon: Multilingual Matters Ltd.

3. I do not intend to put an enormous responsibility on the shoulders of teachers for transforming society. I am aware that the ideology of racism has profound structural roots in society and penetrates all institutions, including educational ones. My intention is to show how racism as an ideology works in the system and makes teachers resistant to the inclusion of the nonethnocentric culture and curriculum in the school system.

4. This was an informal survey conducted by the Etobicoke Board of Education, Race and Ethnic Relations Services, in 1989, in order to find out teachers' needs in relation to the seven statements of the board's race and ethnic relations policy.

5. At present, the word *empowerment* is used by both liberal and radical educators, however, there is a clear distinction between the usages of the term. While for liberal educators the term *empowerment* means personal empowerment, radical and critical educators use the term in a social and political context. Henry Giroux and Peter McLaren define the term as referring to the process whereby students acquire the means to critically appropriate knowledge existing outside of their immediate experience in order to broaden their understanding of themselves, the world, and the possibilities for transforming the taken-for-granted assumptions about the way we live (Giroux & McLaren, 1986:229).

6. I am using here the notion of "organic intellectual" in its most general sense, as expressed by Antonio Gramsci (1971:3): "organic intellectuals [are] the thinking and organizing element of a particular social class. . . . [T]hese organic intellectuals are distinguished less by their profession, which may be any job characteristic of their class, than by their function in directing the ideas and aspirations of the class to which they organically belong."

7. Gramsci's actual words read as follows:

The popular element "feels" but does not always know or understand; the intellectual element "knows" but does not always understand and in particular does not always feel. The two extremes are therefore pedantry and philistinism on the one hand and blind passion and sectarianism on the other. . . . [T]he intellectual error consists in believing that one can know without understanding and even more without feeling and being impassioned (not only for knowledge in itself but also for the object of knowledge); in other words that the intellectual can be an intellectual (and not a pure pedant) if distinct and separate from the people-nation, that is, without feeling the elementary passions of the people, understanding them and therefore explaining and justifying them in the particular historical situation and connecting them dialectically to the laws of history and to a superior conception of the world, scientifically and coherently elaborated—i.e., knowledge. One cannot make politics-history without this passion, without this sentimental connection between intellectuals and people-nation. In the absence of such a nexus the relations between the intellectual and the people-nation are, or are reduced to, relationships of a purely bureaucratic and formal order. (Gramsci, 1971:418)

2

Multicultural Policy Discourses on Racial Inequality in American Education

Cameron McCarthy

Multicultural education emerged in the United States, in part, as a minority response to the failure of compensatory education programs launched by the Kennedy and Johnson administrations in the 1960s. Multicultural education is therefore a product of a particular historical conjecture of relations among the state, contending racial minority and majority groups, and policy intellectuals in the United States, in which the discourse over schools became increasingly racialized.[1] Black and other minority groups, for example, began to insist that curriculum and educational policy address issues of racial inequality, minority cultural identities, and the distribution of power within institutions such as schools themselves (Banks, 1988; Berlowitz, 1984). Proponents of multiculturalism were very much influenced by these radical possibilitarian themes. Indeed, spurred forward by pressure from African-Americans, Latinos, Native Americans, and other marginalized groups for equality of opportunity in education and society, and by the efforts of mainstream educators to provide practical solutions to the problem of racial inequality in the United States, multicultural education has become one of the most powerful educational slogans in the 1990s. Legislation for ethnic studies and bilingual programs has served to underline the federal government's commitment to the promotion of multiculturalism as a viable educational strategy to address the problem of racial inequality in schooling (Grant & Sleeter, 1985a; McCarthy & Apple, 1988). A growing number of school districts and university-based preservice teacher education programs have also espoused various forms of multicultural education (Swartz, 1988; University of Wisconsin–Madison Steering Committee on Minority Affairs, 1987).

Unfortunately, critical curriculum theorists and educators have largely ignored developments in multicultural education. It must also be said that proponents of multiculturalism have paid very little attention to the literature on critical pedagogy—the work of Apple (1986), Ellsworth (1989), Freire (1970), Giroux (1985), Wood (1985), and others. The lack of a critical perspective within the multicultural formulation—one that links school knowledge and the microdynamics of the classroom to structural inequality and differential social power outside the school—has meant that multiculturalism has been in many cases easily incorporated and sucked back (Swartz, 1988) into dominant curriculum and education arrangements. As we shall see, proponents of multicultural policies in education often "claw back" from the radical themes associated with black challenges to the white-dominated school curriculum and school system.[2]

In what follows, I will explore the theory and practice of multiculturalism as a problematic "solution" to racial inequality in schooling. First, I will outline the historical developments in American schooling and state policy towards racial minorities that led up to the events of the 1960s and the emergence of multiculturalism in education. Second, I will closely examine the general perspectives, core ideological assumptions, and desired outcomes of three different types of multicultural policy discourses on racial inequality as embodied in various school curriculum and preservice teacher education program guides as well as in the articulated theories of proponents of multicultural education. There are subtle differences among these policy discourses. These differences, I will argue, have important ideological and political implications. Third, in the final section of this chapter, I will discuss the outlines of an alternative or critical approach to multicultural education.

HISTORICAL BACKGROUND

For over one hundred years and up until two decades ago, a basic assimilationist model formed the centerpiece of education and state policies towards ethnic differences in the United States. Schooling was looked upon as the institution par excellence through which American educational policy makers and ruling elites consciously attempted to cultivate norms of citizenship, to fashion a conformist American identity, and to bind together a population of diverse national origins (Kaestle, 1983; Olneck & Lazerson, 1980). This assimilationist ideology was rooted in the nativistic response of dominant Anglo-Americans to the waves of immigrants from southern Europe who came to work in urban factories at the turn of the century. These southern European immigrants were seen as a threat to social order that was based on the values of earlier settled Euro-American citizenry. The latter traced their ancestry to England, the Netherlands, and other northern European countries.

In 1909, Ellwood P. Cubberley, proponent of "social efficiency" (Kliebard, 1986:223), clearly stated the case for using civil institutions such as schools as vehicles for cultivating dominant Anglo-Saxon values among the new immigrants and their offspring:

Everywhere these people [immigrants] tend to settle in groups or settlements, and to set up here their national manners, customs and observances. Our task is to break up these groups or settlements, to assimilate and amalgamate these people as part of our American race, and to implant in their children, as far as can be done, the Anglo-Saxon conception of righteousness, law and order, and popular government, and to awaken in them a reverence for our democratic institutions and for those things in our national life which we as a people hold to be of abiding truth. (Cubberley, 1909: 15–16)

In addition to promoting highly conformist practices and values in schools, policy makers turned to the coercive apparatuses of the state to control the flow of non-Anglo immigrants into the United States; Highly exclusionary clauses were written into the United States Immigration Acts of 1917 and 1924, which drastically limited the number of immigrants that came from southern and eastern Europe, Asia, and Latin America (Perlman, 1989).

For American minority groups, institutional assimilationist practices were even more stringent and definitively conformist. Efforts were made in educational institutions serving Hispanic, Native American, and black youth to ride these groups of "ethnic traits" (Banks, 1981:4) that were considered inimical to the dominant American culture. Consequently, early twentieth-century institutions such as the Hampton Institute were designed to equip black and Native American youth with "the skills that would bring them to the level of the white middle class" (Kliebard, 1986:126). The course in economics at Hampton, for example, "attempted to get blacks and American Indians to abandon certain undesirable practices in specific areas of practical concern such as the purchase of clothing and the consumption of food" (Kliebard, 1986:126).

For most of the first half of the century, this assimilationist model of education was not seriously challenged, even though black protest groups such as the United Negro Improvement Association, led by Marcus Garvey, championed separatism and pluralism. Indeed, many prominent black as well as white middle-class intellectuals regard assimilation and cultural incorporation of American ethnic groups as a highly desirable social goal. In the 1920s and 1930s, the so-called Chicago School of Sociologists, led by Robert E. Park (a former secretary to Booker T. Washington), outlined the basic assimilation model that was so influential in shaping research and social policy on race relations during the period. Park postulated that all immigrant and ethnic minority group members went through a "race relations cycle," or trajectory, on their way to eventual incorporation into the mainstream of American life. This cycle consisted of four stages: *contact, conflict, accommodation,* and *assimilation* (Omi & Winant, 1986:15).

But for minorities such as blacks and Native Americans, assimilation meant a special kind of cultural incorporation into a racial order in which they were accorded a secondary status. The ideology of assimilation clearly benefitted white Americans. White "ethnics," over time, were able to share in the rewards of the society from which black Americans were systematically excluded (Banks, 1981). Blacks, Native Americans, and Hispanics continued to experience severe discrimination and racial exclusion in housing, employment, and education during the first half of this century. During this same period, European immigrants—Irish, Italian, and Greek—came, settled, and consolidated their status in American society.[3]

By the 1950s and 1960s, policies of assimilation lost credibility among many groups of racial minorities and were subjected to unprecedented challenges by oppositional black groups and the civil rights movement. These challenges were particularly strong in the area of education. Black and other minority groups contended that schools as they were organized in America were fundamentally racist and did not address the needs and aspirations of minority peoples. Minority groups demanded more control of institutions in their communities. They demanded greater representation in the administration and staffing of schools. Even more significantly, black youth and their political leaders demanded a racial redefinition of the school curriculum to include black studies. The latter demand constituted a strategic challenge to the taken-for-granted Eurocentric foundations of the American school curriculum (McCarthy & Apple, 1988).

Essentially then, the assimiliationist approach to race relations and to the education of minorities had become unstuck. Blacks and other oppositional racial minorities had begun to champion a radical pluralism (Berlowitz, 1984). It is in this context of racial black discontent with American schooling that education policy makers and liberal intellectuals began to forge a "new" discourse of multiculturalism. Educators and social researchers such as Baker (1973), Banks (1973), and Glazer and Moynihan (1963) attempted to replace the assimilationist model that undergirded the American school curriculum with a pluralist model that embraced the notion of cultural diversity. Multicultural education as a "new" curricular form disarticulated elements of black radical demands for the restructuring of school knowledge and rearticulated these elements into more reformist professional discourses around issues of minority failure, cultural characteristics, and language proficiency.

MULTICULTURAL POLICY DISCOURSES

Over the years, policy discourses in multicultural education have consistently identified the variable of culture as the vehicle for the resolution of racial inequality and racial antagonism in school (Troyna & Williams, 1986). This central motif does represent a certain continuity with an earlier emphasis on minority culture identifiable in the proposals of liberal scholars for compensatory education. However, unlike the earlier liberal preoccupation with cultural deprivation, multicultural proponents tend to emphasize the positive qualities of minority cultural heritage. Proponents of multicultural education have therefore promoted curriculum models that emphasize the following: (1) *cultural understanding*—the idea central to many ethnic studies and human relations programs that students and teachers should be more sensitive to ethnic differences in the classroom, (2) *cultural competence*—the insistence in bilingual and bicultural education programs that students and teachers should be able to demonstrate competence in the language and culture of groups outside their own cultural heritage, and (3) *cultural emancipation*—the somewhat more possibilitarian and social reconstructionist thesis that the incorporation or inclusion of minority culture in the school curriculum has the potential to positively influence minority academic achievement and consequently life chances beyond the school (Grant & Sleeter, 1989; Rushton, 1981).

In this section, I will discuss, in some detail, the strengths and limitations of these three different multicultural approaches to racial inequality in education. First, I examine the policy discourse of cultural understanding.

Models of Cultural Understanding

Models of cultural understanding in multicultural education exist in the form of various state- and university-supported ethnic studies and human relations programs that place a premium on "improving communication" among different ethnic groups (Montalto, 1981). The fundamental stance of this approach to ethnic differences in schooling is that of cultural relativism. Within this framework, all social and ethnic groups are presumed to have a formal parity with each other. The matter of ethnic identity is understood in terms of individual choice and preference—the language of the shopping mall.

This stance of cultural relativism is translated in curriculum guides for ethnic studies in terms of a discourse of reciprocity and consensus: "We are different but we are all the same." The idea that racial differences are only "human" and "natural" is, for example, promoted in the teaching kit *The Wonderful World of Difference: A Human Relations Program for Grades K–8*, in which the authors "explore the diversity and richness of the human family" (Anti-Defamation League of B'nai B'rith, 1986). In their *Multicultural Teaching: A Handbook of Activities, Information, and Resources* (1986), Tiedt and Tiedt tell teachers and students that there are many different ways of grouping individuals in "our society." Income, religious beliefs, and so on are some of the criteria "we use" in the United States. One of the handbook's many activities requires students to make up a list of cultural traits that would be characteristic of "Sue Wong" (p. 144). Students are also asked to supply the appropriate cultural information that would help to complete the sentence "Sue Wong is . . ." (p. 144). This tendency to focus on the acceptance and recognition of cultural differences has led in recent years to a movement for the recognition of the cultural "uniqueness" of "white ethnic" groups (for example, Poles, Italians, Norwegians, and Swedes) to counterbalance demands for the study of black, Hispanic, and Native American cultures (Gibson, 1984).

But the emphasis on cultural understanding goes beyond the development of communication skills and respect for ethnic differences. Various preservice teacher education programs and state human relations guides emphasize the elimination of racial and sexual stereotypes and the development of positive attitudes towards minority and disadvantaged groups (Wisconsin Department of Public Instruction, 1986). This emphasis on attitudinal change is, for example, reflected in the Ann Arbor, Michigan, Board of Education's regulations of the 1970s:

Beginning in the 1972–73 school year, no student-teacher shall be accepted by the Ann Arbor schools unless he (she) can demonstrate attitudes necessary to support and create the multiethnic curriculum. Each student-teacher must provide a document or transcript which reflects training in or evidence of substantive understanding of multicultural or minority experience. (Baker, 1977:80)

In a similar manner, the University of Wisconsin's Steering Committee on Minority Affairs, in its 1987 report, strongly emphasizes the need for course work that would promote racial tolerance: "The University must implement a mandatory six credit course requirement; and create and develop various Ethnic Studies Programs. These measures will recognize the contributions of ethnic minorities to American society and promote cross-cultural understanding and respect among the entire student body" p. 4).

Cultural understanding models of multicultural education such as the one promoted in the University of Wisconsin's Steering Committee on Minority Affairs (1987) report generally take a "benign" stance (Troyna & Williams, 1986) towards racial inequality in schooling and consequently place an enormous emphasis on promoting racial harmony among students and teachers from different cultural backgrounds. The following are some of the ideological assumptions that centrally inform this approach to racial differences in education.

Core Ideological Assumptions. (1) The United States is a culturally and ethnically diverse nations. (2) This cultural diversity has had a positive effect on the overall growth and development of America as a powerful country (King, 1980; Tiedt & Tiedt, 1986). (3) All of America's ethnic groups have in their different ways contributed to the growth and development of

America (Wisconsin Department of Public Instruction, 1986). (4) The educational system in the past has not sufficiently fostered this multicultural view of American society, and this has contributed to prejudice and discrimination against certain ethnic groups. (5) Schools and teachers must therefore positively endorse cultural diversity and foster an appreciation and respect for "human differences" in order to reduce racial tension and estrangement of minority groups in the school and in society (Tiedt & Tiedt, 1986).

Desired Outcomes. The principal expectation of those who promote the cultural understanding model of multicultural education is that American schools will be oriented towards the "cultural enrichment of all students" (Gibson, 1984:99). It is assumed that teachers will provide such enrichment in their classrooms. By fostering understanding and acceptance of cultural differences in the classroom and in the school curriculum, educational programs based on the cultural understanding approach, it is expected, will contribute towards the elimination of prejudice (Baker, 1977).

Commentary. Proponents of cultural understanding models of multicultural education attach enormous significance to the role of attitudes in the reproduction of racism. Human relations and ethnic studies programs based on this approach pursue what Banks (1981) calls the "prejudiceless goal." The strong version of these programs directly targets white students and teachers. White students and teachers are portrayed as the flawed protagonists in their racial relations with blacks and Native Americans. It is expected that negative white attitudes towards minorities will change if these prejudiced individuals are exposed to sensitivity training in human relations programs. The weak version of the cultural understanding approach emphasizes the promotion of racial harmony and tolerance of social and ethnic differences.

Various pretest and posttest evaluations of multicultural education and human relations programs that emphasize attitudinal change and cultural understanding suggest that these programs have not been very successful in achieving their espoused goal of eliminating majority/minority prejudice. For instance, though in her evaluation of the University of Michigan's human relations program Baker (1973) claims modest changes in white "pro-irrational attitudes" (p. 307), these changes are not reported in the critical area of black/white relations. Thus, according to Baker, the Michigan students' perceptions of blacks remained at the "pretest level" and were not significantly changed by their participation in the university's human relations program: "No statistically significant differences obtained on the black anti-irrational or pro-irrational subscales. Therefore it can be concluded that the change in the perception of blacks held by the [white] students remained fairly constant" (p. 307).

Like Baker, Fish (1981) reports findings of "no significant effects" in his study of the impact of the field experience component of Wisconsin's human relations program on white students' perceptions of blacks and other disadvantaged groups. According to Fish, "Students who completed a fieldwork experience did not over a semester's time show significantly greater positive attitudes towards the population worked with than students who did not complete a fieldwork experience" (p. xi). Instead, Fish indicates a worsening of attitudes towards blacks during the course of the Wisconsin program: "One semester after completion of a fieldwork experience, subjects' attitudes towards the mentally retarded and the physically disabled persisted at the pretest level, whereas subjects' attitudes towards blacks significantly worsened from the pretest level" p. xii). But Fish is not alone in his findings of unanticipated negative effects of attitudinal change programs. Buckingham (1987) draws similar conclusions in his case study of responses to "The Whites of Their Eyes"—a Thames Television educational program on "Racism in the British Media." In his study of the responses of "a number of groups of London school pupils to the program," Buckingham drew the following conclusions:

> In general, for instance, pupils failed to perceive that the program was concerned with racism in the media, and this led many to assume that the program was suggesting that all white people are racist. Likewise few pupils picked up on the program's arguments about the causes of racism, and fewer still seem to have noticed its implicit suggestions about how racism might be eradicated. While the program provides a fairly clear historical context for the discussion of racism, pupils generally failed to make connections between this and the examples of racism in the media today. (Buckingham, 1984:139)

American school critics have raised other concerns about attitudinal change and cultural understanding programs. Writers such as Pettigrew (1974) and Garcia (1974) have argued that the content and methods of these programs are significantly flawed. Pettigrew (1974), Garcia (1974), and Kleinfeld (1975) point to the tendency of proponents of cultural understanding models to overemphasize the differences among ethnic groups, neglecting the differences within any one group. They also draw attention to the unintended effect of stereotyping, which results in multicultural approaches that treat ethnic groups as "monolithic entities possessing uniform, discernible traits" (Gibson, 1984:100). For instance, Garcia contends that advocates of cultural understanding models tend to discuss "Chicano culture as if it were a set of values and customs possessed by all who are categorized as Chicanos or Mexican Americans. . . . This fallacy serves to create the new stereotype which is found in the completion of the statement, Mexican American children are" (quoted in Gibson, 1984:100).

The rather disturbing and contradictory findings of Baker (1973), Fish (1981), and Buckingham (1987) and the complaints about methods and content raised by minority educators such as Garcia (1974) have cast doubt on the educational and practical value of cultural understanding approaches to racial differences in schooling. Some proponents of multicultural education have therefore suggested different curriculum and instructional approaches to race relations in school. These curriculum theorists, led by educators such as Banks (1981, 1988), assert that all students should be able to demonstrate cultural competence in the language and cultural practices of ethnic groups other than their own.

Models of Cultural Competence

Underpinning the cultural competence approach to multicultural education is a fundamental assumption that values of cultural pluralism should have a central place in the school curriculum. This concept of social institutions as representing a plurality of ethnic interests was first formulated by liberal social scientists such as Riesman, Glazer, and Denny (1969) and Glazer and Moynihan (1963). Some educators, such as Banks (1973, 1981, 1988), Cortes (1973), Pettigrew (1974), and Gollnick (1980), contend that there is a general lack of cross-cultural competencies, especially in the area of language, among minority and majority groups in the American populace. These educators argue for various forms of bilingual, bicultural, and ethnic studies programs based on pluralist values. Such programs aim at preserving cultural diversity in the United States, particularly the language and identity of minority groups such as blacks, Hispanics, and Native Americans. Banks (1981) summarizes this pluralist approach to ethnic differences in the following terms:

The pluralist argues that ethnicity and ethnic identities are very important in American society. The United States, according to the pluralist, is made up of competing ethnic groups, each of which champions its economic and political interests. It is extremely important, argues the pluralist, for the individual to develop a commitment to his or her ethnic group, especially if that ethnic group is "oppressed" by more powerful ethnic groups within American society. (P. 62)

The American Association of Colleges for Teacher Education (AACTE), in its often cited "No One American Model," also makes a particularly strong case for cultural pluralism in education. AACTE maintains that

multicultural education is education which values cultural pluralism. Multicultural education rejects the view that schools should merely tolerate cultural pluralism. Instead, multicultural education affirms that schools should be oriented toward the cultural enrichment of all children and youth through programs rooted to the preservation and extension of cultural alternatives. Multicultural education recognizes cultural diversity as a fact of life in American society, and it affirms that this cultural diversity is a valuable resource that should be preserved and extended. It affirms that major education institutions should strive to preserve and enhance cultural pluralism. (AACTE 1974:264)

Proponents of multicultural education as a cultural competence such as the AACTE's Commission on Multicultural Education argue that multiculturalism in education should mean more than the fostering of cultural understanding and awareness about America's ethnic groups. They argue that "teachers (should) help students develop ethnic identities, knowledge about different cultural groups . . . and competence in more than one cultural system" (Grant & Sleeter, 1989:101).

In a related sense, the issue of cultural diversity becomes a matter of white teachers' professional competence rather than an issue of social and educational change. Within this framework, minority students are seen as possessing cultural attributes that the teacher must learn to "handle." The description of the curriculum and instruction course entitled Teaching in the Multicultural Classroom in the general catalogue of a leading U.S. university makes this quite clear. The course listed as EDCI 4800 is described as providing "strategies and resources for teaching students of cultural diversity." Prospective teachers in this area are also informed that they will learn to "develop units and activities of cultural variety."[4] The cultural competence approach therefore emphasizes the need for teachers to help minority students conquer the problems associated with cultural marginalization by initiating these students into the dominant value system, paradoxically through the negotiation of minority languages and cultural heritages themselves. By integrating the language and culture of a plurality of ethnic groups into the curriculum, proponents argue that teachers can help to "build bridges" between America's different ethnic groups (Sleeter and Grant, 1986:4). The target population of this cultural competence approach to multicultural education is mainly minority students. It is expected that minority students will develop competence in the "public culture" and the skills and the attitudes of the dominant white society (Lewis, 1976:35). This familiarity with mainstream culture must not take place at the expense of the minority student's own ethnic heritage—a difficult balancing act indeed.

Core Ideological Assumptions. The cultural competence approach to multicultural education is underpinned by some basic assumptions about race relations in education and society in the United States. The following are some of the principal ideological assumptions and values of the cultural competence approach: (1) Previous assimilationist approaches to education, which characterized the United States as a melting pot of ethnic groups, actually helped to foster the hegemony of Anglo values. This has led to the virtual subordination or exclusion of minority culture from the American mainstream (Banks, 1981). (2) Cross-cultural interaction through bilingual and bicultural education programs will help to guarantee the survival of minority language and minority culture (Banks, 1981; Cortes, 1973; Ramirez and Castenada, 1974). (3) Cross-cultural interaction between America's ethnic groups is regarded as a power antidote to the racial prejudice that continues to limit the presence of blacks, Hispanics, and Native Americans in America's mainstream (Grant & Sleeter, 1989).

Desired Outcomes. Proponents of the cultural competence approach to multicultural education champion a pluralism that has as its principal objective the preservation of minority language and culture. Bicultural and bilingual programs associated with this cultural competence approach aim to prepare minority students for their social and cultural negotiations with dominant white mainstream society. At the same time, it is expected that white students will also acquire knowledge and familiarity with the language and culture of minority groups. It is felt that such cross-cultural interaction will contribute to reduced antagonism between majority and minority ethnic groups.

Commentary. Proponents of the cultural competence approach to multicultural education have attempted to develop programs that go beyond cultural awareness and attitudinal change. This approach to multiculturalism is particularly critical of earlier compensatory education programs, such as Head Start, which worked centrally on the assumption that minority students were "culturally deficient." Instead, proponents of models of cross-cultural competence valorize minority cultural heritage and language and argue for the meaningful inclusion in the curriculum of "aspects of minority culture that a teacher could build on" (Sleeter & Grant, 1986:4).

But the emphasis on cultural competence as a set of curricular strategies for enhancing minority negotiation with mainstream society precipitates a central contradiction. On the one hand, the affirmation of minority culture in various bilingual, bicultural, and ethnic studies programs represents a direct challenge to the centrality of Anglo values in the school curriculum and the notion that minority culture and language are "naturally" deficient (McCarthy, 1988; Banks, 1988). On the other, the closely related objective of "building bridges" (Sleeter & Grant, 1986:4) from minority groups to mainstream society privileges individual mobility over a collective identity politics oriented towards change in the current structure of race relations in schools and society. As such, the cultural competence approach to multiculturalism has a significant unintended consequence. Attempts to have minority students learn how to cross over to the language and culture of the Anglo mainstream also commit these students to a trajectory that leads towards incorporation and assimilation—an educational and social result that is antithetical to one of the principal concerns of biculturalism—the valorization and preservation of minority cultural identity.

In sum, then, despite the emphasis on diversity within the cultural competence model, the minority child is just like anybody else's, free to make his or her choices in the marketplace of culture, ethnicity, and heritage. As Banks (1987) argues, "[Minority and majority] students need to learn that there are cultural and ethnic alternatives within our society that they can freely embrace" (1987:12). Presumably, the responsibility that the enterprising minority youth undertakes in exchange for his participation in the cultural market is that of respecting the society's institutions and the rules that make them "work" for those in the American mainstream.

Within recent years, challenges to the cultural understanding and cultural competence approaches to multiculturalism have led to the reformulation and reconceptualization of multicultural perspectives on racial inequality in education. Proponents of multicultural education such as Suzuki (1984) and Swartz (1988) link the current demands for multiculturalism to a more reformist policy discourse of cultural emancipation and social reconstruction.

Models of Cultural Emancipation and Social Reconstruction

Like proponents of curriculum and educational policies of cultural understanding and cultural competence, educators who promote the idea of cultural emancipation within the framework of multiculturalism attach a positive value to minority culture (Grant & Sleeter, 1989; Suzuki, 1984; Swartz, 1989). These educators argue that multiculturalism in education can promote the cultural emancipation and social amelioration of minority youth in two vital ways. First, proponents of emancipatory multiculturalism argue that the fostering of universal respect for the individual ethnic history, culture, and language of the plurality of students to be found in American schools would have a positive effect on individual minority self-concepts. Positive self-concepts should in turn help to boost achievement among minority youth (Bullivant, 1981b). This first set of claims therefore retraces some of the ground of the cultural deprivation theorists in that it is suggested that minority students do poorly in school because of their lack of self-esteem, among other things. But proponents of emancipatory multiculturalism add a new twist. They link the issue of minority underachievement in the classroom to the attitudinal prejudice of teachers and the suppression of minority culture in the school curriculum. These reformist educators then argue that a reversal in teacher attitudes and curriculum and instructional policies that suppress minority cultural identities would have a positive effect on minority school achievement. Individual minority school performance would improve, since such students would be motivated by a multicultural curriculum and classroom environment in which teachers and students treated minority culture and experiences with respect (Olneck, 1990). For example, Swartz (1988) insists that students who come from family backgrounds in which ethnic pride and identity are emphasized are likely to do well in school, or at least better than those who do not:

A curriculum which values diverse cultures in an equitable way is self-affirming. . . . It makes a statement to students about the importance of their present and future roles as participants and contributors to society. Research findings by Cummins (1986) and Ogbu (1978) point out that significant school failure does not occur in cultural groups that are positively oriented toward both their own and others' cultures. These students demonstrate a higher educational success rate. (P. 6)

The second conceptual strand of this emancipatory agenda is related to the first, but more directly links race relations in the classroom to the economy. Proponents of multicultural education as an emancipatory program suggest that improved academic achievement would help minority youth break the cycle of missed opportunity created by a previous biography of cultural deprivation. The labor market is expected to verify emancipatory multicultural programs by absorbing large numbers of qualified minority youth. This thesis of a "tightening bond" between multicultural education and the economy is summarized in the following claim by James Rushton (1981):

The curriculum in the multicultural school should encourage each pupil to succeed wherever he or she can and strive for competence in what he or she tries. Cultural taboos should be lessened by mutual experience and understandings. The curriculum in the multicultural school should allow these things to happen. If it does, it need have no fear about the future career of its pupils. (Rushton, 1981:169)

This emancipatory or "benevolent" type of approach to multicultural education (Gibson, 1984; Troyna & Williams, 1986) rests, in part, on an earlier curriculum philosophy of "social reconstructionism." Like earlier curriculum theorists such as Rugg (1932) and Counts (1932), proponents of the emancipatory approach to multiculturalism offer the powerful ideology of the "quiet revolution." They suggest that cultural and social changes in minority fortunes are possible if the school curriculum is redefined in response to the needs of minority youth (Grant & Sleeter, 1989; Troyna & Williams, 1986).

Ideological Core Assumptions. Proponents of emancipatory multiculturalism operate on some basic assumptions about the role of education in the reproduction and transformation of race relations. These assumptions can be summarized as follows: (1) There is a fundamental mismatch between the school curriculum and the life experiences and cultural backgrounds of American minority youth (Swartz, 1988). (2) This mismatch exists because schools privilege white middle-class values while simultaneously suppressing the culture of minority youth (Williams, 1982). (3) Thus, schools play a critical role in the production of differential educational opportunities and life chances for minority and majority youth. (4) Educators should help to redress this pattern of inequality by embarking upon multicultural curriculum reform that would provide equality of opportunity for academic success for minority students.

Desired Outcomes. A genuine multicultural curriculum that includes knowledge about minority history and cultural achievements would reduce the dissonance and alienation from academic success that centrally characterize minority experiences in schooling in the United States. Such a reformed school curriculum is expected to enhance minority opportunities for academic success and ensure better futures in the labor market. And, in keeping with this thesis, employers are expected to allocate jobs on the basis of market-rational criteria, namely, the credentials and academic qualifications of prospective employees (Bullivant, 1981b; Rushton, 1981).

Commentary. Proponents of an emancipatory approach to multicultural education offer a "language of possibility" (Giroux, 1985) with respect to the school curriculum—a language that is not present within earlier assimilationist frameworks. In an ideological sense, such a multicultural program allows for the possibility that the scope of current school knowledge would be "enlarged" to include the radical diversity of knowledge, histories, and experiences of marginalized ethnic groups. It is possible, for example, that radical ideas associated with minority quests for social change would also find their way into the discourse of the classroom (Olneck, 1990).

In addition, the powerfully attractive "social reconstructionist" theme running throughout the thesis of emancipatory multiculturalism raises the issue of inequality in the job market itself. Models of cultural understanding or cultural competence tend not to venture so far beyond the textbook, the classroom, and the school.

However, radical school theorists have, with good reason, criticized the tendency of these multicultural proponents to lean towards an unwarranted optimism about the impact of the multicultural curriculum on the social and economic futures of minority students (McLaren & Dantley, in press; Mullard, 1985; Troyna & Williams, 1986). Indeed, the linear connection asserted by multicultural education proponents between educational credentials and the economy is problematic. The assumption that higher educational attainment and achievement via a more sensitive curriculum would lead to a necessary conversion into jobs for black and minority youth is frustrated by the existence of racial practices in the job market itself. Troyna (1984) and Blackburn and Mann (1979), in their incisive analysis of the British job market, explode the myth that there is a necessary "tightening bond" between education and the economy. In his investigation of the fortunes of "educated" black and white youth in the job market, Troyna (1984) concludes that racial and social connections, rather than educational qualifications per se, "determined" the phenomenon of better job chances for white youth even when black youth had higher qualifications than their white counterparts. The tendency of employers to rely on informal channels or "word of mouth" networks and the greater likelihood that white youth would be in a position to exploit such networks constitute one of the principal ways in which the potential for success of qualified black youth in the labor market is systematically undermined. Of course, Carmichael and Hamilton (1967) and Marable (1983) have made similar arguments about the racial disqualification of black youth in the job market in the United States. Expanding this argument, Crichlow (1985) makes the following claim:

In combination with subtle forms of discrimination, job relocation, and increasing competition among workers for smaller numbers of "good jobs," rising entry level job requirements clearly underscore the present employment difficulties experienced by young black workers. Whether they possess a high school diploma or not, blacks, in this instance, continue to experience high rates of unemployment despite possessing sound education backgrounds and potential (capital) to be productive workers. (P. 6)

Besides the issues of naïveté about the racial character of the job market, further criticism can be made of the multicultural thesis. Proponents of multicultural education as an emancipatory formula tend to ignore the complex social and political relations that are constituted in the internal order of the schools. Issues of policy formation, decision making, trade-offs, and the building of alliances for specific reformist initiatives have not really been addressed within multicultural frameworks. For these reformist educators, educational change hinges almost exclusively upon the reorganization of the content of the school curriculum. But as Troyna and Williams (1986) have pointed out, attempts at the reorganization of the school curriculum to include more historically and culturally sensitive materials on minorities have not significantly affected the unequal relations that exist between blacks and whites in schools.

It is criticisms such as those advanced by Troyna and Williams that have seriously called into question the validity of liberal reformist claims about the emancipatory potential of multicultural education and its ability to positively influence minority futures in schools and society in the United States.

TOWARDS A CRITICAL EMANCIPATORY MULTICULTURALISM

Though there are significant differences in emphases in the three different types of multicultural policy discourses explored in this chapter, it is generally the case that proponents invest a shared optimism in attitudinal change models and their capacity to transform race relations in schooling. In my view, the multicultural models of cultural understanding, cultural competence, and cultural emancipation do not provide adequate theories or solutions to the problem of racial inequality in schooling. Within these models, school reform and reform in race relations depend almost exclusively on the reversals of values, attitudes, and human nature of social actors understood as "individuals." Schools, for example, are not conceptualized as sites of power or contestation in which differential resources and capacities determine maneuverability of competing racial groups and the possibility and pace of change. In significant ways, too, the proponents of multiculturalism fail to take into account the differential structure of opportunities that helps to define race relations in the United States. A case in point is the unwarranted optimism that theorists of the cultural emancipation model place in the potential of the multicultural curriculum to help boost minority school achievement and minority job chances in the labor market. As we saw, researchers such as Troyna (1984) and Crichlow (1985) challenge this kind of optimism by pointing to the racially established job ceiling operating in the labor market itself.

Besides this issue, it must be noted that multicultural proponents do not systematically pursue the very premise that set the multicultural project in education in motion in the first place: the interrogation of the discourse of the Eurocentric basis of the American school curriculum that links the United States to Europe and to "Western civilization." Indeed within the past few years, contemporary conservative educators such as Alan Bloom (1987), E. D. Hirsch (1987), and Diane Ravitch (1990) have sought to gain the upper hand in the debate over curriculum reform by reinvigorating the myth of Westernness and the role of Europe in the elaboration of American institutions and culture. No one puts this more directly than George Will (1989): "Our country is a branch of European civilization. . . . 'Eurocentricity' is right, in American curricula and consciousness, because it accords with the facts of our history, and we—and Europe are fortunate for that. The political and moral legacy of Europe has made the most happy and admirable of nations. Saying that may be indelicate, but it has the merit of being true and the truth should be the core of the curriculum" (p. 3).

In response to these frontal attacks on multicultural education, proponents have tended to propose models that emphasize the addition of "new" content about minority history to the school curriculum. But the multiculturalist strategy of adding diversity to the dominant school curriculum serves, paradoxically, to legitimate the dominant Western culture focus of educational arrangements in the United States. Multiculturalists have simply failed to provide a systematic critique of the ideology of "Westernness" that is ascendant in curriculum and pedagogical practices in education. Instead, proponents articulate a language of inclusion. But where does this multicultural strategy of inclusion leave us with respect to the question of race and the curriculum? How should we begin to rethink current approaches to the issue of race and curriculum organization? What are the elements of a new critical approach to multicultural education? Because of space limitations, I will only be able to draw the outlines of a critical approach to multiculturalism.

First, such a new approach must begin with a more systematic critique of the construction of school knowledge and the privileging of Eurocentrism and Westernness in the American school curriculum. The rather philistine assertions of Eurocentrism and Westernness on the part of conservative educators is itself a wish to run away from the labor of coming to terms with the fundamental historical currents that have shaped the United States—a wish to run away from the fundamentally "plural," immigrant, and the Afro–New World character that defines historical and current relations among minority and majority groups in the United States (Jordan, 1985, 1988). To claim a pristine, unambiguous Westernness as the basis of curriculum organization as Bloom, Hirsch, Ravitch, and others suggest is to repress to the dimmest parts of the unconscious a fundamental anxiety concerning the question of African-American and minority identities and "cultural presence" in what is distinctive about American life. The point I want to make here is similar to the one that Toni Morrison (1989) makes about Western literature in a recent essay: there is nothing intrinsically superior or even desirable about the list of cultural items and cultural figures celebrated by traditionalists like Hirsch and Bloom. It is to be remembered that at the end of the last century, the English cultural critic Matthew Arnold did not find it fit to include in "the best that has been thought and said" (Arnold, 1888, 1971; Czitrom, 1983) any existing American writer. This powerfully reminds us that what is "Western" is not synonymous with what is "American," no matter how hard some people may try. It also reminds us that the notion of Westernness is a powerful ideological construct—one thoroughly infused with ongoing struggle over meaning and values (Bernal, 1987). What is Western is therefore highly problematic, as June Jordan (1985) has argued. African-Americans were in the Americas for at least as long as whites; how is it that their history, writings, and culture are non-Western? Who is demarcating the West? Do we, for instance, want to say that Ernest Hemingway is in and Alice Walker is out? Where is the line of the Western to be drawn within the school curriculum? Where does Westernness end and where does Americanness begin? Multiculturalists have tended to counter the Western culture movement by insisting on "diversity" and cultural pluralism. But this approach leaves untouched the very premise of the interchangeability of the culture of the United States and Europe and the notion that there is an easy fit between white America, the West, and Europe. It is this easy fit that needs to be questioned.

This brings us to our second departure from the multicultural models discussed earlier: A critical approach to multiculturalism must not only insist on the cultural diversity of school knowledge but must insist on its inherent relationality. School knowledge is socially produced, deeply imbued by human interests, and deeply implicated in unequal social relations outside the school door. A critical multiculturalism should therefore be more reflexive with respect to the relationship between different social groups in the United States and the relationship of developments in the United States to the rest of the world. This would mean, for instance, that we begin to see the issue of racial inequality in global and relational terms—in the contest of what Terrence Hopkins and Immanuel Wallerstein (1980) and Andre Gunder Frank (1981) call world system theory. The links between America's development and the underdevelopment of the Third World and the links that African-Americans have had in terms of their intellectual and political engagement with the peoples of the Caribbean, Africa, and Asia must be emphasized. For example, the civil rights movement in the United States has had profound multiplier effects on the expansion of democratic practices to excluded groups in Australia, the Caribbean, Africa, England, and the United States itself (McCarthy, 1990). In a related sense too, a world systems approach would call attention to the fact that the development of "Western" industrialized countries is deeply bound up in the underdevelopment and the exploitation of the Third World. C.L.R. James (1963), for example, points out that in the 1770s, at the time when the French government was helping to bankroll the American Revolution, its West Indian colony in Haiti was generating two-thirds of France's overseas trade.

A third consideration is the status of the conceptualization of the race category within a multicultural paradigm. Current multicultural formulations tend to define racial identities in very static or essentialist terms. By this I mean that proponents tend to treat racial identities as a settled matter of cultural and linguistic traits. Minority groups are therefore defined as homogeneous entities. For example, as discussed earlier, Tiedt and Tiedt's (1986) fictional character Sue Wong is presented in their handbook for preservice teachers as a generic Chinese-American. She is defined by the presumed invariant characteristics of the group. A critical approach to multicultural education requires a far more nuanced discussion of racial identities of minority and majority groups than currently exists in the multicultural literature. This critical approach would call attention to the contradictory interests that inform minority social and political behavior and define minority encounters with majority whites in educational settings and in society. These discontinuities in the needs and interests of minority and majority groups are, for example, expressed in the long history of tension and hostility that have existed between the black and white working class in this country. Also of crucial importance within this framework are the issues of the "contradictory location" (Wright, 1978) of the "new" black middle class within the racial problematic and the role of neoconservative black and white intellectuals in redefining the terrain of contemporary discourse on racial inequality towards the ideal of a "color-blind" society (McCarthy, 1990). Just as important for a nonessentialist approach to race and curriculum is the fact that minority women and girls have radically different experiences of racial inequality than their male counterparts, because of the issue of gender. A nonessentialist approach to the discussion of racial identities allows for a more complex understanding of the educational and political behavior of minority groups.

As Michael Burawoy (1981) and Mokubong Nkomo (1984) make clear with respect to South Africa, economic divides that exist between the black underclass from the Bantustan and their more middle-class counterparts working for the South African State (police officers, nurses, etc.) often serve to undermine black unity in the struggle against apartheid. Similar examples exist in the United States, where some middle-class minority intellectuals have spoken out against affirmative action and minority scholarship programs in higher education, suggesting that such ameliorative policies discriminate against white males. A case in point is the recent ruling by the U.S. Department of Education's assistant secretary for civil rights, Michael Williams, that has made it illegal for a college or university to offer a scholarship only to minority students (Jaschik, 1980). The irony of this situation is underlined by the fact that the assistant secretary for civil rights is an African-American. The tragic fact is that without these scholarships, a number of very indigent minorities would not be able to pursue higher education. Here again, the "point man" on a policy that effectively undermines the material interests of African-Americans and other minority groups is a neoconservative member of the emergent minority middle class. The point that I want to make here is that you cannot read off the political behavior of minority groups based on assumptions about race pure and simple. Different class interests within minority groups often cut at right angles to racial politics. In a related sense, to predicate multicultural education on the basis of static definitions of what white people are like and what minorities are like can lead to costly miscalculations that can undermine the goal of race relations reform in education itself.

But a new approach to multicultural education must go much further than a critique of current definitions of racial identity. A critical approach to the fostering of multiculturalism must also seek to promote democratic initiatives in curriculum and pedagogical practices and social relations in schools. In this matter, certain facts have become painfully clear. There is now considerable documentation in both the mainstream and radical literature indicating stagnation and, in some cases, reversals in the educational fortunes of black, Hispanic, and Native American youth in the emerging decade of the 1990s (Gamoran and Berends, 1986; Grant, 1984, 1985; Sudarkasa, 1988). These studies also draw attention to some of the most pernicious ways in which current curriculum and pedagogical practices—not simply content—militate against minority success and alienate minority students from an academic core curriculum. For instance, studies show the following: that minority girls and boys are more likely than their white peers to be placed in low or nonacademic tracks (Fordham, 1988;

Grant, 1984); that teachers' encouragement and expectations of academic performance are considerably lower for black and Hispanic students than for white students (Ogbu & Matute-Bianchi, 1986); that black students have access to fewer instructional opportunities than white students (Gamoran and Berends, 1986); and that, ultimately, black, Hispanic and Native American youth are more likely to drop out of school than white youth (*Education Week* staff, 1986). These racial factors are complicated by dynamics of gender (black girls fare better academically than black boys but are more likely to be denied the academic and social status accorded to white girls and white boys in the classroom [Grant, 1984, 1985; Ogbu, 1978]) and dynamics of class (increasingly, black youth from professional middle-class backgrounds are abandoning predominantly black institutions and opting for white-dominated state colleges and Ivy League universities, thereby imperiling the autonomy and the survival of black institutions and raising disturbing questions about cultural identity [Marable, 1985]).

As we have seen, multicultural proponents have stressed attitudinal models of reform. In this manner, these proponents have tended to paste over the central contradictions associated with race and the curriculum, promoting instead a professional discourse of content addition. These approaches to curriculum and educational reform have consequently had the effect of stabilizing rather than challenging the modus operandi of schooling and the curriculum practices such as ability grouping and tracking—the principal mechanisms through which minorities are culturally excluded from an academic core curriculum and "prepared" for the secondary labor market. These practices of curriculum differentiation—the teaching of different types of curricula to different groups of students—also constitute the core processes or racial marginalization and subordination of minority students in the institutional culture of the school. In fundamental ways, then, mainstream educators and policy makers have failed to engage teachers and students in a sustained examination of the sociological and racial dimensions of current curriculum and pedagogical practices of tracking and ability grouping (Bastian et al., 1986). All students should have access to an academic core curriculum. The fact that disproportionate numbers of America's black, Hispanic, and Native American youth are now alienated from such a curriculum in the public schools is both intolerable and indefensible.

But the idea of a general academic core curriculum also poses direct political questions about the selective tradition in curriculum organization. As school populations become more ethnically diverse, and minorities become the numerical majorities in many school districts across the country, the moral and practical support for the hegemony of Eurocentrism in the curriculum has been imperiled (Schmidt, 1989). The hegemonic truce that has existed over the years between school authorities and the rapidly diversifying constituencies they serve has become frayed. Minority youth and women have begun to offer a more systematic challenge to the existing structure of school knowledge and the assumptions and practices that undergird the curricula of colleges and universities in the United States. Questions are being raised about "traditional dichotomies such as the division between the hard 'masculine' subjects like mathematics and the sciences, and the soft 'feminine' art subjects" (Sarupt, 1984:17). Minority students are once again mounting "new" demands for democratization and diversity in the curriculum and course offerings of dominant educational institutions across the country. It is at this point of rupture within the dominant curriculum paradigm that more radical demands for critical anti-racist and anti-sexist curriculum materials and pedagogical practices can be introduced. As school critics such as Connell (1987) and Sarupt (1984) have argued, the school curriculum for minority and majority youth should have an organic link to other experiences and struggles within the society, with respect to such issues as the loss of infrastructural supports and jobs in minority communities in the inner cities. Such a new critical approach to the multicultural curriculum would also "celebrate the contributions of working people, women, and minorities to our general cultural pool" and would be the point of departure "for providing students with their own cultural capital" (Wood, 1985:107). By insisting on the introduction into the school curriculum of radically diverse cultural knowledge(s) rooted in the social basis and experiences of oppressed groups, we can move beyond the "benign pluralism and cultural relativism of mainstream programs as embodied in certain innocuous forms of multicultural education. For as Abdul JanMohamed and David Lloyd (1987) argue, "Such pluralism tolerates the existence of salsa, it even enjoys Mexican restaurants, but it bans Spanish as a medium of instruction in American schools" (p. 10).

But merely moving beyond simplistic models of cultural relativism is not enough to "invert the hegemony" (Connell, 1987:15) of Eurocentrism in the curriculum. We must go further than the compensatory strategy of simply adding diverse cultural knowledge onto the dominant curriculum. A critical approach to the transformation of school knowledge requires a second strategy, one aimed at promoting difference and heterogeneity as what Bob Connell (1987) calls a program of "common learnings." Such a strategy aims at reconstructing the dominant curriculum—which we now know legitimates the experiences and practices of the white middle class—by bringing the uninstitutionalized experiences of marginalized minorities and working class women and men to the center of the organization and arrangement of the school curriculum. The ultimate objective of a "common learnings" educational strategy is to seek the generalized diffusion throughout the whole system of schooling of counterhegemonic knowledge based on the experiences and perspectives of the disadvantaged. Connell argues for such a proactive and generative approach to "universalizing" the heterogeneous experiences of oppressed groups in the curriculum.

Connell's argument rests on two important principles. First, he suggests that a political and ethical principle of positive social justice should inform the selection of knowledge in the school curriculum. In advancing the notion of an expanded approach to educational and social justice, Connell also suggests that a "new" critical curriculum should privilege the human interests of the least advantaged. Second, he maintains that the racial transformation of the school curriculum should be based on the epistemological principles that affirm the validity of the points of view of marginalized minorities and working class men and women. It is useful to quote him in some detail here:

In principle there are many possible common learnings programs, though in a particular historical setting only a few are likely to be of great practical importance. A minimal criterion for choice among them, and a minimal defense of the strategy of inverting hegemony, is the criterion of social justice. We can accept with Rawls that social justice means taking the standpoint of the least advantaged, though we can do without his fantasy that this might occur in ignorance of one's social position. . . . But this is only a minimal defense. There are stronger reasons for seeking an educational program constructed in this way. Different standpoints yield different views of the world and some are more comprehensive and powerful than others. . . . If you wish to teach about ethnicity and race relations, for instance, a more comprehensive and deeper understanding is possible if you construct your curriculum from the point of view of the subordinated ethnic groups than if you work from the point of view of the dominant one. "Racism" is a qualitatively better organizing concept than "natural inferiority," though each has its roots in a particular experience and embodies a social interest. [Another] case is provided by the growth of knowledge about gender. There has long been a body of information and discourse about the family, women's employment, children's social development, masculinity and femininity, which remained for decades a backwater in social sciences hegemonized by the interests of men. The standpoint of the least advantaged in gender relations, articulated in feminism, has transformed that. Modern feminism has produced a qualitatively better analysis of a large domain of social life through a range of new concepts (sexual politics, patriarchy, the sexual division of labor, etc.) and new research informed by them. The implications of this conceptual revolution are still to be felt across much of the curriculum. (Connell, 1987:16–18)

Connell's arguments for reconstructing the curriculum from the standpoint of those "carrying the burdens of social inequality" (p. 17) are well founded. It is true that "the marginalized or the oppressed are the only ones who can understand the full significance of oppression" (Edgerton, 1989:3). A critical multicultural curriculum, which emphasizes anti-racist and anti-sexist change and social reorganization and utilizes the points of view and experiences of oppressed minorities and working class women and men as the primary bases for a core curriculum, would constitute a fundamental step in the direction of preparing students for democratic participation in a complex and differential world. Of course, we must be ever mindful of the dangers that Freire pointed us to in his volume *Pedagogy of the Oppressed*—that is, the oppressed "are at one and the same time themselves and the oppressor whose consciousness they have internalized" (1970:32). There are no simple guarantees in political or educational life, and critical multicultural educators must avoid the tendency to reify the oppressed through an activism shrouded in "monologues, slogans, and communiques" (p. 52). Multicultural changes in the curriculum to address the present and the future of race relations in the United States must therefore be founded in dialogue among subordinated groups and in the recognition that knowledge is socially produced and is systematically relational and heterogeneous.

CONCLUSION

In this chapter, I explored the conceptual and practical claims of three approaches or discourses of multicultural education. I described these approaches as "models" of cultural understanding, cultural competence, and cultural emancipation. As we saw, each of these approaches represent a subtly different inflection on the issue of what is to be done about racial inequality in schooling. Thus, proponents of cultural understanding advocate sensitivity training and appreciation of cultural differences—a model for racial harmony. Cultural competence proponents insist on the preservation of minority ethnic identity and language and "the building of bridges" between minority and mainstream culture. Finally, models of cultural emancipation go somewhat further than the previous two approaches in suggesting that reformist multicultural curriculum can boost the school success and economic futures of minority youth. As I tried to show, these approaches are predicated on attitudinal change models that place a great emphasis on transforming white intolerance and boosting the self-concepts of minority group members. Proponents of these traditional models do not contest the underlying rules of the game of American society or its existing structures of exploitation and oppression. Finally, I made the case for an alternative approach, what I called a critical multiculturalism, that links the microdynamics of the school curriculum to larger issues of social relations outside the school. It is my view that a critical approach to multicultural education must involve a radical rethinking of curriculum and pedagogical practices in schooling in ways that begin to take seriously the heterogeneous populations now present in urban school systems and in higher education in the United States.

NOTES

1. The 1960s represented a period in which minority challenges to inequality in American society focused centrally on educational opportunity as well as the very

construction of what was good knowledge in the school curriculum. When school critics influenced by Latino and African-American organizations such as SNCC (the Student Non-violent Coordinating Committee) began to draw attention to the racial exclusion of minority history from the textbooks used in schools, a whole new avenue of curriculum and pedagogical critique opened up—one that called attention to the way in which the organization of the school curriculum reproduced inequality in society by delegitimating the culture, history, and language of minority groups. Minority school critics maintained that existing curriculum and pedagogical practices helped to foster a highly racially selective tradition that valorized white, middle-class values. These critics therefore sought to emphasize the way in which U.S. schooling itself constituted a racial order. It is in this sense that I am contending that debates over the organization of schooling were "racialized."

2. By "claw back," I am referring to the way in which proponents of multiculturalism tend to articulate the negotiated central concerns and values in society— the values of possessive individualism, occupational mobility, and status attainment—leaving completely untouched the very structural organization of capitalism in the United States. Within this framework, the emancipation of the minority individual is fulfilled when he becomes a good capitalist. It is the nonthreatening social centrality of "the good bourgeois life" for minorities that the multiculturalist ultimately seeks to promote.

3. For a fuller discussion of the historical emergence of white ethnic immigrant groups in the United States, see Joel Perlman's *Ethnic Differences* (1989).

4. See Louisiana State University's *1988–1989 General Catalog* (1988).

3

Multicultural and Anti-Racist Teacher Education: A Comparison of Canadian and British Experiences in the 1970s and 1980s

Jon Young

Since the publication of the National Indian Brotherhood's policy paper *Indian Control of Indian Education* (1973) in the early 1970s and the initial work of the Toronto Board of Education's Work Group on Multicultural Programs, questions of race/racism, ethnicity, and culture have occupied a central place in the Canadian discourse on schooling and (in)equality. The last two decades have witnessed an ongoing struggle by some to name and contest the sources of inequality built into Canadian school systems and to prescribe and effect changes within these systems. This struggle has seen a debate couched in an evolving language of various versions of multicultural education, anti-racist education, and sovereignty and self-determination in education and a plethora of initiatives designed to reform or transform the existing school systems.

In all these debates, the central role of teachers in the construction of school experiences and the production of school outcomes is clearly recognized. Despite this, faculties of education have contributed little to this struggle and have received little attention in the multicultural or anti-racist education literature in Canada. While some faculty members have taken part in the critique of school practices (and have built academic careers theorizing about such practices) our own worksites and practices have been virtually ignored and left beyond critique. Only twelve citations directly related to "multicultural teacher education" appear in *The Canadian Index of Journals in Education* for the last ten years, and there are none related to "anti-racist teacher education." Of the twelve articles cited, only two were more than six pages in length, only two appeared in "scholarly journals," most were written by white educators, and none reported on any substantial Canadian research.

In this chapter, in order to begin the examination of the role of faculty members and faculties of education in the transformation or reproduction of inequalities in education and public schooling, attention will be given to two sources where, it is argued, there is a relevant and developing body of literature: teacher preparation in Britain, and First Nations, or Native, teacher education in Canada. This literature will be used both to critique the lack of activity within education faculties in Canada and to discuss the dismantling of racist structures within those faculties.

THE CONTEXT OF INITIAL TEACHER TRAINING IN BRITAIN

Initial teacher education in Britain generally takes place in either university departments or schools of education, polytechnics, or colleges of higher education, and consists of either a three- or four-year bachelor of education degree or a one-year after-degree Post Graduate Certificate in Education (PGCE).[1]

Over the last two decades teacher training has undergone considerable restructuring. Early in the 1970s, 180 public sector institutions and 27 universities produced 40,000 teachers a year. By 1983 this had shrunk to 56 public sector institutions and 27 universities admitting fewer than 16,000 students a year. The small "monotechnic" college of the early 1970s had virtually disappeared, either closed, amalgamated, or merged with polytechnics, and most institutions had expanded their programs to include other vocational training and vocational degree courses (Department of Education and Science, 1987:7). Thus, at the same time that teacher training institutions were being asked to substantially review their programs in the face of changing societal needs, they were themselves undergoing a radical restructuring in the face of financial cutbacks and declining enrollments. A consequence of these changes, Craft (1981) suggests, has been an institutional environment highly inconducive to the scope of change called for and a system characterized by low morale among faculty; fewer appointments; the closure of many urban colleges, affecting the number of sites available for practical work; and an increasing proportion of initial teacher training taking place via the least flexible option, the one-year PGCE.

THE PROVISION OF MULTICULTURAL EDUCATION IN INITIAL TEACHER TRAINING IN BRITAIN

Over the last decade there have been a number of attempts to assess the extent to which teacher training institutions in Britain have developed courses and programs that address in some way the realities of teaching in a multicultural and multiracial society. Following on early surveys by the National Committee for Commonwealth Immigrants (NCCI) in the 1960s

Table 1
Multicultural Education Courses and Elements in
British Teacher Training Institutions

		Institutions with					
	N	*Compulsory Courses*	*Optional Courses*	*Total*	*Compulsory Elements*	*Optional Elements*	*Total*
Colleges and Institutes	64	4	10	14	--	--	17
Polytechnics	31	5	9	9	--	--	
Universities	52	1	3	4	6	3	9

Source: Adapted from Cherrington and Giles (1981), pp. 76–78.

and Her Majesty's Inspectors in the 1960s and 1970s (reported in Ambrose, 1981), the first national survey of initial teacher training in Britain's colleges of higher education, polytechnics, and universities was carried out in 1979 (Cherrington & Giles, 1981). This survey was followed by other surveys in 1980–1981 (Watson, 1984) and 1985–1986 (Watson and Roberts, 1988).

Attempting to provide some baseline data for charting the development of multicultural teacher education in Britain, the Commission for Racial Equality commissioned a survey of all initial teacher training institutions (some 147 institutions). The survey was carried out in 1979.[2] Reporting on this study, Cherrington and Giles (1981) found that 14 colleges and institutes of education, 9 polytechnics, and 4 universities reported having a total of 48 courses on multicultural education, 9 of which were compulsory. In addition, 17 colleges and institutes identified a total of 46 different courses that contained "elements related to multicultural education," and 9 universities identified 13 courses that contained similar elements (pp. 76–78). (See Table 1.)

Offering a somewhat more positive commentary on the Cherrington and Giles data than is suggested in Table 1, Craft (1981) suggests that "getting on for half of the 64 colleges, two-thirds of the 31 polytechnics and one-third of the 53 universities approached offered *something* in a multicultural field" (p. 12) (italics added).[3] If this interpretation is accepted, it would indicate that in over half of Britain's teacher training institutions, no specific attention to multicultural education could be identified in 1979, with universities being the least responsive.

Reporting on a similar survey conducted in 1980–1981, Watson (1984) described the situation regarding the preparation of teachers for work in a multicultural society as "at best an unsatisfactory picture . . . and at worst an ostrich like lack of interest" (p. 385). Most courses or elements related to multicultural education were restricted to institutions located within urban centers with substantial black populations, overwhelmingly optional, and "frequently came towards the end of the period of training and, thus, attract only those who are already psychologically committed or interested" (p. 397).

Commenting on the state of British multicultural teacher education in 1984, Lynch (1986) offered the following assessment:

What is know is that by 1984 few institutions of teacher education had undertaken a systematic reappraisal and revision of their epistemological and organizational Aufbau, to make them more congruent with the norms and values deriving from an ethic appropriate to a multicultural and multiracial society, let alone altered the "economic" and power-political make-up to wider policies expressive of those values. What little action had been taken in teacher education by that time was at first additive, often folkloric, and optional to the mainstream epistemology of the curriculum. More recently the commitment to multicultural teacher education was dissipated, sometimes to the point of invisibility, by means of a so-called "permeation" curricular approach. . . . Teacher education could not escape a strong impression of tissue-rejection, and evasion strategies of innovation in response to the need and demand for fundamental change. (P. 150)

Of considerable importance in informing the public debate around multicultural education in Britain was the work of the Committee of Inquiry into the Education of Children from Ethnic Minority Groups (the Rampton/Swann Commission), whose final report, *Education for All*, published in 1985, was highly critical of existing teacher education programs. During the 1985–1986 academic year a further study was conducted (Watson & Roberts, 1988) to investigate the extent to which the recommendations of this report had impacted upon teacher education institutions, and to look at the changes that had occurred since their previous study five years earlier (Watson, 1984). The study sent questionnaires out to all 105 teacher training institutions in Britain and received responses from 73 of them. These responses indicated that all but 4 included multicultural education as a compulsory element within their programs and that the majority of institutions provided their students with over ten hours of multicultural experience. (See Tables 2 and 3.) Of the 73 institutions responding, 43 indicated that they offered optional courses in multicultural education, and 17 institutions stated that their courses were permeated to a great extent with multiculturalism. This finding, the authors suggest, indicates that:

somewhere around 20 percent of institutions are fully committed to multicultural education and are positively following the recommendations of the Swann and Rampton reports regarding permeation of courses. On the other hand, there is a significant number of institutions whose students' experience of multicultural education is limited to a few hours during the period of their course. (P. 350)

Table 2
**Location of Multicultural Education within the Core
of British Initial Teacher Programs**

Area	Universities	Polytechnics	Colleges	Total
Educational studies	14	7	13	34
Name section in core	8	2	6	16
Method (subject)				
Course	1	0	1	2
Permeation	2	3	9	14
Not identified	1	1	1	3
	26	13	30	69

Source: Watson and Roberts (1988), p. 344.

Table 3
Hours of Multicultural Education in Initial Training Courses

Hours	Universities	Polytechnics	Colleges	Total
0	3	0	0	3
5–10	6	1	2	9
10–20	12	3	6	21
Over 20	6	6	22	34
Unassessed	1	5	0	6

Source: Watson and Roberts (1988), p. 345.

THE SUBSTANCE OF MULTICULTURAL TEACHER EDUCATION IN BRITAIN

The preceding data, attempting to provide some approximate measure of the amount of attention given to matters of race/racism, ethnicity, culture, and schooling in British teacher training institutions, offer little insight into the substance of that attention: a topic of considerable importance, given the confused and contested nature of "the interminable debate" (Modgil, Verma, Mallick, & Modgil, 1986) in Britain (and elsewhere) between proponents of alternative versions of multicultural education and between proponents of anti-racist education (ARTEN, 1988; Brandt, 1986; Cole, 1989; Sarupt, 1984).

Cherrington and Giles (1981), in their survey of British teacher training
institutions at the end of the 1970s, described the approach taken to multicultural teacher education—where it occurred at all—as a "purely prob-
lem-oriented, subject based approach" (p. 83).

Without exception, they concluded, the terms "multicultural" and "multiethnic" education

were employed to develop approaches equalizing educational opportunities for
children presumed to be disadvantaged because of cultural and/or linguistic
differences; or for teaching about the culture of ethnic minority groups, either to
members of those groups in order to improve self-image, or to other groups and to
the wider populations in order to create cultural awareness and to improve race
relations. (P. 81)

Furthermore, "in the relatively few teaching training institutions which
have responded to the challenge of multicultural classrooms by offering
specialist courses, most titles suggest that the 'problem' lies with the school
children, rather than the severely limited capacity or willingness of either
the school or most teachers to respond to a new situation" (p. 82). In a
similar vein, Watson (1984) concluded from his survey:

Most teacher education in the United Kingdom is essentially ethnocentric and very
practical. "Specialists" are expected to deal with multiracial/cultural aspects of
education which, in any case, are not considered essential for all students. The idea
of multiculturalism "permeating the whole of the curriculum" as advocated by the
Rampton Report and The Commission for Racial Equality, is virtually unheard of.
(P. 398)

The first half of the 1980s saw considerable pressure exerted from a
variety of sources, including Her Majesty's Inspectors, the Council for
Accreditation of Teacher Education, as well as the Rampton and Swann
Reports (DES, 1981; DES, 1985), upon teacher training institutions to radically improve their programs in the light of the multiracial nature of British
society and British schools. That this pressure resulted in some increased
attention has already been noted in findings of Watson's 1985 Survey
(Watson & Roberts, 1988). Without suggesting that developments were
even across the country, Watson reported that virtually all institutions (96
percent) reported specific changes over the previous five years in their
provision of multicultural teacher education. These changes included:

- The introduction of new courses
- The change from an optional element to a compulsory one
- The appointment of personnel with specific responsibility for multicultural
  education
- The movement towards a more anti-racist stance

- The appointment of honorary research fellows
- The placement of students in multiracial schools
- The appointment of external evaluators to monitor multicultural programs
- The improvement of links with external bodies such as the Commission for Racial Equity
- Increases in the extent of permeation
- The setting up of working parties with the aim of improving staff awareness and encouraging staff development
- The establishing of support services to work with departments to implement multicultural practices

Providing a framework for evaluating the scope of these developments, Lynch (1986) suggests a seven-stage typology for multicultural teacher education moving from ethnocentric captivity through curriculum-centered multiculturalism and institutional multiculturalism to systemic multiculturalism. (See Table 4.) With few exceptions, he would suggest that British initiatives have not extended beyond curriculum-centered multiculturalism.

PRESCRIPTIONS FOR MULTICULTURAL AND ANTI-RACIST TEACHER EDUCATION IN BRITAIN

Multicultural Teacher Education

Critiquing the efforts of most British teacher education institutions to date for being narrowly curricular in their focus and "resting on the dubious assumption that staff [most of whom derive their cultural biography from an Anglocentric socialization of many years duration and manifest efficiency (p. 154)] have the cultural and intellectual, social and moral prerequisites already [to prepare teachers for a multiracial and multicultural society] and that structures, procedures, and governance are not on the agenda" (p. 154), Lynch (1986) goes on to lay out a preliminary agenda for the development of institutional and systemic forms of multicultural teacher education.

Discussing six essential dimensions, which he labels cultural/contextual, moral/affective, cognitive, pedagogical performance, consequential, and experiential, Lynch outlines elements of each in relation to individuals, institutions, and educational systems. Contextually, he argues, an indispensable element of a truly multicultural teacher education system is a heterogeneous staff and student body accompanied by direct and potent representation from ethnic minority communities at all levels of decision making. His moral dimension requires that teacher training institutions formulate "norm-encouraging" policy statements that articulate a commitment to "the ethics of multicultural education" and develop activities that

Table 4
A Typology of Multicultural Teacher Education

Stage VII	Systemic Multiculturalism	Norms and values of system and all components attuned to core ethic of multicultural education
Stage VI	Total Institutional Multiculturalism	All variables and factors in total environment permeated by multicultural ethos
Stage V	Institutional Multiculturalism	For example, multiethnic staff, student bodies, involvement in governance
Stage IV	Holistic Policy Multiculturalism	For example, policy formation at system and institutional level
Stage III	Curricular Multiculturalism	For example, new programs
Stage II	Ad Hoc Multiculturalism	For example, isolated initiatives (mainly addressing cognitive gains)
Stage I	Ethnocentric Captivity	For example, predominantly monist culture, epistemology, structure, including staff, students, evaluations, and few if any links with ethnic minorities

Source: Lynch (1986), p. 162.

allow staff and students to examine and, where appropriate, change their race, class, and sex values. Cognitively relevant components of a multicultural teacher education program that Lynch identifies include:

a knowledge of the micro-cultures of society, of ethnic minorities and their cultures, alertness to bias, ethnocentrism, stereotyping, prejudice and racism, and their educational, social and economic impact, an understanding of race relations and the impact of nationality legislation; a knowledge of the pedagogical implications of work on prejudice acquisition and reduction, cognitive styles of research on field dependence and independence, and vocational guidance; an awareness of the issues associated with testing, assessment and examinations in a multicultural society, of educability and achievement as social constructs deriving from specific cultural assumptions; the implications of cultural diversity for curriculum and teaching methods of schools; the availability of materials to support the multicultural curriculum and of criteria to evaluate them for their fidelity to that concept. (Lynch, 1986:156)

Combining the categories of pedagogical performance and consequential needs, Lynch argues for the outcomes of multicultural teacher education to be demonstrable in professional action that would include a broad intercultural competence, teaching methods and practices that would manifestly value diversity and challenge racism and prejudice, the critical evaluation of curriculum materials for their compatibility with the goals of multicultural education, the expansion of the cultural criteria used for assessment, and the ability to critically reflect upon one's own practices. Finally, he argues for the importance to both staff and students of the regular experience of working within a variety of multiracial and supplementary school settings.

Anti-Racist Teacher Education

Within the British educational debate, considerable attention has been given to separating anti-racist education from multicultural education (Sarupt, 1984; Cole, 1989; Troyna, 1987) as well as other efforts to synthesize the two perspectives. Rejecting the notion that the marginalization of black people and culture in Britain is "an error of history [rather than] a product of power relations" (Brandt, 1986:128), anti-racist education starts from the premise that society is institutionally racist and that "there exists a complex 'race'/sex class hierarchy located within an exploitative male power structure and that part of the role of education in *all* educational institutions is to attempt to dismantle that structure both through the hidden curriculum and the active curriculum" (Cole, 1989:149). Theoretically, this requires that the discourse of racism be located within a broader framework of the political, social, and historical production of inequality. Mullard (in Brandt, 1986) makes this point in maintaining that

no understanding of racism in society or in its social institutions, such as education, can be attained without employing a theoretical framework which explicitly and structurally recognizes and accounts for the connections between the oppressions, exploitations, and inequalities associated with the notions of race, class and gender. But to state that should be so is, of course, a lot easier and quite different from explaining how it is the case. (P. viii)

The development of this framework, anti-racists agree, has to be informed by black formulations based upon black experiences of racism. Politically, anti-racist education requires that dismantling racism within white society is the priority and it therefore values collective action that forges links across and outside the school system as the appropriate strategy for achieving this end; racist practices are to be dismantled not through individual conversion but by reconstructed power relations that carry with them sanctions and disciplinary action against racist practices (Cole, 1989:150).

In this political struggle, the significance of those institutions that regulate entry into teaching cannot but command critical attention. Active in taking these concerns up within "the closed world of teacher education" in Britain has been the Anti-Racist Teacher Education Network (ARTEN) established in 1984 to "assist in the implementation, monitoring and evaluating of anti-racist strategies at all levels of teacher education, and to seek the support of people in institutions of teacher education and the communities for this purpose" (ARTEN, 1986:1). In a series of occasional papers reporting on national seminars, the network begins the task of articulating and developing an anti-racist critique of, and agenda for, teacher preparation in Britain.

Central to this critique is the virtual exclusion of a black voice within national and local governance of teacher education. The network's second occasional paper notes: "The national Advisory Body of Public Sector Higher Education and the Council for the Accreditation of Teacher Education reflect a white social, intellectual and professional monopoly and the Department of Education and Science has proved as yet impervious to suggestions that appointments to them should reflect the multiethnic nature of British society" (ARTEN, 1986:22).

Further, at the local level it concluded that things were little different and that "while a small number [of institutions] have black representation and consult regularly with black communities, many have still to make the anti-discriminatory, equal opportunities commitment" (p. 23). Consistent with Cole's (1989) assertion that "it is absolutely essential . . . that all institutions draw up and implement an anti-racist policy" and Brandt's (1986) imperative that anti-racist education be enshrined within a legal system that includes critical appraisal, the third ARTEN occasional paper devotes its attention to the development of anti-racist policies for teacher education institutions.

A second central tenet of the anti-racist agenda in teacher training has been the recruitment of black teachers and teacher trainers into a school system within which traditionally the recruitment of a virtually exclusively white workforce has served to perpetuate white interests and authority and black subordination. Evidence to date suggests not only that few black staff are being recruited into teacher training institutions, but also that without changing existing hiring criteria and practices in teacher training as well as challenging the racism that black teachers experience within the career structure of the larger school system, efforts to change this situation will meet with little success. While ARTEN calls for the establishment of more appropriate selection criteria that facilitate the hiring of black teachers who have demonstrated a proven ability to motivate, communicate with, and relate education to a wide range of students (ARTEN, 1986:53), it also recognizes the need for a number of short-term strategies to bring black educators into current teacher training as paid resources. In advocating this role (as paid consultants and not free advisors), ARTEN acknowledges the potential for abuse if this approach is used as a substitute for institutional change and the hiring of black staff (ARTEN, 1986:52).

Within the formal curriculum of teacher preparation programs the anti-racist agenda requires that *all* students come to understand racism as a structural phenomenon and to recognize the forms of inequality of educational opportunity that confront black children, both in its historical and contemporary dimensions. Furthermore, students should be required and helped to question their own racism, recognize the need to challenge school practices that sustain inequality, and develop the skills to build on the range of experiences that their students bring to the classroom (ARTEN, 1988:12–13). While advocating that such requirements be articulated through an institutional code of practice, anti-racist educators are critical of the concept of "permeation" that sees "issues" of racism introduced across the curriculum. Such an approach within the current structures of teacher education, they argue, is likely to constitute a theoretical and token treatment that "holds anti-racism hostage to the limited levels of awareness and commitment of most staff members" (ARTEN, 1988:5).

"School experience" or "teaching practice" is a part of initial teacher preparation widely viewed by students as the most useful part of their programs, yet it is an activity that is currently more likely to be driven by the pragmatics of finding willing sites for students than by the quality of the school experience and the existence of well-developed anti-racist practices within the school. Such a situation may not only provide an inappropriate socializing experience for students but also present serious problems for those who have committed themselves to anti-racist principles. For student teaching to be consistent with anti-racist ideals, ARTEN (1988:46) suggests, requires an essentially new working relationship between teacher training institutes, the school, and local authorities. This relationship would include a clear statement that issues of race, class, and gender are major concerns of all school experiences; that the teaching/learning model for the student be interactive, reflective, and critical; and that clearly defined assessment procedures be developed that would include an element of self-assessment.

THE PROVISION OF MULTICULTURAL EDUCATION IN INITIAL TEACHER EDUCATION IN CANADA

The picture developed so far in this chapter of the development of multicultural and anti-racist teacher education in Britain during the 1980s might be characterized by substantial external pressure for change, a considerable amount of descriptive and prescriptive literature devoted to the issue, heated debate between advocates of multicultural and anti-racist education, and measurable change, albeit it often piecemeal and curriculum focused. While teacher training institutions (especially those housed in universities) have generally shown themselves to be resistant to change, they have not been immobile, and individual institutions would appear to have initiated substantial changes. The picture in Canada would appear quite different,[4] and while the call for multicultural (and, to a much lesser degree, more recently anti-racist) education has been sustained within the school system, its entrance into faculties of education and into a debate around the training of teachers has been conspicuous only in its absence.

Consistent with the neglect that has been afforded the issue of multicultural teacher education in Canada is the lack of any comprehensive description of the extent of program offerings across the country. The only national survey that parallels those conducted in Britain was carried out by Masemann and Mock in 1985, but it suffers from a disappointingly low response rate (63 percent). The development over the last thirty years by faculties of education across Canada of a number of special First Nations/Native teacher education programs designed to improve the education provided to First Nations children and to increase the number of First Nations members trained as teachers constitutes the most concrete and important response to Canadian cultural diversity and racism, and is more fully documented (Allison, 1983; More, 1980). These sources, combined with a cursory examination of faculty of education calendars across the country (Henley & Young, 1987), provide the fragmentary evidence on which the following description is based.

Within the preservice curriculum of Canadian faculties of education, specific attention to issues of race/racism, ethnicity, and culture have been afforded varying degrees of attention both in terms of how, when, and to whom it is presented, in part mirroring approaches already described in relation to British institutions and in part reflecting a uniquely Canadian context. Different approaches include the integration of materials into foundations courses; the provision of elective and/or required courses such as multicultural, cross-cultural, and intercultural education, or more focused courses addressing particular aspects of Canadian diversity or particular ethnic groups; the integration of material into methodology courses and field experience; the provision of minor or major areas of specialization in either the education of specific minority groups or in various general dimensions of minority education; and the availability of special preservice (First Nations) programs.

An examination of Canadian university calendars, supported by the findings of the Masemann and Mock survey (1986), suggests the following generalizations. First, the most common response in Canadian faculties of education is to include some material in foundations courses and to offer one or two elective courses that relate generally to issues of ethnic, cultural, and racial diversity in Canada, such as Teaching English as a Second Language or Native Education. Masemann and Mock concluded: "the most notable finding is the prevalence of elective courses and the dearth of compulsory courses. In only two provinces are there any compulsory courses. Moreover, many courses offered are half courses or units" (Masemann & Mock, 1986:4). Second, a few universities have developed a considerable number of electives that address issues of diversity. They have also developed more specialized courses dealing with either specific ethnic groups (for which aboriginal peoples provide the most common but not exclusive focus) or issues of diversity viewed from a particular orientation, for example, the Education of Selected Minority Groups in Western Canada: A Historical Study (University of Alberta). Third, very few faculties have developed small undergraduate programs around multiethnic/multicultural/intercultural education. An example of this initiative would be the University of Calgary's bachelor of education program in intercultural education, which includes academic courses in anthropology, sociology, and/or linguistics, a minor in Intercultural Education, teaching practice in a cross-cultural setting, and a full course in a special interest area such as English as a Second Language, Native Studies, and Latin America or Far Eastern Studies. Finally, a considerable number of First Nations/Native Indian teacher education programs provide another significant response to ethnic diversity, a response that Allison (1983) provocatively argues is distinguished primarily by issues of access rather than issues of curriculum content. While students in most programs may pursue courses related to specific cultural agendas, the primary rationale for such programs tends to be focused upon graduating more First Nations teachers.

The variety of different approaches that can be documented within Canadian faculties of education should not be mistaken as an indication of any widespread recognition of the importance of culture and race/racism to the task of preparing Canadian teachers. On the contrary, it is questionable whether the majority of faculties of education could justify a location other than that of ethnocentric captivity within Lynch's typology or whether any could claim any developments beyond that of curriculum multiculturalism. Furthermore, it would seem that the late 1980s and beginnings of the 1990s have witnessed a stagnation in the pursuit of this kind of reform in Canadian teacher education (Allison, 1983; Henley & Young, 1990). Masemann and Mock (1986) concluded their recent survey of Canadian faculties of education with the following assessment:

While several key institutions have some well developed programs in multicultural teacher education in place, generally speaking there is a lack of well entrenched programs across the country. It is quite possible for students in several provinces never to encounter the concepts of muticulturalism at all in their teaching training. It is possible for almost all teachers in training in Canada to avoid taking an elective course in multiculturalism. . . . The most significant finding of this first phase of the study is how little multicultural teacher education really exists in Canada. (P. 9)

FIRST NATIONS/NATIVE TEACHER EDUCATION PROGRAMS IN CANADA

For advocates of multicultural teacher education in both Britain and Canada, the increased representation of marginalized groups within the teaching professional has become an important concern; for anti-racist it is a sine qua non. While some steps have been taken in Britain by way of access courses for ethnic minority students (DES, 1985:644–45), substantial steps have been taken in Canada, primarily by way of special programs, to increase the representation of Indian, Inuit, and Métis people within the Canadian teaching force. Because of the unique legal position of status Indians within Canadian society and the complex bureaucracy that has been established to administer their relationships with the Canadian state, group-specific data have long been available to document their conspicuous absence from the teaching force. More (1980:32), for example, noted that in 1974 in British Columbia there were some 26 Native Indian teachers in a teaching force of 26,000, whereas if they were represented in proportion to their presence within the British Columbia population as a whole, there should have been around 1,300!

Currently there exist some twenty special First Nations/Native/Indian Teacher Education Programs across the country. These programs have without doubt had a significant effect over the last two decades in reducing, but by no means eliminating, the underrepresentation of First Nations/Native teachers within federal and band-controlled schools. (According to the Education Directorate of the Department of Indian and Inuit Affairs, in the school year 1982–1983 in federal and band-operated schools, there was a total of 2,216 teachers, of whom 684 were Native and 1,532 were non-Native, teaching 37,727 students.) Within the provincial school systems (where some 50 percent of Native children are educated along with 95 percent of non-Native students), this advance would appear to have been significantly more slow and difficult (Saskatchewan Human Rights Commission, 1985; Winnipeg School Division, 1989).

More (1980) suggests that despite the unique characteristics of each program, it is possible to group them into three broad types: *orientation and support programs* that provide on-campus preparation and ongoing counselling for students; *significantly altered programs*, where programs are based largely on the regular program but with significant alterations such as the inclusion of Native studies courses, off-campus courses, and greater amounts of student teaching time; and *community-based programs*, where the locus of control is one or more communities and the content of the program is likely to be even more modified than the significantly altered program. For proponents of the latter programs, it is important that they do more than "train teachers who just happen to be Native" (Wyatt, 1978:27), that the curriculum of the programs reflects the distinctive needs of Native children as defined by Native communities themselves, and that the programs are "specialized" as well as "special" (Allison, 1983:112). Such aspirations have often led to conflicts with faculties of education and universities over control of the curriculum and who should be approved to deliver it, and with most programs funded jointly by the federal and provincial governments, separately from the main university funding processes, these programs have continually been marginalized by their host institution.

IN SEARCH OF A CANADIAN ANTI-RACIST TEACHER EDUCATION PERSPECTIVE

Racism (particularly institutional and systemic racism) and the role of faculties of education in confronting and challenging, as opposed to reinforcing, racist structures within society and schools are not topics that have received a lot of attention in Canadian educational writings. Neither have faculties of education generally provided a hospitable environment in which to pursue an anti-racist agenda. In looking for Canadian anti-racist initiatives in teacher education, and at the same time looking for explanations for the lack of attention that these issues have received to date, it is useful to make some comparisons between the development of "special" First Nations/Native teacher education programs (which, while usually not rooted in a radical tradition or language of critical pedagogy, surely represent the most serious efforts to address institutional racism in Canadian teacher education) and the mainstream programs of main campus.

Community Involvement and Accountability

A central tenet of anti-racist education is that oppressed groups of people need to exercise greater control over the education of their children and the systems within which they are educated (Cole, 1989; Thomas, 1987). In this sense community control—with the ambiguities that it brings with it—has become a critical issue for proponents of anti-racist education and for First Nations/Indian education in Canada over the last two decades. As stated clearly by the National Indian Brotherhood, "If we are to avoid the conflict of values which in the past has led to withdrawal and failure, Indian parents must have control of education with the responsibility for setting goals" (p. 3). Fifteen years later, the Assembly of First Nations restated this commitment as follows:

Since 1973, under DIAND's definition of "Indian Control" another generation of First Nations young people have been subjected to provincial, territorial, and federal educational programs which refuse to acknowledge the importance of First Nations languages, cultures, and spiritual beliefs. First Nations have struggled to exercise jurisdiction over these programs in order to make education more relevant to their people. If First Nations truly believe that their children are their most important and precious resource, they must exercise jurisdiction over their education programs. (Assembly of First Nations, 1988:2)

In pursuit of this goal, many First Nations/Native teacher education programs have been able to develop strong ties with the communities they serve through their community-based locations, community advisory committees (which may exercise significant power over the viability of the program), the use of community resources, and their links with the schools where students practice teach and where they may work upon graduation. Such collaboration and power sharing, which serve to increase the accountability of the program to the constituency that it serves, are something that becomes much more problematic on main campus. The claim of powerful interest groups within the university to autonomy and the privileges of tenure constitute a two-edged sword that significantly reduces the ability of outside constituencies to exert a direct influence upon faculties of education.

Divorced from this influence by their relatively recent migration onto the university campus, and with considerable freedom to chart their own course, large faculties of education (with a doctorate as the entrance credential for their faculty and peer review as the basis for progress through the professorate) have tended to become distanced physically and professionally from the schools they are meant to serve. Rather than being supportive of the efforts of progressive teachers to address issues of racism, they have proven to provide chilly climates for people and forms of knowledge that lie outside of the confines of the white, male, middle-class figure in dominance.

While some First Nations/Native teacher education programs have succeeded in employing elders as faculty members, and since these programs' marginal status within the university community has generally denied their faculty the rites of tenure, such programs have generally had more open hiring practices than other programs. However, on main campus, the 1970s and 1980s have not been a period of increasing the representativeness of faculty members within faculties of education. Given the lack of outside accountability, the lack of strong links to practicing teachers, particularly those most involved in anti-racist education, and a faculty deriving "their cultural biography from an Anglo-centric socialization of many years duration and manifest efficiency" (Lynch, 1986:154), it is probably not surprising that they have contributed little to the development of the anti-racist agenda.

Curriculum

Anti-racist education requires that teaching be conceived as a political and moral activity before it is regarded as a technical or vocational one. As such, a task of anti-racist education thus becomes the analysis of the political, historical, and social processes of society that have institutionalized and worked to sustain unequal power and the ways in which schools and the people who work in them are implicated in, and may contest, those power relationships (Cole, 1989:148). Such curricular agendas may increasingly be taken up in some First Nations/Native teacher education programs, but Allison's (1983) analysis of these programs suggests that some vary little in substance from the offerings of main campus, other than being more restricted in terms of course offerings. Within faculties of education, generally such a "foundation" perspective is oppositional to the rationalist agenda that tends to hold sway (Kirk, 1986), and where priority is given to a narrowly defined vision of technical mastery in the teaching-learning environment—"the glorification of technique at the expense of real human substance" (Henley & Young, 1989a:27). Within Canadian faculties of education, such attention as is afforded these issues is often crowded into a single core course and a few elective courses that are poorly subscribed to, or, to use Lynch's phrase quoted earlier, "dissipated to the point of invisibility" across a fragmented and inchoate curriculum. Linkages with other faculties, such as those of sociology, political science, economics, and social work, that might support these analyses are usually informal and poorly developed. Critical reflection on the role of faculties of education is not usually a part of the formal curriculum, nor are substantial considerations of the role of teachers.

Nor have faculties of education generally made problematic the craft of teaching other than in a technical manner. Liston and Zeichner (1987) argue that "radically orientated teacher educators must serve as living examples of the kind of critically orientated pedagogical practices that they seek to have their students adopt. This means that teacher educators need to reflect critically and act strategically upon the nature of their own pedagogical practices and the institutional contexts within which they work" (p. 133).

While there is a developing literature on what such pedagogic practices might look like (Brookes, 1990; Kelly, 1990; Ellsworth, 1989; Troyna, 1987), such practices currently appear highly marginal to the main ethos of the faculty of education.

Students

Equally central to the anti-racist agenda is the increased representation of minority teachers within the school system. First Nations/Native teacher education programs have clearly had an impact here, as has been noted earlier. What is also worth noting is that such programs have well-developed admissions procedures that target and actively recruit students into their programs based upon criteria of potential such as community sponsorship as well as a variety of support mechanisms designed to see that once admitted, students find a climate conducive to success. This is a radically different approach to the passive recruitment practices of main campus, with its preoccupation with grade point average and the bureaucratic and alienating procedures that students generally face on entry into teacher education programs. Outreach activities and affirmative action initiatives, which have become quite common across American campuses, have not become a prominent feature of Canadian universities.

CONCLUSION

Canadian faculties of education in the last two decades, isolated from and inaccessible to those parents, children, and communities whose educational needs they are supposed to be addressing, have generally proven to be either apathetic or hostile environments for those seeking to understand and challenge racism within Canadian schools and Canadian society. Without more representation from and accountability to traditionally excluded groups of people, and without more faculty involvement in community action against racism, faculties of education and the professors who work within them are likely to remain ill informed and ill equipped for, and increasingly irrelevant to, the task of dismantling and transforming a racist school system.

For those people, within and outside of faculties of education, concerned to change this situation, this chapter has attempted to elaborate something of the shape and magnitude of the task that awaits. For white, male faculty members such as myself, whose careers are built within these same institutions and who seek to be a part of their transformation, Ng (1989) reminds us:

While we begin from a recognition of the fundamental inequality between women and men, between people of different racial and ethnic groups, at the everyday level we have to recognize that we are part of those institutions. We must pay attention to the manner in which our own practices create, sustain and reinforce racism, sexism and class oppression. . . . We need to re-examine our history, as well as our own beliefs and actions, on a continuous basis, so that we become able to better understand and confront ways in which we oppress others and participate in our own oppression. (P. 19)

NOTES

1. Since writing this chapter, there have been a number of important changes in higher education in Britain. In 1992 polytechnics were given university status, removing the previous distinctions made between these two types of higher education institutions (*Times Higher Education Supplement* Staff, 1992:8). In addition, in June of 1992 the Department of Education in its Circular 9/92 (and Circular 35/92 from the Welsh Office) required that schools play a much larger part in initial secondary teacher training "as full partners of higher education institutions" (Department for Education, Initial Teacher Training (Secondary Phase), 1992:1). Many higher education institutions are still in the early stages of working out new programs and relationships in light of these changes, and their impact on multicultural teacher education has yet to be seen.

2. The inadequacy of an available data base upon which to base either informed debate or educational policy in the area of teacher education was emphasized in the Swann Report. In surveys such as those attempted by Cherrington and Giles, Watson, and Watson and Roberts, their findings were limited by (1) a less than 100 percent response deciding rate, (2) the conceptual ambiguity inherent in any respondent deciding what does and doesn't constitute a component of "multicultural teacher education," and (3) a survey method that requires a single informant to appreciate accurately the content of other people's courses. The same limitations apply to the only attempt at a national survey carried out in Canada, that conducted by Masemann and Mock in 1985.

3. While neither the Cherrington and Giles article (1981) nor the Craft commentary on it elaborate in detail on the data they present and discuss, this discrepancy would appear to be related in part at least to the fact that some of the institutions, particularly the universities, did not have teacher training programs associated with them and therefore should properly be excluded from a discussion of those institutions that had responded in some way with multicultural teacher education initiatives.

4. The discussion of multicultural teacher education in Canada is frequently clouded by questions of audience: does multiculturalism really include British and French culture or Native culture? If it does, to what extent does it recognize the unique histories and special status of these groups? Masemann (1981) has noted how in those countries where multiculturalism has become a "thinkable thought," attention to aboriginal people has tended to be in large part overlooked. Bagley argues a similar case for Britain when he notes:

The aboriginal people of the British Isles are the despised "Celtic fringe" ruthlessly suppressed and exploited by the Anglo-Saxon ascendency for many centuries. The struggle of Celtic people for autonomy and justice is continuing. This struggle is totally ignored in the multicultural curriculum in Britain. Schools have accepted without question the ideology that the Irish struggle reflects the aspirations of contemptible and evil man who shall not be admitted to the halls of civilization. (Bagley, 1986:74, n.1)

II

Reflections on Critical
Approaches to Education

4

Warrior as Pedagogue, Pedagogue as Warrior: Reflections on Aboriginal Anti-Racist Pedagogy

Robert Regnier

> It is not possible to divorce the process of learning from its own source
> in the lives of the learners themselves
>
> Paulo Freire, *Pedagogy in Process*

This chapter proposes an anti-racist pedagogy by considering aboriginal opposition to the Meech Lake Accord and the Mohawk standoff at Oka in Canada during the spring and summer of 1990. It offers an analysis of political struggle as pedagogical struggle in which "pedagogue as warrior" is presented as a model for anti-racist teaching. Warriors act to reveal contradictions between dominant ideologies and aboriginal subjugation, act out the world as it could be, inspire the subjugated to oppose their subjugation, and call upon the public to support aboriginal struggles for mutual survival and justice. They address long-standing oppression. They seek preservation and restoration of language, customs, and culture; recognition of sovereignty; return of surrendered and illegally dispossessed lands; the granting of promised but never transferred land; recognition of aboriginal rights; and improvement of social and economic conditions. Pedagogues as warriors criticize racial injustice and enact the possibility of a reconstructed order within school. In school, where the hidden curriculum of racism is to be rooted out in structure and ideology, the pedagogue as warrior inserts the self into a position that confronts structures and provokes critical reflection.

CONFRONTING CONSTITUTIONAL RACISM: THE ELIJAH FACTOR

The image of Elijah Harper stalling the passage of the Meech Lake Accord in the Manitoba legislature burned into the consciousnesses of aboriginal students across Canada in the spring of 1990. The event constituted a ready codification for unravelling meaning and possibility. Terry Pelletier, the student who thanked Elijah Harper for his public address at the University of Saskatchewan, expressed the deep pride and profound thankfulness that he and other aboriginal people felt about Harper's stand. Chief Elijah Harper, with the Assembly of Manitoba Indians and its phalanx of legal advisors and consultants, turned the task of resistance and opposition into a forum to educate the public. Through it, Chief Harper and the Assembly of Manitoba Chiefs were presented as "subjects" with the force to resist, oppose, and transform the dominant order. This "no" inserted aboriginal constituencies into a federal redistribution of power that they were otherwise being excluded from.

The Meech Lake Accord was initially intended to alter the Canadian Constitution to recognize Quebec as a "distinct society" within Canada. Quebec had not signed the Constitution when it was repatriated by Prime Minister Trudeau in 1982 because the Constitution did not protect what the government of Quebec claimed to be Quebec's distinct rights. After several first ministers' meetings, provincial premiers sought alterations to the accord. Its passage would have significantly altered the way provincial and federal governments share powers, but it did not address the outstanding concerns of Canada's aboriginal people. Through the accord, Quebec could preserve and promote its character as a distinct society, the provinces would be financially compensated for programs that matched federal programs, they could provide lists from which the prime minister would appoint Supreme Court justices and senators, and provinces would be allowed to set immigration policy and provide an amending formula to the constitution.

The federal government had set June 23, 1990, as the date by which the provinces had to agree on the terms of the accord. The accord had to be passed unanimously in each of Canada's ten provincial legislatures. The federal government warned that the death of the Meech Lake Accord could be a threat to national unity and have serious and irreversible consequences for the country. Without it Quebec might separate from the rest of Canada. About ten days prior to the deadline, the first ministers met in highly publicized rounds of negotiations to formulate a mutually acceptable agreement. After these meetings, Newfoundland, New Brunswick, and Manitoba brought the accord to their legislatures to obtain the unanimous consent required. Canada's officially recognized aboriginal representatives of the Assembly of First Nations, the Métis, the Inuit, and the Prairie Treaty Alliance were not part of the process of considering the Constitution in spite of growing government and public support for aboriginal self-determination.

The aboriginal drive for political rights in Canada for the previous twenty years was being sidelined by the accord-making process. After aboriginal people obtained the right to vote federally in 1961, aboriginal political influence grew dramatically in Canada with the Red Power movement and government funding of Indian organizations in the late sixties and early seventies. In 1975, the Dene of the Northwest Territories became the first group to assert nationhood within Canada with their manifesto, the Dene Declaration. As a result of intensive National Indian Brotherhood lobbying, the Trudeau government recognized "existing" treaty and aboriginal rights in the Constitution Act of 1982, proposed a conference to define aboriginal rights, and defended aboriginal rights against the individual rights section of the Charter (Purrich, 1987:195). Although the Constitution did not restore rights taken away before the Constitution was proclaimed, the fact that any rights for aboriginal people were recognized in the Constitution, in light of Canada's past treatment of aboriginal people, was a significant development. The failure of a series of first ministers' conferences between 1983 and 1987, when aboriginal groups met with federal and provincial leaders, to resolve issues of aboriginal rights left aboriginal groups frustrated. Furthermore, by 1990 the 1983 recommendation of the all-party Special Parliamentary Committee on Indian Self-Government in Canada that "the federal government recognize native people's right to self-government and that such a right be entrenched in the constitution" (Purrich, 1987:p. 201) had still not been implemented. Instead, the federal government sought to amend the Constitution without addressing aboriginal self-government, by attempting to pass the Meech Lake Accord in June of 1990.

In Manitoba, Elijah Harper participated with the Assembly of Manitoba Chiefs to stop the accord through a series of tactics to delay debate in the legislature. One tactic was to let the clock tick to the June deadline without allowing a final vote to take place to counteract federal government strategies to build public consensus in favor of its passage. To delay passage, the plan was to have hundreds of Indians address the Manitoba legislature, a right provided by law. Before the hearings began, Chief Harper withheld his approval for the unanimous consent to begin public hearings immediately and thereby delayed them for two days. Then he pointed out a technical procedural error that delayed the hearing until June 20. After this date, hundreds of aboriginal and nonaboriginal people registered their intention to speak at the public hearings. When, in the final hours before the June 23 deadline, a vote was taken, Elijah Harper stood alone as the sole member to say "no."[1] Without this consent, the Manitoba legislature could not approve the Meech Lake Accord. That night, both the Newfoundland and the Manitoba legislatures did not approve the accord.

By means of strategies to defeat the accord, Harper made the politics of constitutional amendment pedagogical. With the Manitoba Assembly of Chiefs, he turned the Manitoba legislature into a national forum that gave voice to aboriginal interests. He showed that the accord did not represent the best interests of aboriginal people and excluded them from constitutional debate. He also demonstrated that reshaping aboriginal political identity beyond the historical limitations of the Indian Act and the previous political practices required a shift to active participation by aboriginal people in the dominant modes of parliament representation. Through these actions, Harper showed how aboriginal peoples can use provincial legislatures as forums of counterhegemonic leverage. Teachers and students can now open and engage in an entirely different and "positive" domain of discourse possibilities. Any aboriginal person elected to a legislature in Canada can deny consent to further constitutional proposals if aboriginal claims are not made part of future negotiating arrangements. This factor, dubbed "the Elijah Factor . . . demonstrated that a person working in the legislature can be an effective voice for change ("Elijah Factor," 1990). The national aboriginal confrontation had been preceded in a much more violent manner in Canada during the thirty-fourth opening of Parliament in 1974 when, on the steps of the Parliament buildings, an RCMP riot squad attacked members of the Red Caravan that had travelled to Ottawa from Vancouver. During the early 1970s, a pan-Amer-Indian militancy had emerged with the rise of the American Indian Movement and the anti-war movement. Ideas of red nationalism fed dreams of Indian nations that would throw off neocolonial and assimilationist education strategies. Histories of genocide against American Indians, analyses of corporate and state exploitation of first peoples around the world, and the common experience of being administered in Canada's colonial structures provided all-embracing frameworks for political, cultural, and educational criticism and a basis for solidarity. The caravan symbolized and publicized the beginning of this new era as it passed through Canadian cites with its manifesto of demands for recognition of treaty and hereditary rights.[2] The caravan brought aboriginal people from across the country together within a pan-Indian ideology. Pan-Indianism could take what was common from all Indian groups to organize a unified struggle. Common understandings, various Indian-based non-Western cosmologies, rituals, and explanations and the common culture of exploitation in a capitalist society brought Indians together in a unified eclecticism. The common desire for self-determination, shared experiences within the colonial administration, and the commonality of uniquely different non-Western cosmologies, ceremonies, and awarenesses offered the ideological foundation for aboriginal unity.

This spirituality had a revolutionary force because it was grounded in aboriginal subjectivity, which visualized the emancipatory possibility of constructing an aboriginal national identity that could be self-determining. Even without land, food, or shelter, this spirituality gave purpose, direction, and energy that fueled initiatives when all else was gone. It extended each person into the past through the ancestors and into the future through the possibilities it generated. For the present, it brought identity in the Indian cosmos. It was the means of moving out of self-destructive lifestyles and limiting situations. Children imbued with Indian spirituality would recognize their Indianness, their place in the Indian world and be filled with existential purpose and identity. Schools could be the means to build a new generation of Indians committed to cultural revival, nationhood, and Indian personhood. Out of the beatings on the steps of Parliament and in response to the overt discrimination their children experienced at school, Pauline and Vern Harper, two Caravan participants, led the formation of the Wandering Spirit Survival school, Canada's first survival school.[3] Committed to understanding Indian cultures within Canada as a racist society, the school was open to all children, supported by many aboriginal and nonaboriginal groups. It became the inspiration for other survival, Native Way, and Indian-controlled schools in Canada.

When Chief Elijah Harper confronted Canada's constitutional racism, he moved Indian opposition from the reserve hinterland to the living room television. The event transmitted an image of Indian identity liberated from inevitable political determinism to political participation and possibility. This victory carried the hope of restructuring social relations and renewing self-esteem. Given that pedagogical enterprises arise out of political struggle, the constitutional struggles reflect and set the stage for new educational enterprises, the way the Red Caravan did.

WARRIOR AS PEDAGOGUE

On August 31, 1990, a caption underneath a photograph on the front page of the *Globe and Mail* read: "A 7 year-old Mohawk boy wears camouflage mask and hat while playing at an Oka Barricade." The close-up photo focused on two eyes peering through torn knitted fabric pulled tightly over the boy's head under a green and brown army hat. Within the summer media images of masked Mohawk warriors, this picture presented negative and positive possibilities of knowledge and power. What self-image, what emancipatory identity, what personal subjective self-consciousness did the Mohawk struggle teach aboriginal youth throughout Canada? How many of them imagined this mask on their faces in the summer of 1990? This picture contrasts sharply with images of aboriginal students sitting in classrooms eager to learn about Canadian citizenship. Classrooms are rarely chronicled as sites of aboriginal liberation from the cultural domination, political dependency, chronic unemployment and underemployment, hunger, and incarceration of Canada's racial and class structure. Classrooms have seldom been heralded for confronting the weight of Canadian history that hedges against transformative change. The clandestine identity concealed behind the mask is not the result of enlightened dialogue within a society of equitable power relations. Instead, the mask codifies alienation and reflects an option aboriginal people visualize for the future of their children.

The warrior image punctures the liberal ideology that all Canadian children have equal opportunities. In contrast to images of resignation, domestication, colonization, or assimilation, it reflects a resolve to confront a coercive and ideologically hegemonic state.[4] The image reflects an impatience with land claims delayed into an indefinite future of deteriorating and stagnating social and economic conditions. It is frustrated with unresolved aboriginal rights while aboriginal cultures are lost to industrial intrusion, eco-disaster, and stonewalling. Within the Western emancipatory tradition, enlightened human action guided by moral reasoning may seem contradictory to the role of the warrior. However, the warrior who confronts the overwhelmingly oppressive irrationality of a justice system, police, army, media, and set of governing institutions over aboriginal people offers a substantive liberating option.

The summer of 1990 was a pedagogical triumph for Canadian aboriginal people in their counterhegemonic efforts to bring various Canadian sectors into solidarity with their causes. On June 23, when Elijah Harper, eagle feather in hand, said "no" to ratification of the Meech Lake Accord, he stood alone in the Manitoba legislature to oppose a constitutional amendment that excluded participation by aboriginal people. Defeat of the Accord opened the possibility for aboriginal people to participate in renegotiating Canadian confederation. When Mohawk warriors began their standoff at Oka, they reflected the interests of Canadian Indian bands who seek settlement of as many as one thousand land claims and recognition of sovereignty. The standoff followed the actions of several aboriginal groups who acted as warriors to protect their rights. The Innu of Labrador entered into restricted military areas of the Canadian Forces base at Goose Bay, where they were arrested for protesting low-level training flights of military aircraft and the proposed construction of a NATO base. The Haida confronted loggers at Moresby Island in British Columbia, where they were arrested. The Setton band north of Vancouver beat their drums and sang as they were arrested for blockading rail traffic into northern British Columbia. Hunger strikers opposed the Department of Indian Affairs E–12 guidelines to cap funding of postsecondary education for status Indians in the spring of 1989 (Stevenson & Lanceley, 1991). These confrontations have touched the conscience of Canadians, resulted in stopping a proposed NATO base in Labrador, halted logging at South Moresby Island, and brought hope to aboriginal people throughout the country. With the events of 1990, aboriginal leaders agree that never before in Canada have Native organizations experienced such solidarity and unity (Harper, 1990). These counterhegemonic struggles offer teachers and students the opportunity for broader political and economic leadership within which to formulate critical pedagogies.

Major political changes throughout the world demonstrate two contrasting tendencies within which ideological and pedagogical change is possible: the collapse and the strengthening of states and superstates in response to economic and social forces. The fall of the Berlin wall and the demise of East European communism, the creation of western Europe's superstate, the press for autonomy in the "ethnic" regions of the Soviet Union, the free trade agreement between the United States and Canada, and the death of the Meech Lake Accord augured an era of political possibility. Within this context of change, aboriginal demands for self-determination, increasingly refined, rationalized, documented and justified through research and litigation, have begun to enter public consciousness. Over the years several critical accounts of repressive government policies and the systematic domination that have shaped Canadian relations with aboriginal peoples fortified aboriginal self-consciousness and increasingly informed Canadian public consciousness.[5] In the realignment of political and economic forces and the growing critical consciousness of aboriginal conditions, new possibilities emerged for aboriginal constitutencies. And while no unanimity or homogeneous consciousness exists about how aboriginal sovereignty can be expressed, several aboriginal constituencies have recommended proposals.[6]

In the summer of 1990, Mohawk warriors declared suppressed truths about their subjugation by locating themselves politically and culturally into contradictions between dominant ideologies and apparent injustices. Because these contradictions are maintained by taken-for-granted force of law or military force, warriors named and confronted them to reveal their oppressiveness as part of a racist system. Through this naming and confronting, warriors risked the possibility of criminalization and incarceration. Since these injustices are concealed in what has become socially and culturally acceptable practice and discourse, the warriors faced the possibility of rejection, isolation, and rebuke. Distinct from other political leaders, bureaucrats, and participants who operate within institutional constraints and definitions of a coercive state system that has become part of their working culture, the warriors addressed the very coerciveness of the system that others have come to assume as natural. They appealed to followers to address denied values and beliefs, and focused public attention on the injustice of contradictions by "performing" justice, by prophetically asserting the world as it should be, by calling upon the like-minded to follow their own consciences, and by forcing the system of hegemonic control to play out its injustice in the hope that this unveiling would motivate the enlightened to transform it.

In the subjugation of Canadian plains Indians and Métis in the late 1800s, the Canadian government hanged warriors and imprisoned defenders who fought for nationhood, cultural preservation, and sovereignty.[7] The government then instituted a pass system, discredited indigenous leadership, imposed regulatory controls, denied Indian religion, and instituted policies to detribalize.[8] The pass system, which had no legal foundation in Canadian law, required that Indians obtain permission to leave the reserve for any activity, including hunting, fishing, trapping, shopping, visiting another reserve, or visiting their children at an industrial school (Carter, 1990:149–58). It was used from 1885 to the mid-1930s, initially to "control and confine what was perceived to be a potentially hostile population" (p. 154) and eventually became a method of "expunging" "Indians, who came to be viewed as more a source of irritation and annoyance," and preventing them from "loafing about the towns" (p. 158). Through the "permit" system, Indians on reserves were required to obtain permission from an Indian agent to sell crops or other produce. "The restrictions had enormous impact on the agricultural activity of the Indians" (p. 158). Through other policies Indian leadership was not recognized and religion was restricted.

The force and symbolism of these government acts militarily, politically, culturally, and economically disarmed the defenders of aboriginal culture. If aboriginal people cannot imagine themselves as being warriors and defending a version of their culture, then are they not dominated and defeated? The hegemonic strategy of cultural and political disarmament resides partially in discrediting the notion of warrior. Pronounce the notion of warrior dead or unsavory, and defense of aboriginal claims to sovereignty is gone. This surrender of aboriginal sovereignty is then played into eternal recurrence through the popular culture of comic books, arcade games, and movies. The Indian warrior, once trivialized as an anachronism at the cigar store door and on the automobile hood, is even played out by aboriginal children, who select the role of cowboy only to reenact this racism anew. While the American notion of soldier, cowboy, and cavalry is socially constructed through imperialist adventures into Central America and Vietnam and the conquering of Indians in the wild West, the aboriginal notion of warrior is associated with resistance and defense of land and culture. Contrary to the soldier image of aggression, domination, and genocide in its relation to aboriginal peoples, the aboriginal warrior symbolizes survival, hope, and possibility. Although the conqueror views survival from cultural and political genocide as subsistence existence, the victim idealizes survival as victory.

ABORIGINAL ANTI-RACIST STRUGGLE AND CRITICAL PEDAGOGY

"People do not fight because of beautiful ideas that they have in their heads, they fight in order to get a better way of being, of existing" (Freire, 1978b). Systemic racism is embedded in the history of aboriginal relations with Canada's dominant economic and political stakeholders.[9] The Canadian state along with the cultural imperialism of schools and churches has facilitated and participated in this racism. Hegemony over aboriginal interests continues to be achieved where the dominant classes control society through their intellectual and moral leadership. This leadership articulates principles to incorporate aboriginal meanings and practices that do not contradict the dominant culture.[10] The economic and political stakeholders continually seek and reinforce acceptance about this incorporation through the media and state structures, including schools. The dominant classes reformulate and rearticulate ideological support for changing economic structures, which aboriginal constituencies consent to through compliance by not resisting. The emancipatory initiatives of teachers interested in an aboriginal anti-racist pedagogy would take these issues up as part of counterhegemonic struggles.

Canadian aboriginal opposition to systemic racism is grounded in economic claims to one half of Canada's land mass, to timber, mineral, and fishing rights and the right to regulate their economies, including high-stakes bingo and importing cigarettes, and in political claims to sovereignty and cultural self-determination. These claims have carried them into direct conflict with ruling economic and political interests. The force of aboriginal counterhegemonic struggle arises from the truth of their claims, from contradictions and tensions in the dominant consensus or ideology, and from the substantive campaigns to confront, oppose, lobby, and negotiate the dominant group. These campaigns have included research, public education, negotiations, and court challenges to establish land claims and recognition of aboriginal rights (Wilson-Smith & Allen, 1990), to entrench aboriginal rights in the Canadian constitution, and to control cultural institutions that can reconstruct a nexus of power and knowledge within aboriginal spheres of influence.

These struggles are the basis of frameworks of a critical, anti-racist education for teachers and educators. A critical, anti-racist education may be constructed upon the following presuppositions:

1. Aboriginal constituencies throughout Canada view themselves politically and culturally as self-determining nations. The right to self-determination has been recognized in various ways through international organizations, including the United Nations (Purrich, 1987:202–8), the Canadian courts, and in the Penner report of the all-party parliamentary commission of the House of Commons (Purrich, 1987:200–202). Nevertheless, Canada's relation with aboriginal nations within its boundaries has been historically one of domination and dependency, particularly as constructed through the Indian Act.[11] Anti-racist aboriginal education must be founded upon recognition of the legitimacy of aboriginal claims to political self-determination.

2. Racism against aboriginal people in Canada has been structured through the expropriation of aboriginal land and economic domination. Anti-racist aboriginal education means advancing legitimate aboriginal claims to land and economic development.

3. While nonaboriginal immigrants to Canada have an external mother country to protect and refurbish their language and culture, aboriginal people do not. If their cultural "disk" is erased or lost, none exists to back it up. Aboriginal-centered anti-racist education not only seeks to recreate culture in the contemporary politic, it is preoccupied with cultural survival.

4. Aboriginal people have been referred to as the class of the permanently unemployed, surplus population, and the lumpen proletariat because they have been fixed at the bottom of Canada's class structure. An anti-racist education must be founded on recognition of the internal class structures of aboriginal societies in relation to the class hierarchy of Canadian society.

5. Unlike other Canadians, most aboriginal people have been subject to a history of educational policy designated specifically for them by the federal government. Aboriginal policy is dominated by the relations of aboriginal people directly to the federal government, particularly as agreed to in treaties and controlled through the Department of Indian Affairs. Anti-racist aboriginal pedagogy must recognize the specific and unique features of aboriginal relations with state structures.

Aboriginal anti-racist pedagogy could be conceptualized within a broader emancipatory cultural vision for education in Canada without compromising the aspirations and agendas of aboriginal people. Immigrant cultures to Canada, for example, share with aboriginal peoples in being victimized by dominant ideologies and material structures that keep them oppressed. However, aboriginal constituencies are cautious of participation with multicultural educational associations, for example, to avoid being identified or defined in ethnic or cultural minority terms that do not recognize claims to sovereignty, to land, to aboriginal rights, and to socioeconomic obligations as spelled out in treaties. This unique history of subordination is the basis for an aboriginal anti-racist education.

Furthermore, immigrant constituencies within Canada's ethnic mosaic have benefitted directly from racist government policies to terminate aboriginal self-determination and to expropriate aboriginal land, a factor that has put them in direct economic and ideological conflict with aboriginal people. Immigrant settlement of the prairies is directly related to the subjugation of aboriginal peoples there, the appropriation of their land through treaties, and the maintenance of the pass system that kept them confined to reserves. To associate with immigrant constituencies, aboriginal groups run the risk of supporting policy that does not sufficiently address, and ultimately pre-empts, their concerns. Emancipatory anti-racist pedagogies formulated with multicultural frameworks run the risk of supporting policy that does not sufficiently address, and ultimately pre-empts, their concerns. Emancipatory anti-racist pedagogies formulated within multicultural frameworks run the risk of utilizing ideologies of cultural pluralism to revise rather than criticize strategies of assimilation. For critical multicultural pedagogies to substantively reflect aboriginal interests, they would have to reflect aboriginal locations within the historic construction of Canada's "cultural" mosaic, and they would have to be formulated within clearly distinctive possibilities for coliberating initiatives.

SOVEREIGNTY AS ANTI-RACISM

On March 11, 1990, Mohawk warriors blockaded a road to the town of Oka to stop expansion of a golf course on land claimed by the Mohawk residents of Kanesatake. When the mayor of Oka called upon the police to enforce a Quebec Superior Court injunction to tear down the barricades on July 10, the Mohawk fortified their barricade. The next day one hundred provincial police raided the barricade and surrounded the Kanesatake reserve. The Mohawk of nearby Kahnawake then blockaded highways on their reserve leading to the Mercier Bridge into Montreal and threatened to blow up the bridge if a second police assault occurred. For seventy-seven days Mohawk warriors maintained an armed standoff with Quebec police and the Canadian Army. The standoff constituted a declaration of sovereignty over thirty-nine hectares of disputed land and of the right to undertake economic projects within the jurisdiction of the Mohawk nation, including high-stakes bingo at Kahnawake. It was a demand for commitment from the Canadian government to negotiate creation of Kanienkahaka (a unified Mohawk nation) within three years as a means of resolving outstanding land claim and sovereignty issues (Picard, 1990). This action was a means not simply to bring the Canadian government to the negotiating table but to redefine "the basis of relationship and dialogue between aboriginal people and the Canadian state ("Native Self Rule," 1990). The standoff brought aboriginal grievances directly to public attention unmediated by the federal government, disturbing the complacent view that the "Indian problem" was being handled.

The standoff made it possible for the Canadian public to theorize, question, and debate aboriginal sovereignty and land claims within forums not controlled by the federal government. It inspired sympathetic action and educational strategies across Canada, sent out the call for aboriginal people to act in solidarity with the Mohawk, revealed how the historical compliance of aboriginal people could not be taken for granted, and solicited nonaboriginal public support. The standoff provided a forum for raising questions about political subjugation centered in the Indian Act, which has prevented and discouraged aboriginal government and self-determination; about the limits of aboriginal organizations' negotiations through the forums of the first ministers' conferences; and about the inadequacy of land claim procedures.

During the standoff, for example, George Erasmus, national chief of the Assembly of First Nations, used media time to explain what native organizations were calling for:

- Policies that "recognize and affirm our rights," and act more fairly and quickly on claims.

- An "independent claims commission to end the government's conflict of interest created by a constitutional duty to defend Native rights while acting in an adversarial role when Natives make claims."

- The government to stop seeking extinguishment of aboriginal rights to about fifty-five comprehensive claims filed by groups such as the Dene and Inuit, who have never signed a treaty.

- The government to deal more quickly with more than one thousand specific claims, since only an average of two are settled each year.

- The government to act more fairly instead of rejecting claims it thinks Natives may lose in court and instead of offering discounted compensation where a court case is likely to succeed. ("Ottawa Must Change," 1990)

Aboriginal peoples across Canada demonstrated the support through public rallies, vigils, protests, the toppling of electrical power towers, and blockades of railways and roads. The civil disobedience paralleled the black civil rights movement in the United States in the 1960s. Support by the Canadian public for aboriginal land claims was unprecedented. The Toronto *Globe and Mail* reported: "Rail companies, unions, and shippers are blaming the federal government, not Native people, for the rail blockades that are causing havoc in the transportation industry" (Lalonde, 1990). The president of the Canadian section of the United Transportation Union, which represents fourteen thousand rail workers in Canada, said union members supported the legal means to get Native land claims resolved, but they blame a "total abdication of leadership by the federal government for the Indian recourse to civil disobedience" (ibid.). On September 6, 1990, an advertisement sponsored by the National Action Committee on the Status of Women, Greenpeace Canada, and the Canadian Peace Alliance and signed by fifty Canadian church, union, peace, and other organizations supported government action on claims. Many organizations committed to social justice emerged from their trenches, from their own positions of resistance, and responded to their democratic impulse to support the Mohawk. The crisis of legitimacy for the federal government prompted it to act. With the opening of parliament, the prime minister announced an agenda with which to address aboriginal concerns about "land claims; economic and social conditions on reserves; the relationship between aboriginal peoples and government and concerns of aboriginal peoples in contemporary Canadian life" (Fraser, 1990).

The Mohawk warriors made the politics of land claims and sovereignty pedagogical. The standoff became a public forum through which long-standing issues were grieved to the Canadian citizenry. Canadian and Quebec governments revealed how social control and political decisions are enforced through armed force, a move portrayed through the reconquering of aboriginal peoples into a repressive state system. By making the state use of force public, the warriors changed the politics of coercion into critical knowledge. The standoff was part of the aboriginal anti-racist struggle to reclaim their aspirations for sovereignty and to construct their identity liberated from the constraints of political domination.

SURVIVAL EDUCATION AS CULTURAL POSSIBILITY

The Mohawk claim to self-determination and sovereignty is grounded in their view of themselves as the Kanien'kehaka and their relationship to the Haudenosaunee. According to their own accounts, the present-day Haudenosaunee (Iroquois Confederacy of the Mohawk, Onendaga, Cayuga, Oneida, Seneca, and Tuscarora) began a thousand years ago when a man called the Peacemaker travelled the northeast of North America to bring peace among warring factions ("History," 1991). By 1600 this confederacy embraced 157 nations, who came together to uphold "a unified belief in the principles of peace promulgated by the Peacemaker" (ibid.). Since the invasion of Europeans, the Haudenosaunee have not been defeated militarily, have maintained a strong sense of nationalism, and have steadfastly viewed themselves as allies and separate nations rather than as subjects. Furthermore, they initially maintained their separate status through the Two Row Wampum Treaty with the Dutch, French, Americans, and British. Nevertheless, the Canadian government has interpreted its relationship with the Mohawk in Canada within a colonial model established through the Indian Act, has degraded their political status, and has refused to recognize treaties and agreements. As part of recent efforts to establish recognition of their sovereignty, in 1977 the Haudenosaunee began issuing passports that they claim are recognized by twenty-eight countries (ibid.).

The Mohawk of Kahnawake's solidarity with the warriors at the Oka barricades was reflected in twelve years of teaching at the Kahnawake Survival School. Since 1978 they had been teaching that Mohawk survival depends upon achieving sovereignty and self-sufficiency. To this end, they designed school curricula to increase control over their own affairs and their participation in the world. The social studies program raised the consciousness of the new generation of Mohawk in the struggles of their predecessors. In contrast to previous courses, which ignored or incorporated Indian history into the dominant paradigm, this course resists the pitfalls of incorporation and integration into the dominant culture. The course introduces students to a history of their reserve, other Mohawk reserves, the Iroquois confederacy of which they are a part, and their relationship to the rest of the world from the perspective of Mohawk-originated research. Students study how the school was established and learn about their community and Iroquois culture, the Mohawk nation with attention to features of Mohawk territory and environment, the human geography, and aboriginal cultures of North, Central and South America (Blanchard, 1980).

The Survival School was started when Kahnawake students and eight hundred supporters marched from Chateauguay to Kahnawake on September 6, 1978, the first day of school, to protest their loss of control over education. The students refused to register at Howard S. Billings School in Chateauguay, the town adjacent to Kahnawake, where the students had attended through Department of Indian Affairs arrangements since 1968. The march was a direct response to Quebec Bill 101, the Charter of the French Language, which made French the language of instruction in schools. The bill legally required Indian students who went to school off their own settlements to fill out a blue form on the first day of school to apply for permission to be schooled in English instead of French. This language requirement was an indignity that directly contradicted the Kahnawake view of their basic rights and sovereignty. They viewed this requirement as recognition of Quebec's legal authority over their own education and culture. Following this withdrawal from registering, community members assumed authority for high school education, another step in assuming self-determination for their community.

PEDAGOGUE AS WARRIOR

Anti-racist pedagogues who construct or teach in educational institutions must confront racism in curriculum goals, content and structure, in the hidden curriculum of attitudes, predispositions, cultural expectations, methodology, discipline and classroom organization, in institutional contexts, expectations, policy, and practice, and in the public's conventional wisdom about education. The pedagogue as warrior confronts the entrenched racist hegemony of educational establishments by inserting the self into the hidden curriculum that reinforces and conceals racism. These confrontations reveal, objectify, and name the contradictions, while acting out possibilities that address them.

An emancipatory aboriginal pedagogy needs to bridge the dualism between structure and agency advanced in theories of social and cultural reproduction that view schools as sites of domination. The pedagogy must establish conditions for aboriginal students to reclaim their own voices to engage in critical discourse that leads to social action. It moves beyond the view that "ideas and meanings are merely a reflex of the economic structure of society" (Giroux, 1983:124) as characterized in orthodox Marxism's base-superstructure model. Reproductive theories of aboriginal education have focused upon how schools mediate between students and capital to reproduce attitudes and social relations necessary to maintain the social structures needed for production (Adams, 1989). While exposing assumptions about ideology by stressing the determinate nature of the economy and state, these theories do not develop the conditions for counter-hegemonic struggle. By failing to acknowledge the degree to which "human agency" remains unaffected by capital, they preclude the formulation of radical pedagogy. Theories of cultural production that view schools as relatively autonomous institutions by distributing the dominant culture also do not ground transformative possibilities.

Aboriginal counteridealogies and power can be expressed through various forms of resistance, opposition, and possibility. Resistance theories like that of Paul Willis in his book *Learning to Labour* (1977) demonstrate that some forms of resistance and opposition are not necessarily counter-hegemonic but actually serve domination. Few works about aboriginal education (e.g., Haig-Brown, 1988; Jones, Stamp, & Sheehan, 1979) recognize theories of resistance, while many other critical educational theories may propose emancipatory pedagogies but do not recognize aboriginal cultural resources. The educator as warrior opens the possibility of an aboriginal pedagogy of possibility.

Through the lens of Antonio Gramsci's notion of organic intellectual, the warrior may be viewed as an emancipatory pedagogue who addresses structural racism. Committed to freedom, cultural survival, and democracy, this warrior conducts counterhegemonic struggles that refuse consent to ruling social sectors and build oppositional alliances. As organic intellectuals, warriors are "mediators, legitimators, and propagators of ideas and social practices; they perform a function eminently political in nature" (Giroux, 1988:151). They formulate their experiences and their understanding of aboriginal aspirations and limit-situations[12] into ideological constructs, material practices, and critical pedagogies. They provide an evangelical morality and intellectual leadership as well as the pedagogical and political skills to engage in collective struggle.

The pedagogue as warrior is a concept similar to that of pedagogue as transformative intellectual developed by Henry Giroux (1988) and that of pedagogue as prophet developed by David Purpel (1989). Both of these concepts of teacher are committed to human emancipation. Giroux's teacher as transformative intellectual follows the Greek tradition inherited from Socrates. Socrates persistently confronted the statesmen and orators of Athens and the dominant ideas in Greek society in efforts to lead its citizenry to practical moral action. These confrontations in pursuit of the truth involved great personal risk, as demonstrated in the decision of the Athenian democracy to put Socrates to death for allegedly corrupting the youth through his questioning. His efforts to allow a new ethical order to emerge required a conviction and commitment beyond the ideas and organization of the existing state. Henry Giroux advances the notion of teacher as a transformative intellectual who, in the Socratic tradition, courageously questions moral contradictions in the public sphere. Emancipatory education consists of challenging the anti-intellectualism of society and schools by acting courageously to construct new public spheres that foster critical rationality and ideological critique. Construction of these spheres is itself a form of critical action from which comes the possibility of further transformative action. Both the Elijah Harper and the Mohawk actions can be interpreted as courageous efforts to challenge contradictions in the public sphere.

David Purpel draws the notion of teacher as prophet from the biblical tradition of the Old Testament prophets, who castigated and censured, intensified responsibility, were impatient of excuse, were "contemptuous of pretense and self pity" (Heschel quoted in Purpel, 1989:151) and sought to wrench "one's consciousness from a state of suspended animation." They did not have exceptional powers but rather combined "deep devotion to sacred ideals with a determination to speak out vividly and loudly on the profane" (Purpel, 1989:80). The spiritual dimension of the prophets arose from a preoccupation with sacred beliefs and their meaning in current historical, economic, social, and political affairs. "Their prophecy lay in their deep understanding of the severe consequences that were in store for a people flaunting and rejecting their own deepest aspirations. Prophets were passionate social critics who applied sacred criteria to human conduct, and when they found violations of the criteria they cried out in anguish and outrage" (Purpel, 1989:80). The prophetic warrior's standoff comes from a compassionate understanding of the suffering, oppression, violence, and hunger in aboriginal communities. The sacred beliefs arise in the ceremonies and traditions of aboriginal spiritual practices. Teachers as warriors play a prophetic role when they articulate the deepest aspirations of aboriginal communities, which are in conflict with the consequences of neo-colonial schooling.

The task of warriors to protect aboriginal nationhood was already inherited by teachers in the 1970s Indian control of Indian education movement in Canada. Through this movement, Indian bands across Canada began to undertake administrative control of their schools. Although the pace and direction of this change has been clearly managed by the state, and the state has relinquished neither management control nor sovereignty, the Indian control movement was the beginning of increased self-determination. The 1973 National Indian Brotherhood paper, *Indian Control of Indian Education*, called for federal initiatives to be undertaken in collaboration with people to educate them as teachers by using experimental approaches and structures that would accommodate mature persons. It advocated increased aboriginal participation and control as the means of defining education away from the hegemonic interests of the Canadian state and the social, political, and economic interests of the aboriginal people. One result of the movement was the rise of aboriginal teacher education programs across Canada designed to offer teaching opportunities to aboriginal people who could bring knowledge of aboriginal language, social conditions, and culture to aboriginal children. Today, Indian bands administer education programs on their own reserves through a contract with the federal government. While the federal government in effect manages these programs through budget control, this band participation is a significant departure from the federal government's 1969 plan to turn aboriginal education over to provincial governments.

As schools moved from federal to Indian administrative control and as provincial governments recognized the inadequacy of provincial schools in the 1980s, band councils, reserve school committees, and provincial educators were faced with questions about what to do with the schools. What curriculum should be implemented? If reserves are to be sovereign and autonomous, what does this sovereignty mean and how should schools advance it? What are the plans to link schools to employment, economic development, social improvement, and cultural restoration? Many bands preferred the security of Indian Affairs control. Band councils and school committees were faced with decision making in unfamiliar areas such as curriculum and staffing. Alternative curricula for Indian schools were limited. Questions of discipline or shaping the hidden curriculum in an alternative system were unresolved. Many students were age-grade displaced, had not learned basic skills, and had developed resistance to schooling. Most students lived below the poverty line. Band councils wanted their students to learn English well, and they were concerned initially that teaching Indian languages (which many thought would disrupt English learning) was not necessary.

Most Indian schools assumed provincial curriculum guidelines and standards, infused cultural content, and used culture-sensitive pedagogies. Educational initiatives shifted from the politics of achieving control to using this limited but significant control to recreate a meaningful and relevant education. Schools became viewed as places to heal, to affirm, and to generate possibility, places where individuals were willing to reveal themselves and participate in the curriculum of the community. In this revelation and participation, members were able to address and recover self as well as recreate communities shattered by decades of repressive and divisive policies and practices. Probably the most publicized and dramatic reflection of this consciousness occurred at the Alkali Lake reserve in British Columbia, where the band, in critical reflection of its lost spiritual culture and community life, recovered from a 100 percent alcoholism rate to 95 percent dry, then proceeded to address the community's history of sexual abuse (Alkali Lake Indian Band, 1985). The band has become internationally recognized for its work in assisting others.

A significant aboriginal critical pedagogy advance with and for urban youth in Canada was pioneered by Kelly Murphy at the Saskatoon Native Survival School (now the Joe Duquette High School) in Saskatoon, Saskatchewan (Murphy & Smillie, 1986; Regnier, 1988; Mackie, 1989). Kelly

Murphy constructed this pedagogy upon Cree speaking traditions, the writing of Paulo Freire, and the work of Constance Stanislovsky. She experimented with strategies using story circles and collective improviza-tion to move urban aboriginal youth beyond the cultures of resistance into creative social cultural possibilities. For a decade, she has confronted her own teaching practices and structures to develop a pedagogy that enables students to engage cooperative, supportive, and imaginative social rela-tions, to significantly improve language and communication interaction, and to construct elements of an Indian mythos for living in the urban context. Her pedagogy has given authentic artistic expression to urban aboriginal youth, who have produced as many as ten plays for public presentation. These plays address their real issues and problems associated with the justice system as well as incarceration, prostitution, urban and reserve life, street warfare, schooling and education, and family life. The story circle and improvizational pedagogy acknowledge the complexity of urban aboriginal youth culture, popular culture, the domination of aborigi-nal cultures, and the aspiration to recreate that culture as a form of self-de-termination. It is committed to disciplined, substantive English teaching through aboriginal students' experience, and demands rigorous attention to development of a socially imaginative praxis within the students' life world.

Increased participation of aboriginal students in higher education and more relevant, less alienating schooling present new problems and strug-gles for the 1990s. In the spring of 1989, hundreds of Aboriginal students and their supporters across Canada were arrested and charged as they conducted hunger strikes, protests, and sit-ins in opposition to the federal Department of Indian Affairs and Northern Development's new policy on the Postsecondary Assistance Program. Students criticized the policy for being developed without consultation with them, for capping the total assistance budget so that fewer students would receive postsecondary assistance (Stevenson & Lanceley, 1991), and for restricting funds for higher degree programs to areas of study and to places of study. Elders from various parts of Canada who fasted for many days became the spiritual anchor point for confronting an entrenched bureaucracy, for calling like-minded supporters into the struggle, and for sustaining morale and com-mitment to the struggle. The fasts framed the protests within the power dynamics of an aboriginal cosmology that challenged the knowledge and legitimation of the dominant rationality. Within this cosmology, many student protestors faced the prospect of criminal charges for acts like chaining themselves to the doors of the Department of Indian Affairs offices.

In the summer of 1990, these students were part of coalitions in Canadian cities that supported Mohawk demands at Kanesatake. The coalitions conducted public rallies, marches, vigils, and other events in support of the

Mohawk. In Saskatoon, Saskatchewan, for example, the coalition drew aboriginal and nonaboriginal people together under aboriginal leadership, which included students who had opposed the E–12 guidelines. The support work was characterized by close social relationships, sacrifice of time and finances, direct activism, and a high level of organization (Regnier, 1990). This activism was committed to building aboriginal community beyond aboriginal factionalism and to constructing aboriginal and non-aboriginal solidarity in support of anti-racist structural and ideological transformation. At both the E–12 guidelines and Oka rallies, students served as parade marshals and poster makers in a process where the political was being made pedagogical and the pedagogical political.

CONCLUSION

The liberation of aboriginal education, implicit in Chief Elijah Harper's opposition to the Meech Lake Accord and in the Mohawk warriors' confrontation at Oka, was acted out by many students in the summer of 1990, not by sitting in their desks bound to the standard curriculum but by helping to turn the streets of some Canadian cities into forums for anti-racist education. Their confrontations, conducted in solidarity with nonaboriginal supporters, held the seeds of a reconstructed social order. In the school of the streets, students grieved the historic tragedy of punishment and discipline meted out on the aboriginal body politic, resisted the educational genocide of complacency and manufactured satisfaction, and called upon the Canadian public and government to transform its relations with aboriginal peoples. This is an anti-racist pedagogy that reflects Freire's admonition that authentic learning finds its source in the experience of the learner, in this case the experience of the aboriginal warrior.

NOTES

1. Not all aboriginal peoples agreed with Harper or the strategy of the Manitoba Assembly of Chiefs to stop the Meech Lake Accord. The Manitoba Métis Federation believed that from 1983 to 1987, during the period when aboriginal peoples participated in the first ministers' conferences, Native people made substantial progress. Furthermore, the accord committed them to participate in first ministers' conferences every three years. See J. MacDonald, "One Little Man," *WEST*, Sept. 1990.

2. For a discussion of the Red Caravan, see Harper, 1976.

3. For an overview of five survival schools in Canada, see R. H. Regnier (1987), Survival schools as emancipatory education, *Canadian Journal of Native Education*, 14(2), 42–54.

4. For an accessible discussion of hegemony read M. Apple, On analyzing hegemony, in Apple (1979), pp. 1–25.

5. National attention accorded to the discrimination of aboriginal people through the justice system has been highlighted in Canada, especially through extensive media attention accorded to the Donald Marshall Inquiry and the Manitoba Justice Inquiry. The dramatic increase in aboriginal publishing, newspapers, and other media over the years has given the public access to aboriginal views. And the continuing significant increase in aboriginal people attending institutions of higher learning and entering the professions has created a class of aboriginal intellectuals willing to advocate aboriginal interests.

6. See Purrich (1987). Even Bob Rae, the NDP Premier of Ontario, stated that his government would be willing to negotiate provincial rights to minerals and forests on Indian reserves with the federal government. Proposals for sovereignty range from requiring powers equivalent to municipalities and dependent nations to requiring those of independent nation-states.

7. For a discussion of the time, see Barron and Waldram (1986).

8. For a history of the politics of Indian subjugation in western Canada, especially see Carter (1990); York (1990); Goodwill and Sluman (1984); Titley (1986); Tobias (1983).

9. See, for example, World Council of Indigenous Peoples, "Transnational Corporations and Their Effects on the Resources and Lands of Indigenous Peoples," paper presented to the International Conference on Indigenous People and the Land, September 1981.

10. As the main agencies of the dominant culture, schools establish what may be called a "selective tradition," where certain meanings, practices, and content are included in or excluded from school culture. Through the process of incorporation "some of these meanings are reinterpreted, diluted or put into forms which support or at least do not contradict other elements in the dominant culture" (Apple, 1979:5).

11. On November 21, 1990, the Canadian Human Rights Commission called upon the Department of Indian Affairs to scrap the Indian Act. This "devastating" critique, presented after the Mohawk crisis, states that "the pace of change is simply too slow. . . . For every community where headway has been made on land claims, self government or economic development there are dozens of others with grievances still outstanding and aspirations still to be realized" (Indian act, department condemned," [Toronto] *Globe and Mail*, Nov. 22, 1990).

12. In his book *Pedagogy of the Oppressed* (1970), Paulo Freire discusses limit-situations as those conditions that appear impenetrable and beyond which one cannot go. For Freire these situations "imply the existence of persons who are directly served by these situations, and of those who are negated and curbed by them." The liberating potential in these situations consists of the "untested feasibility" through which critical action can change the participants from "being to being more human" (pp. 92–93).

5
Connecting Racism and Sexism: The Dilemma of Working with Minority Female Students

Goli Rezai-Rashti

Canada's policy of multiculturalism was introduced more than two decades ago. Yet the meaning of the term and its implications for education remain obscure and problematic.

Multiculturalism was to depart from the cultural assimilation ideology practiced prior to 1971 to become a national ideology that accepted and tolerated cultural diversity. In practice, however, the policy had little of the impact that was anticipated. If anything, it has been found wanting. Since the early 1980s, state-sponsored multiculturalism has come under considerable criticism by educators and social scientists. These critical views of multiculturalism are not unique to Canada. In the United States, and especially in England, similar criticism has arisen. In both societies, a growing number of educators have taken issue with the traditional approaches to multiculturalism. They came out with a more novel model of pluralism: one that is geared to bringing about a greater degree of egalitarianism in society while giving greater relevance to issues of class and gender. Similarly, this new school of thought, known as the anti-racist approach, made a radical theoretical departure from mainstream multiculturalism. The latter's emphasis had been on the transformation of individuals' attitudes and prejudices; the former, however, shifted that focus to the study of institutionalized forms of racism. It maintained that racism is manifested in the policies and practices of larger institutions. Henry Giroux, a well-known representative of this new critical approach, said it bluntly: "mul-

This chapter first appeared as an article in the Spring 1994 *Canadian Woman Studies*, 14, (2), 76–82.

ticulturalism should mean analyzing not just stereotypes but also how institutions produce racism and other forms of discrimination" (1992:10).

Multicultural education also came under criticism for its liberal rhetoric, its additive and supplementary character, and, more important, for its lack of analysis of power relations. Critics stressed the point that multicultural education failed to integrate itself into the school curriculum and everyday educational activities. For them, such activities as Black History Month and Heritage Week were attached to, but not part of, the educational experience.

In my own work as a practitioner in the field of anti-racist education, I have become fully aware of the marginal nature of such programs. After all these years, they still have not become an integral part of the ongoing, mandatory school curricula.

The contributions made by anti-racism educators are to be commended. They certainly touched a cord with their criticisms of the conceptual short-comings of multicultural education. To discuss those valid criticisms goes beyond the scope of this article. My goal here is to initiate a debate on an important issue ignored by both multiculturalism and anti-racism advocates: the analyses of the complex interrelationship between racism and sexism in the education system. True, anti-racist educators can claim to be concerned about gender issues; however, their concerns have not developed into a comprehensive and convincing argument. Race, class, and gender are categories that have been used in a rhetorical sense as categories that can be studied and discussed separately. The exception to this theoretical vacuum in what is otherwise a very sound approach has come from the works of two Canadian scholars. In effect, both Himani Bannerji and Roxana Ng have concerned themselves with this issue, only at the level of institutions of higher learning or within the context of immigrant communities. Roxana Ng has helped to develop a framework in which race, class, and gender are not exclusively used because of their theoretical value but are treated as relations that are discoverable in the everyday world of experience (1989:50). A similar analysis is needed of the ways the interrelationship between racism and sexism is approached in the official discourse of anti-racist education within schools, boards of education, and the Ministry of Education.

As a feminist and a practitioner in the field of anti-racist education, I constantly find myself dealing with complex issues involving racism and sexism. These issues are largely problematic in my work with minority female students. These students have to deal not only with the institutional racism present in the school system and in society at large but sometimes with sexist practices prevalent within their own communities and the racialization of the gender issues at the school level.

My intention in reflecting upon my experiences with minority female students does not aim at providing an essentialist perspective. I am fully aware that students' existential reality varies greatly in accordance with their social class location and national origin. It is possible, however, to find some striking similarities within that greater diversity.

On the one hand, there is the racialization of gender issues as practiced at the school level by school administrators, counselors, and teachers. Here we find that in many respects the ways in which the education system looks at Third World female students are permeated by the remnants of what I should call "colonial discourse." This discourse has a long history that dates back to colonial domination, in which the issues of women and culture were fused by the colonizers.[1] On the other hand, there is also a manipulation of the policies of multiculturalism by some of the families of minority female students. Reflecting the sexism within their own communities—which is usually hidden under the rubric of "culture"—there are parents who are demanding special provisions for their daughters from the school system. Not surprisingly, some educators who still cling to a colonial past appear too willing to comply with those parents' demands.

In brief, to attribute the discriminatory situation faced by minority female students only to the racism of the school system and society, while remaining silent and ignorant of the sexism present within the student's community, is to be found wanting. Such a narrow focus fails to provide a meaningful explanation of what is, by all means, a very complex process. The complexity of the lived reality of minority female students, accompanied as it is by the marginal nature of the work of the practitioner, makes the latter's intervention and advocacy on behalf of such students a very difficult task. In order to understand this better, it is necessary first to discuss the racism present in the school system and then to provide an analysis of the mechanisms by which racism and sexism become articulated in the lives of minority female students.

RACISM AND SCHOOLING

The research demonstrating the existence of racism in the education system is both exhaustive and compelling. As a practitioner involved in the field of anti-racism education for the past decade, I have come to recognize the existence of structural/institutional racism as well as a form of commonsense, everyday, cultural racism. Racism is embedded in the normal individual interactions and institutional practices of schools. This fact has been acknowledged by the Ministry of Education in Ontario. On July 1993, in Policy Memorandum Number 119, it claimed that

there is growing recognition that the educational structure, policies and programs have been mainly European in perspective and have failed to take into account the viewpoints, experiences, and needs of Aboriginal people, and many racial and ethnocultural minorities. As a result, systemic inequalities exist in the school system that limit the opportunities for Aboriginal and other students and staff members of racial and ethnocultural minorities to fulfill their potentials. Educators, therefore, need to identify and change institutional policies that are racist in their impacts, if not in intent. In this regard, anti-racist and ethnocultural equity education goes beyond multicultural education, which focuses on teaching about the cultures and traditions of diverse groups. (1993:45)

As of now, it is still too early to evaluate the success of the new government policies. But if experience with previous attempts is as good an indicator as any, then it can be claimed that those boards of education that have had an anti-racist policy for a number of years do not appear to have had much success in implementing them. This is confirmed by the research conducted by Carol Tator and Frances Henry:

There appears to be a significant increase in the level of activity as it relates to the policy development over the last few years. This is reflected in the number of policy documents produced by different educational institutions. . . . However, both the review of the documents and dozens of interviews suggest that little in the way of concrete, measurable programs and organizational change has taken place. (1991:117–18)

Equally important in terms of highlighting the limitations of government-sponsored policies is the fact that in the new guidelines for the development of anti-racism policies, the Ministry of Education failed to include issues of gender and social class in the school curricula. Once again, anti-racism is devoid of gender and class connotations in the official discourses in the same ways that class and gender were glaringly absent in the official discourse of the old multicultural education policies.

THE ARTICULATION OF RACISM AND SEXISM

In dealing with a large number of female students mainly from the Middle East, South East Asia, and Africa, I have found that the actions of many school principals, teachers, and guidance counselors are still very much influenced by the ideology of colonization. There is a strong belief in Western superiority among some educators at school levels. Their image of Third World countries is still stereotypical and ethnocentric: poor, underdeveloped, and uncivilized. Likewise, women from such countries are construed as individuals who are truly oppressed, powerless, and submissive. They are seen as victims who must be rescued from the oppressive influences of their families and culture. Often, that implies suggesting that they adapt to the Western way of life. In pursuing this approach, educators seem bent on racializing gender issues pertaining to minority students. This perspective creates several interrelated problems.

Sometimes, problems that are perceived by school personnel as being related to a student's "home culture" in fact have little to do with specific cultural practices. They may well be the types of problems encountered by any typical adolescent. I was once called to go to a school and talk to a Muslim student who, according to her counselor, was experiencing "cultural conflicts." Upon my arrival at the school, the school principal introduced me to the student in question. Before leaving the room, the principal looked at me and said that the girl's parents wanted to follow the "old country's rules." Then he added that the parents needed to learn that there are rules and regulations in Canada that work against sexism. After talking to the student for an hour, I found that her problems had nothing to do with her country of origin or her culture. Her school failure was the result of jealousy among siblings due to the preferential treatment that her parents gave to an older sister—nothing different from a situation that could also be found in any Anglo-Saxon household. There are numerous cases such as this one that are uncritically attributed to the cultural inferiority associated with a student's background.

A correlate to this ethnocentric attitude occurs in those cases when minority female students go and talk to school administrators, teachers, and guidance counselors about the conflicts that they are experiencing with their parents. These conflicts usually involve dating, going out after school hours, and/or instances of physical punishment. Rather than bothering to ask parents to come to school, much less offering to visit the student's home in order to discuss the student's complaints, the individuals in authority accept the student's claims as a matter of fact. Again, this view is largely related to the preconceived ideas about the inferior status of minority culture in relation to gender issues. In numerous cases that I have dealt with, I found there was more to the story than appeared at first. Students can be very skillful at pitting their parents against the educational system. Consequently, it has always been my recommendation to school authorities that every situation should be investigated and worked out cooperatively with the student's parents. Doing this does not imply denying that there is no sexism within minority communities. On the contrary, it implies rejecting as simplistic, if not ignorant, the tendency to interpret the student's problems as arising exclusively from the sexism attributed to the student's racial and cultural background.

I agree with the assertion made by Avtar Brah (1992), who, in studying the women of South Asian origin in England, said that there is no evidence to suggest that conflicts among South Asian families are much different from those in white families. Asian parents tend to be portrayed as "authoritarian," "conservative," and supposedly "opposed to the liberating influences of schools." Yet there is as much variation among Asian parents on issues concerning the education of their children as can be expected in any other group of parents (p. 74).

In my observations of the school system, I have come to understand the tremendous amount of pressure that is placed upon minority female students to assimilate into the dominant Western culture. I see such demands as the result of systematic racism resulting from the colonial experience. Sometimes, the attempts to assimilate may lead to students' alienation and a loss of identity (i.e., the anglicization of one's name; the rejection of one's first language or of the language spoken at home; the contempt for one's parents because of accent, religion, and/or culture; the need to date boys in order to prove that one is different from one's parents; and so on). This, in turn, may lead to conflicts between the students, their parents, and their larger cultural community. When these conflicts reach the school, educators are likely to see students as rebelling against the perceived repressive culture of their communities. Seldom are students' problems seen within the context of the systemic racism present in the relationship between educators and students. There is, in short, a need to explain the difficulties of minority female students by engaging in a more comprehensive analysis that situates their lives in the two worlds that constitute their existential reality: that of their communities, and that of society and the education system at large. Both worlds exhibit racism and sexism. Both worlds are not without contradictions and conflicts.

It is very common, when dealing with minority female students in Canadian schools, to see how the discussion concentrates on the oppressive, sexist nature of their culture and religion. The sexism prevalent in Canadian society suddenly leaves center stage and is placed on the back burner. The discussion then proceeds in a way that indicates that Canadian women have somehow already achieved the equality that is eluding their sisters in the Third World. This perception has little to do with the reality faced by Canadian women. In discussing how Western feminists present Third World women as underdeveloped and economically dependent, Mohanty has said that there is an underlying implication that Western women are secular, liberated, and in control of their lives. She argues that this is a discursive self-presentation and not necessarily the material reality. If this were a material reality, there would be no need for Western women to organize in the strong political movements that one sees emerging in almost every country nowadays (1988:74).

It is important for educators engaged in the discourse of sexism across different communities (especially Third World women) to give serious consideration to a statement made by Marnia Lazreg (1988). This author has brought the subject of intersubjectivity into the analysis of women's studies on a cross-cultural basis. She argues that when studying Third World women, it is important to see their lives as meaningful, coherent, and understandable instead of as being infused "by us" with doom and sorrow. What this means is that their lives, just like "ours," are structured by similar economic, political, and cultural factors. It means that these women are, just like us, involved in the process of adjusting, shaping, and, at times, resisting and transforming, their own environments (pp. 81–107).

In the anti-racist workshops that I often conduct in schools, typical concerns of teachers and administrators revolve around gender issues in different cultures. Questions will be asked as to why women from such and such a culture walk a few steps behind their husbands and whether or not we should prevent our students from learning that behavior, or what we can do when a student or a parent from such and such a culture has no respect for us because we are female teachers. These questions bring out, once again, the alleged passivity attributed to women from those cultures and make issues related to sexism culture-specific. Moreover, they oversimplify the whole range of possibilities that may be open to women within a given culture. By taking into account intersubjectivity, we can challenge the sexism of any community, because it allows us to see the expressions of society's hidden colonialist, Eurocentric, and racist attitudes.

An excellent example, from which we Canadians can learn a great deal about the shortcomings in anti-racist literature in dealing with gender issues, can be found in the debate among educators that took place in England in the 1980s. The debate surrounded the opening of segregated schools for Muslim girls, as demanded by Muslim communities (Walking & Brannigan, 1986; Troyna & Carrington, 1987). Troyna and Carrington provided an excellent analysis of the various expressions of racism, misunderstanding, and stereotyping of the Muslim culture by most of British society. They were not able, however, to fully grasp the issue of the sexism present within the more fundamentalist Islamic community. In combatting racism, they and others forgot or ignored the sexism that Muslim women and girls face within their own cultural milieu. The emergence of an organization such as Women Against Fundamentalism in England is probably a result of such inconsistencies in the analysis of gender issues by anti-racist educators. It calls our attention to the fact that reducing problems of sexism to forms of institutionalized racism and/or individual stereotypes does not, in any meaningful way, help minority women who are the subject of discriminatory practices by some radical elements with the fundamentalist movements (see Gita Sahgal and Nira Yuval-Davis, 1992). In discussing the fundamentalist groups' demands for an only-Muslim girls' school, author Saeeda Khanum (1992) shows with great lucidity how male Muslim leaders abused England's policy of multiculturalism to achieve their goals. She decries the fact that anti-racist educators and practitioners failed to acknowledge the "hidden agenda" behind the demands of religious fundamentalists: an attempt to stifle dissent and exert absolute control over the lives of Muslim women within the Islamic community (p. 138).

Since Canada is by no means immune to the spread of religious fundamentalism, and given the fact that increasing numbers of studen⟨ from families who have migrated from Third World countries, it is ⟨ to be aware of situations similar to those developing in England interaction with Third World students, we need to develop the techniques needed to successfully challenge both the racism and the sexism of the education system as well as the sexism, tensions, and conflicts present within the minority female students' own communities. As religious fundamentalism rises in many parts of the world,[2] it becomes more and more important that everyone concerned with the negative impact that such a movement has on women's lives be ready to challenge fundamentalism head-on.

An example of this occurred not too long ago. A request was made by a father that his 13-year-old daughter be exempted from participating in physical education and music classes as well as from attending school assemblies. The man stated that his request was in line with the Canadian policy of multiculturalism, which guarantees respect for diverse religions and cultures. Since the school authorities did not know how to respond to the father's request, I was asked to intervene as a mediator because my cultural and religious backgrounds are similar to those of the girl's family. I met the father, who gave me a very rigid interpretation of his religion; according to him, it specifically forbids girls from coming into contact with boys and from listening to music or attending school assemblies. Interestingly enough, the same man had no qualms whatsoever with regard to his 12-year-old son, who attended the same school as his sister. The boy was not constrained by any of the demands that the father was imposing upon his daughter. School administrators were quite willing to accommodate the father's request and minimize the daughter's contacts with boys during physical education classes, but the father was in no mood to compromise. He threatened to keep his daughter at home, because according to him, there was no need for her to go to school if the school was not willing to comply with his demands. He was told that his daughter must attend school in accordance with Canadian law, but he remained adamant about upholding his religious beliefs. I suggested to him that his interpretation of his religion was not shared by other religious scholars, who do not see learning music as a sinful act. I even referred him to a religious authority in the city with whom we could discuss the problems, but he would not listen. A few days later I found out that he had placed his daughter in a religious school. This example clearly shows that the public education system should be better prepared to deal with fundamentalism across a variety of religions.

To successfully meet the challenge, a more democratic education system is needed. This is the site where the struggle to resist racism, sexism, and classism must be situated. It is there that the tensions, conflicts, and the gap that characterize the relationship between the school system and the home environment must be bridged. As discussed earlier, our education system is found wanting when it comes to the ways in which minority female students are treated. The presence of a colonial discourse among some of our own Canadian educators signals the need to completely uproot institutionalized racism and sexism. Only through the elimination of the old colonial attitudes will the education system be able to deal with gender issues pertaining to minority female students and develop the knowledge and understanding needed to identify and successfully challenge the demands of the more religious fundamentalist groups.

WHAT IS THE DILEMMA?

Anti-racist practitioners do the kind of work that is not part of mainstream education. In fact, their work is seen as marginal to whatever the business of education is supposed to be. Accordingly, anti-racist practitioners are faced with insurmountable difficulties when dealing with the racism and sexism present in institutional structures. While anti-racism is becoming mandatory, there appears to be little concern with anti-sexism education. Only a few boards of education offer programs and policies regarding gender issues. There are still no mandatory requirements for anti-sexist education. Moreover, it appears that at the structural level, a distinct separation between the work of anti-racist and anti-sexist educators continues to be made.

As I mentioned earlier, in the new guidelines for the development of anti-racism policies, there are no references to gender issues. Each specialist is expected to work within his or her own boundaries. For some of us who are interested in combining anti-racism and anti-sexism work, the crossing of those boundaries is a must. Yet when we cross the boundaries, we are likely to face some other contradictions and tensions in our work. The workshops that practitioners lead in order to sensitize school personnel are not sufficient (usually not more than two hours) to deal with complex issues such as colonization, capitalist expansion, school knowledge, power, and curriculum reform. In addition, the clear differentiation between anti-racism and anti-sexism does not allow the practitioner to provide the necessary input to bringing about needed changes at the structural level. On the contrary, given the nature of their work, practitioners are more likely, although unwillingly, to facilitate and reinforce the normal state of affairs that characterize the existing larger structure. This is not to say that structural constraints completely disable practitioners and prevent them from doing progressive work in the area of racism and sexism. They still find the means with which to overcome the limitations and resistance that they constantly face from the education system. Under extremely difficult circumstances, they are constantly looking for allies in order to be able to carry on the business of making the school system more democratic. Much of their energy is consumed by choosing words that won't antagonize their audience or hiding the fact that if they could they would be providing a more critical analysis of the education system, one in which words such as capitalist exploitation and colonial domination are presented within their real historical dimensions. The reality of the context within which practitioners operate is very different: the dominant ideological discourse is still so strong that some teachers and administrators believe that Canada is a socialist country because of the existence of the universal health care and welfare system. Time constraints and the marginal nature of anti-racist work do not allow practitioners to take issue with such misinformation. All that some "educators" want is to talk mainly about individualized forms of racism and what kinds of "prescriptions" the practitioner can give them so that they can be used right away in the classroom. Any attempt to bring into the discussion other crucial issues such as institutionalized racism, sexism, classism, capitalist exploitation, colonialism, and so on, are found to be "too academic" (i.e., useless) and of no practical relevance to their classroom experience.

Practitioners can take solace in the fact that the most rewarding part of their jobs is the contributions they are making towards students' empowerment. Unlike the uniformity of the educational bureaucracy, which continues to be mainly Anglo-Saxon, the diversity of the student population makes it possible to work consistently with large numbers of students who are eager to understand—and who can relate to—those complex interactions between racism and sexism and the ways of dealing with them. Concerns about racism and sexism among Canadian students have a sense of urgency that neither the institutional structure nor educators appear able to grasp at the present time.

The growing number of immigrants to Canada, the increase in racial and ethnic diversity, and the growth of religious fundamentalism are making the diverse Canadian student population even more aware of the challenges that many of them face in dealing with the scourges of racism and sexism. Sahgal and Yuval-Davis (1992) put it excellently:

Issues of racism and sexism are intricately interwoven. However, this is no reason always to prioritize one struggle in favour of the other. The task ahead is to find ways to confront the contradictions and conflicts within minority communities as well as oppression and racism in the state and society at large. To find ways to resolve the tension between autonomy and tolerance, diversity and equality. To have the right to dissent and oppose both racism and sexism—and, of course, fundamentalism. (P. 25)

NOTES

1. Leila Ahmed (1992:151–53) provides a very good account of this discourse in regard to Muslim Middle East. She states that the discourse of patriarchal colonialism captured the language of feminism and used the issue of women's position in Islamic societies as the spearhead of the colonial attack on those societies. Imperialist men, who were the enemies of feminism in their own societies, abroad espoused a rhetoric of feminism, attacking the practice of other men and their "degradation" of women. They used the argument that the cultures of colonized

peoples degraded women in order to legitimize Western domination and justify colonial policies of actively trying to subvert the cultures and religions of the colonized people.

2. My use of the term fundamentalism departs from that often used in the mainstream media. In the latter, the word is usually used in relation to the Islamic world. My understanding of fundamentalism is closer to the definition used by the organization Women Against Fundamentalism and to the meaning given to it by Edward Said in his recent work, *Culture and Imperialism*. The rise of fundamentalism should be seen in relation to colonization and the search for an original, authentic identity. The Women Against Fundamentalism organization identifies fundamentalist groups in accordance to two traits: they believe that their version of the religion is the only correct one and therefore feel threatened by any pluralistic system of thoughts, and they use political means to impose their version of the truth on all members of their religion. These beliefs, in turn, translate into their attacking the notion of secularism, since the very idea of a public sphere not controlled by organized religion is unacceptable to them.

6

Aboriginal Teachers as Organic Intellectuals

Rick Hesch

Most teacher education programs in North America serve to maintain a social system based on inequality and injustice (Popkewitz, 1987; Ginsburg, 1988). Graduates from these teacher education programs also tend to be politically conservative citizens (Lortie, 1975). Furthermore, comparative data suggest that aboriginal teachers will oppose or limit militant or radical trends within indigenous organizations or social movements (Marable, 1984, 1985; Sarupt, 1984). An alternative to this scenario exists, however, if aboriginal teachers can use their academic experience to develop a broad, critical understanding of Canadian indigenous history and social conditions, including racist schooling. Such teachers have the potential of integrating their own cultural experience and memories of racist schooling with a new theoretical consciousness in order to contribute to movements for progressive social change, at least in the field of education. This chapter shows how a university course that focused on anti-racist education and critical pedagogy was used by eight aboriginal women to develop their capacity as "organic intellectuals"—preservice teachers with a commitment to anti-racist education.

Antonio Gramsci (1891–1937) has contributed much to current theorizing in the sociology of education (Apple, 1985; Giroux, 1988; Sharp, 1980; Weiler, 1988). Although Gramsci lived and wrote in Italy in the 1930s, his commitment to the advancement of relatively powerless people and his brilliant analyses of the state, culture, ideology, and the process of fundamental political change make his insights of specific and current value to those working in the field of aboriginal education who are dissatisfied with the status quo and seek a transformation in existing power relations between the state and aboriginal people. Gramsci's first commitment was to the Italian working class. While not all aboriginal Canadians are located within the working class, they do share a relative lack of political power and access to capital, which I argue makes Gramsci's arguments and analyses useful. With reference to the role of intellectuals, Gramsci argued that each social class "creates together with itself, organically, one or more strata of intellectuals which give it homogeneity and an awareness of its own function not only in economic but also in the social and political fields" (quoted in McLellan, 1979:101). According to Gransci, fundamental social change will arise, in part, from the work of organic intellectuals from the working class. Organic intellectuals from aboriginal communities, then, use the language of their culture to express the real experiences and feelings of their people. In order to express and truly understand these experiences, they must feel the same passions as the people (Kolakowski, 1985). The responsibility of these or-ganic intellectuals is to draw out and make coherent the latent aspirations and potentialities already inherent in their people's activity. The relationship of organic intellectuals and their social group is thus a dialectical one: they draw knowledge from their social community's experience at the same time as they provide "clear theoretical consciousness of. . .practical activity" (Gramsci, 1971:333) back to them. Organic intellectuals have a capacity and promise that go beyond the potential of the most theoretically developed and committed members of the middle-class intelligentsia: they speak both from and to their own communities.

This chapter is a review of my experience in teaching a course that focused on the themes of anti-racist education and critical pedagogy to a group of eight aboriginal women enrolled in the Saskatchewan Urban Native Teacher Education Program (SUNTEP). It examines the theory that informed the course design and delivery and the process for course deliv-ery, and presents conclusions from reflections on the work of doing anti-racist education with aboriginal preservice teachers. Initially, the proposed focus of the course was resisted by the students, who argued for a more conventional course consistent with dominant forms of teacher education. My own abstract theoreticism, abstract language, idealism, and limited understanding of the women's lived culture contributed to their resistance. The result was a near inversion of more common conflicts between the conservative ideologies of teachers in authority and the cultural forms of minority and working-class student populations (McLaren, 1989; Weis, 1985; Willis, 1977). However, a dialogical strategy underlying the pedagogy of the course led first to a space and a sense of trust where sources of conflict could be taken up; second, to the relatively democratic negotiation of the terms for the course; third, to an appropriation by the students of at least elements of critical pedagogy; and fourth, to the continuing education of a radical teacher educator.

Since the course was designed to introduce theory drawn from the fields of both anti-racist education and critical pedagogy, the dialogical process also encouraged the students to reflect together on their own earlier school-ing experience and its relationship to racism in their broader community. As their collective consciousness became more coherent, they also moved towards an increasingly more sophisticated articulation of aboriginal peo-ple's experience and oppression in the social and economic realms. The students' expressions in class often resonated with the anger motivated by both the memory and the currently lived effects of racism. However, we did not restrict our mutual analysis and learning to critique alone. The students also moved towards a "language of possibility" (Aronowitz & Giroux, 1985).[1]

SUNTEP is an affirmative action teacher education program for students of Métis ancestry in Saskatchewan. A contractual arrangement with the local district chiefs, however, meant that two of the students were Cree. All of the eight students were women, a condition not entirely unrepresentative of the SUNTEP student population in general, and the North American teaching workforce as a whole (Apple, 1987; Marshall, 1987).[2] SUNTEP operates at three provincial sites, and had an enrollment of 187 students in the 1989–1990 academic year. Although all of the students are aboriginal people, none of the teaching faculty at the center where this case study was set were aboriginal.[3] I had been employed by the University of Saskatche-wan to teach EdCur 380.3: Senior Methods in Teaching Elementary Social Studies for the program at its site in Forestland.

Methodologically, the reflections represented here were developed in two stages. First, field notes were kept of plans that were developed for delivering the course, elements of student discourse during the progress of each class meeting, and ethnographic summaries written at the completion of each meeting. Documents written for presentation to the group and excerpts from students' written papers were also kept. Second, after the completion of the course all field notes and documents were reviewed and analyzed, as were students' final exams and a typed copy of their course evaluations. Data were analyzed and were presented from the perspective of critical sociology in education (Weiler, 1988; McCarthy & Apple, 1988). Personal and place names used here are fictional. Students gave written permission for use of data from the class for this chapter. Its personal and subjective style is meant to acknowledge that each person's pedagogic style is both personal and creative, that there are no recipes, and that I take personal responsibility for the limitations of the course and its pedagogy. The attempt to map out my pedagogy in some detail is a response to what I sense as a lack of concreteness in much of the literature.

Given the historic relation between Métis and white people in central Canada and the fact that all of the students were women, the pedagogic and research relationships were problematic. Therefore, some space and effort need to be given to my own social location in the production of this chapter. Explicit consciousness and recognition of my subject position may make visible the limitations of the analysis that follows and enable me to use the strengths I bring to this work.

My social location can best be explained by my history (Hall, 1988; Spivak, 1990). I have lived most of my life in the inconsistent and unpredictable location characteristic of many middle-class radical intellectuals in advanced capitalist countries of the late twentieth century. That is, as a socialist, I have intentionally spent most of my working life attempting to effect social change in the interests of those without property. On the other hand, I have accumulated relative privilege both by chance of birth and as a result of benefits that often accrue to those with a university education. My historical trajectory begins in a settler economy established through the dispossession of aboriginal people. Ultimately, the same historical dynamic that colonized aboriginal people on the prairies, that is, capitalism on a world scale, also produced economic conditions where it was impossible for me to become an independent commodity producer on a Saskatchewan farm. It was necessary to borrow money to attend university; yet I could train and work as a teacher and simultaneously for social change without creating long-term rupture to my life chances within the middle class. As the Métis occupy a social location between treaty Indians and white society, I occupied a social location between the working class and the sons and daughters of the professional class.

My location in relation to gender is not quite analogous. Racism was a silent issue in the formative years of my youth, whereas I had a ready-made setting for the learning of patriarchal gender relations within my family. This early sexist learning has never been completely divorced from my mature consciousness or practice. An introduction to Marxism and the student politics of the 1960s did contribute to a more secure and long-lasting alignment with the interests of those without power and property, however. Furthermore, my employment as a classroom instructor on a Saskatchewan Indian reserve in the 1970s moved me from a position of moral and political support to personal investment in the improvement of conditions for aboriginal people. To work as a radical teacher educator within SUNTEP, then, is to engage with a tension between ideology and material position. This contradiction could not help but affect the reciprocal relations I developed with my students. For their part, the students may have seen less difference than I did between myself and the many other male, white university teachers they had listened to and written papers and exams for. On the other hand, the fact that most students were "mixed blood" people may have mediated our racial difference.

THEORETICAL FRAMEWORK

The idea of teaching a Social Studies Methods course with a conventional structure and content was not something I considered. As Paulo Freire advises, "There are no neutral 'methodologists' who can teach how to teach history, geography, language, or mathematics neutrally" (1983:102). Teaching a methods course in a college of education setting is a political act that most often asks the instructor to unproblematically transmit the behaviorist and empiricist ideology represented by most North American teacher education programs (Ginsburg, 1988; Popkewitz, 1987). Specifically, social studies methods text and courses usually reflect the Tayloristic principles of scientific management and assume that social studies classrooms operate principally according to an ethic of control (Grundy, 1987; McNeil, 1988; Schiro, 1978). To replicate these models for social studies teaching would be to reinforce the notion that aboriginal and other students resist or refuse social studies school work because of inherent limitations in either students or teachers, or both. It would at the same time accept the notion of the hegemonic social studies curriculum and the idea that problems in social studies classrooms can be repaired through implementation of the appropriate value-neutral technique.

Rather, an approach to teachers' work that acknowledged that "education must be understood as producing not only knowledge but also political subjects" (Giroux, 1991:47) was necessary. I assumed that a commitment to and understanding of anti-racist education and critical pedagogy could most effectively be built out of students' theoretical comprehension of their personal schooling history and a critique of a dominant state ideology with reference to racist schooling: multicultural education. From a theoretical consciousness of the limitations of what exists, we would move to the formation of a theory for change constructed on strategies for anti-racist education and critical pedagogy. I do not want to suggest here that the theoretical framework utilized in the course is the only legitimate construct for promoting the well-being of aboriginal students. Teacher educators should be conscious that "thought is nothing more and nothing less than a historically locatable set of practices" (Rabinow, 1986:239), so that traditional aboriginal "styles of thinking" (ibid.:237) have as much purchase on "truth" as any Eurocentric modes of rationality (Amin, 1989). Certainly my fundamentally Marxist framework originates within one tradition of European rationality.

Five major concepts formed the basis for developing students' language of critique (Aronowitz & Giroux, 1985): social reproduction, resistance, cultural reproduction, cultural production, and (ideological) hegemony. Each of these major concepts enjoys currency within the critical sociological literature (Weiler, 1988). They can be summarily defined as follows:

1. *Social reproduction*: The replacement of a relationship between social classes or groups. In a number of ways, Saskatchewan schools exclude aboriginal children from the potential benefits of formal education. Through these practices, social reproduction is realized, ultimately, in the "racial" division of labor, whereby some people are school executives and others are janitors, for example.

2. *Resistance*: The oppositional practices of some children to the racist or otherwise oppressive practices and attitudes exercised against them in schools. The precise meaning of the concept is currently under debate (Weiler, 1988; Carnoy, 1989). However, it serves as an alternative explanation for student "misbehavior" to the concept of deviance.

3. *Cultural reproduction*: Minority and working-class children are in some ways implicated in the processes that result in their own subordination. Partly as a result of their own resistance, some children become consigned to live out their lives at the bottom of the social hierarchy in some ways, similar to the lives of their parents and kin. Thus, cultural reproduction occurs both through the actions of the victims of racism and through the overt practices of personnel in the field of public education (Ogbu, 1988; Weis, 1985). Practices that are culturally reproductive are often reflections of ideas and attitudes inherited through the culture of the family, kin, or social group. Cultural reproduction of the dominant society also occurs through the historical practices of the school in its privileging of bourgeois cultural forms (Giroux & Simon, 1989).

4. *Cultural production*: To the extent that the students' resistance takes the form of creating new forms of cultural attitudes and practices, such as the wearing of nose rings in symbolic opposition to mainstream cultural norms, cultural production has transpired.

5. *Ideological hegemony, or hegemony*: Refers to the ways in which the state works to ensure that oppressed and exploited populations give consent to their own domination and that of others. Hegemony depends, in large part, on people accepting the ruling ideas in society as "common sense." One of the major institutions in society for gaining ideological hegemony is the school (Althusser, 1971). Hegemony is never completely secured by the state, however, so policies and practices are constantly shifting to secure it.

Hegemony is maintained through the operations of the institutions of civil society, such as the church, trade unions, schools, and the press. Civil society is the site of ideological production. It is civil society that supports the persistence of workers' "common sense," that is, those views "inherited from the past and uncritically absorbed" (Gramsci, 1971:333). In contrast, workers also produce a view of the world "which emerges from the real activity of each man [*sic*]" (p. 326). That is, because subordinate populations are daily engaged in practical activity in a world of oppression and exploitation, consent to rule is never passively given. Elements of "good sense," of the working class's "own conception of the world, even if only embryonic, manifests itself in action, but occasionally and in flashes—when, that is, the group is acting as an organic totality" (p. 327). However, the worker has "no clear theoretical consciousness of his practical activity . . . which in reality unites him with all his fellow-workers in the practical transformation of the real world" (p. 333). The result of the transmission and partial acceptance of "common sense," which conflicts with "good sense," is a "contradictory consciousness" or "too theoretical consciousness" (p. 333). This is the terrain for the cultural and ideological work of the organic intellectual. Organic intellectuals seek to "refashion and transform" common sense through the propagation of "organic ideologies" in order to create "a new form of national-popular will . . . to interrupt, renovate, and transform in a more systematic direction the practical consciousness of the masses" (Hall, 1988:55).

SUNTEP was created on the basis of multiculturalist assumptions, to produce "role models" (Hesch, 1989b), and the program's primary nonaboriginal support comes from those who understand SUNTEP graduates as fulfilling a multiculturalist mandate (Hesch, 1989a). Therefore, the ideology of multicultural education was central to the identity of "teacher" that my students were engaged in constructing. In this analysis, multicultural education can be viewed as a strategy of the state to secure hegemony in the field of race relations. Troyna and Williams (1986) argue that multiculturalists define educational problems that arise from a multiracial society as stemming from the existence of minority children. These problems include "underachievement," poor motivation, indiscipline, both cultural and psychological alienation, low self-esteem, damaged personal identities, and cultural differences. The origins of problems for multicultural educators lie in the following: (1) the relationship between minority students and the dominant society produces a lack of self-respect, self-esteem, and/or identity problems; (2) as with multiculturalism's predecessor, assimilation theory, parents continue to be blamed for the child's performance in school, due to both lack of stability and educational, especially language, backwardness; (3) minority cultures are not acknowledged or respected in school settings; (4) disadvantaged or deprived material conditions for families limit the possibilities of learning. To confuse the effects of racism with perceived causes located in the minority family is to understand minority experience as a pathology (Lawrence, 1983). In each case, the gaze of the policy maker falls on the subjects, the victims of racism, rather than its perpetrators.

Following from this identification and analysis of minority education, multicultural education policy recommendations are aimed at compensatory solutions designed to remedy linguistic, cultural, and psychic deficits. A great deal of stress is placed on the development of a multicultural curriculum aiming to increase students' motivation and commitment to educational achievement. Since racism is perceived as a problem of attitude, the multicultural curriculum is also intended to educate white students out of their prejudices (Manicom, 1987). Hazel Carby's (1982) description and analysis of multicultural education policy in Britain during the 1970s also provides a very useful summary of the multicultural education strategies. Amongst these, multicultural educators are concerned about culturally biased testing and "progressive methods" of teaching, but the concern remains with improving the performance of the individual child rather than with examining schooling as a means of social reproduction.

Multicultural educators share common assumptions with multiculturalists in general. The two most frequently made criticisms of multiculturalism
are: first, that it casts the experience of victims of racism purely within a
culturalist theoretical framework; second, that multiculturalism usually
reifies culture. That is, in relying on a culturalist framework, multiculturalism fails to recognize the ways in which class (Buchignani, 1980; Ng, 1987;
Osborne, 1987) and gender (Ng, 1987; McCarthy & Apple, 1988; Witt, 1984)
contribute to the reality experienced by racial and ethnic groups. To reify
culture is to turn it into a dead, static thing. Rather than understanding
culture as lived experience, we are asked to honor cultural heritages in the
form of traditional songs and dance (Ng, 1981; Rizvi, 1986; Simon, 1987).
Ethnicity or cultural groups are socially constructed and historically variable, not fixed in time (Mullings, 1984). These two limitations of multiculturalism have a single ideological utility for the state and capital, a point
made both clearly and succinctly by Jackie Wilson:

The Canadian multiculturalism policy seems to guarantee that we can each do our
little dances and flash our pretty, lacy petticoats while we drink our ethnic drinks
and admire each other's handicrafts, as long as we realize that in reality the mosaic
is vertically organized. It says little about meeting the needs of those of us whose
place is at the bottom of that vertical column, who can not find decent employment
or housing, where creative spirit is crushed by poverty and incessant insecurity,
whose children are destined only to replace us in our bottom slots. It does not speak
to the injustice that pervades our daily lives if our hair style or skin colour is unlike
that of the members at the top of the column. (Quoted in Bullivant, 1981a:12)

As others argue in this collection, much of what passes for anti-racist
education is, in fact, multiculturalism in new clothing (Brandt, 1986;
Hatcher, 1987). Anti-racist education can, however, serve as a counterhegemonic strategy or set of strategies in which the effects of racist education are challenged, struggled against, and at least partially changed.
Troyna and Williams (1986) argue that in contrast to multicultural education, anti-racist educators define educational problems for minority children as arising from the normal operations of capitalist schooling in a racist
social order, rather than from the presence of aboriginal children in the
schools. Rather than being concerned with the presumed deficiencies or
pathological nature of aboriginal children, anti-racist educators focus their
analyses on the origin and perpetuation of racism and the production and
reproduction of "racial" inequality. Instead of developing programs and
curricula to change children so that they adjust to the school, anti-racist
educators are concerned with changing institutions, through such measures
as the politicization of the formal curriculum, attention to the "hidden"
curriculum, changes in the ways children are streamed and assessed, the
hiring of more minority staff, and the promotion of those already hired. The
minority teachers are not expected to serve as models of accommodating

behavior and simply reduce minority student resistance, but to contribute to the achievement of "racial" justice and equality and to affirm lived minority cultural practices and attitudes.[4] Schools do not conduct their business in social isolation, but are part of a complex and systematic process at work in society at large. Therefore, anti-racist educators must also be active in the social/public arena (Brandt, 1986). Anti-racist education debunks multiculturalist conceptions of culture by examining culture as it is lived, and incorporates factors of class and gender into notions of aboriginal culture.

The idea of "race" lost all credibility as a concept with any scientific validity some fifty years ago (Miles, 1989), and is therefore placed within quotation marks in this chapter, following Robert Miles (1989). However, the ideology of racism always reflects real observable phenomena in some distorted way (Miles, 1989). The notion of the "lazy Indian," for example, is related to high unemployment rates amongst aboriginal Canadians and particular cultural practices amongst some aboriginal people who resist capitalism's requirement for a low-paid, menial labor force to do the "dirty work" in the economy. Therefore, anti-racist education is futile if it restricts its aims to changing the attitudes of racists. The aim must be to attack the conditions that produce racism (Miles, 1989).

The Social Studies Methods course was aimed to help produce pedagogues rather than skilled classroom technicians. That is, borrowing from Giroux and Simon (1989), I take pedagogy to be a deliberate attempt to influence how and what knowledge and identities are produced in a particular society. Pedagogy attempts to influence the occurrence and qualities of students' experiences. Pedagogues assume that knowledge is constructed by individuals in a social context. That is, knowledge does not exist in books or on the air waves. Rather, we each interpret words differently, based largely on the nature of our own previous experiences in life. Thus, the same structured learning experience leads to different "ownership" of knowledge of individuals. A pedagogue must attend to all of the following: (1) curriculum content and design, (2) classroom strategies and techniques, (3) a time and space for the practicing of these strategies and techniques, and (4) evaluation purposes and methods. Moreover, pedagogy is not neutral. What actually takes place in a classroom is a reflection of a view about the nature of teachers' work within a classroom and the outcomes of that work. What work a teacher does in a classroom will tell us much concerning what that teacher believes about: (1) what knowledge is most valuable; (2) what kinds of desire we can have; (3) what it means to know something; and (4) how we can develop our own identities, our views of others, and our views of our physical and social environment. A teacher's answers to these questions reflect an understanding of who has power in society, both legitimately and actually, and also who should have power. Politics in society is concerned with the question and problem of power.

Therefore, to develop a preferred form of pedagogy is to develop a political view. The concept of critical pedagogy asks, To whom are we committed if, as teachers, we want to work in such a way that our students can develop their abilities to live and participate in a more socially just and democratic society? Further, if we want to work in such a way that our students can develop all of their personal potential, then our pedagogy must be linked to the goals of educating students: (1) to understand why things are the way they are and how they got to be that way; (2) to ask questions about the nature of their everyday lives; (3) to take risks and to challenge unequal forms of power; and (4) to have a vision of a world that doesn't exist yet in order to strengthen the possibility for creating a better society. To be committed to this approach to teaching is to be committed to critical pedagogy. Critical pedagogy incorporates student experience and lived culture as a curriculum concern. In the sense that critical pedagogy is implicated in the construction of identities and engages in a study of lived culture, it is itself a cultural practice.

One of the central concepts of critical pedagogy is the notion of dialogue, or dialogical education. This means considerably more than the conventional "class discussion" format popular in some humanist classrooms. At a theoretical level, dialogue is best articulated by a leading founder of critical pedagogy, Paulo Freire:

> Parallel with the reorganization of the means of production, an essential task for critical understanding and attention in a revolutionary society is the valorization—and not the idealization—of popular wisdom that includes the creative activity of a people and reveals the levels of their knowledge regarding reality. What is implied is not the transmission to the people of a knowledge previously elaborated, a process that ignores what they already know, but the act of returning to them, in an organized form, what they have themselves offered in a disorganized form. In other words, it is a process of knowing with the people how they know things and the level of that knowledge. This means challenging them, through critical reflection, regarding their own practical experience and the ends that motivate them in order, in the end, to organize the findings, and thus replace mere opinion about facts with an increasingly rigorous understanding of their significance. (1983:24–25)

This style of work comes very close to the cultural work outlined for organic intellectuals by Antonio Gramsci (Hommen, 1986).

COURSE DESIGN

This section outlines the major assumptions, goals, and requirements of the course. This overview of the course will show how these assumptions, goals, and requirements contributed to the development of organic intellectuals. In the Gramscian sense that every person is an intellectual, the students came to the program as intellectuals. Their capacity to think and act analytically had been strengthened in previous courses in the program as well, notably a Native Studies course with Métis radical nationalist Howard Adams (1989). Planning the goals and requirements for the present course was an important stage in its limited achievements. This section also provides a necessary foreground for understanding the dialectic between the structure of the course and the cultural politics at play as we moved through the term.

The course was designed with the understanding that critical pedagogy lends itself well to a project of facilitating the further development of organic intellectuals and shares fundamental goals with anti-racist education. The power relations between students and teachers that are reflected in educational practices are as political as explicit curriculum content (Giroux, 1983). Thus, a pedagogy aimed at democratically restructuring the classroom relations between the students and myself was planned. Since anti-racist education includes a critical analysis of curriculum content and its method of transmission, as well as an examination of the "hidden curriculum" (Brandt, 1986), an alternative to a lecturing method seemed preferable. That is, if schooling and capitalist society create a "culture of silence" (Freire, 1970) amongst victims of racism, then a teaching style directed against silencing of students was in itself an anti-racist measure. Anti-racist education's affirmation of life histories and the lived experience of those silenced by racism (Brandt, 1986) could be validated by the practice of dialogical education and attention to "generative themes" (Freire, 1983) from students' everyday and historical existence. In brief, critical pedagogy's commitment to "education for critical consciousness" (Freire, 1973) could be satisfied by meeting the anti-racist goal of examining the reproduction of racialized divisions of labor, economic wealth, and cultural privilege (Carter & Williams, 1987).

With limits imposed by the university as a state institution and employer, the course was designed to facilitate the development of intellectuals who would become more familiar with the limitations of racist and capitalist schooling and would be prepared to speak and act against these limitations and for progressive alternatives. The course was designed to move from a critique of the problem of racist education to the development of practical possibilities for anti-racist education. There were four evaluated assignments for the course. In the first course assignment, I asked the students to write brief papers critically analyzing a local education policy based on multiculturalist assumptions. The assignment was intended to show the limitations of multiculturalism as a solution to aboriginal concerns about schooling, to identify multiculturalist policy as a local phenomenon affecting the lives of aboriginal children in the community, and to demonstrate the relevance of policy to the nature of teachers' work. For their second and major assignment, students were asked to develop an anti-racist project that would be utilized in some public way. The intent was to allow the students to apply anti-racist education theory to practice and to establish the link between social action in the community and classroom practice, a principle of both anti-racist education and critical pedagogy (Brandt, 1986; Giroux, 1988). The third assignment, which was a concession by me to the expressed interests of my employer, asked students to construct a learning center using ideas drawn from the text *Open Minds to Equality* by Schniedewind and Davidson (1983). Both the major anti-racist project and the learning center were to be completed through group work in order to encourage group identity and collective consciousness, and to undercut the individualistic ethos of conventional schooling. Finally, the students were required by university regulation to write a final exam. The very fact that there were requirements that would be graded and entered into the students' permanent university transcripts underlined the structural limitations imposed on the course, the students, and myself.

PEDAGOGY FOR ORGANIC INTELLECTUALS

The process through which the course developed was the most critical feature for its success. Three features of the course helped clarify the "good sense" of the organic intellectuals by the end of term: dialogue, negotiation, and the selection of anti-racist education as a "generative theme" (Freire, 1970). Both dialogue and negotiation contributed to our sharing of power over the content, process, and evaluation of student work during the course. One effect of this limited but significant empowerment was to enhance students' sense that the social relations of the classroom are problematic and can be changed. Dialogue also encouraged students to collectively focus on the manifestations of racism in their personal and community lives. The theoretical and practical consciousness that a classroom can be a place for the legitimation of students' own knowledge, a place for discussion and critique of their cultural lives and local forms of oppression, was reinforced. Initially this aspect of the course seemed rather fruitless for their purposes; however, as the process continued, students became more committed to the need for change. The selection of anti-racist education as a theme for the course, generated by their prior experience and practical concerns (as I understood them), meant that course content developed students' theoretical understanding of racism and anti-racist education. It also meant that space was created in the classroom for the generation of their own theoretical consciousness.

Dialogue and Negotiation

A dialogic approach to anti-racist education with the direct victims of racism is superior to a lecture method for the integration of theoretical with practical knowledge of the world. On the other hand, teacher educators should not be ashamed to offer their own theoretical and practical resources to students (Freire, 1983). In our case, classroom dialogue usually preceded informal lectures. I established the overall direction of each class discussion through selection and assignment of appropriate course materials. The process of generating a critical discussion of assigned readings was initiated by my asking students, "What issues arose for you from the reading?" This question recognizes that knowledge formation is not only a social process but is also highly personal, and that it involves an integration of studied theoretical content with the biography of the reader. The question can also serve to reinforce democratic relations in the classroom, as it directs the "ownership" of discussion back to the students. Finally, students' anticipation of the question encourages an active and practical reading of the material to be studied.[5]

At least three difficulties can arise in the process of dialogical education: (1) moving beyond "class discussion" towards the development of meaningful theory, (2) breaking students' ingrained dependence on teachers for the "right" answer, and (3) creating a democratic classroom where dominant student personalities do not exclude the voices of the more reticent. At the beginning of the term, the students' initial responses to the readings sometimes failed to converge into mutual dialogue. One of two processes unfolded as the class meeting progressed, however. Either the students would find their own grounds for dialogue as time passed, or I would identify emerging issues by actively "reading" their discussion. That is, acting as facilitator of the meeting, I would attempt to "read" students' talk for emerging contradictions in lines of thinking, quickly summarize the contradiction, and return the problem inherent in the contradiction to them for further discussion and theorizing of their own. It was not unusual for students to directly ask for my views on an emerging theoretical difference between themselves or for a reference to theory. I tried always to return the question to the student in order to encourage the generation of theory rooted in the students' own experience. When I was not delivering a planned lecture, I tried to limit my answer giving to the clarification of theoretical concepts, responding to problems with assignments.

Even within a group of students who were relatively homogeneous in terms of nationality, class, and gender, it became important to watch for the unconscious silencing of some by more talkative others and to intervene as facilitator in response to the smallest sign that a less dominant student was interested in speaking. My own practices of silencing were less visible to me, although I usually attempted to surrender space to students whenever an opportunity for students' critical reflection became apparent. For example, the group once deviated into a discussion of how, as children, they had learned to avoid staff rooms because they had experienced them as hostile terrain. One of the students in the course remarked how "that feeling sticks with you for a long time," since, as a preservice teacher in field experience and mother, she became nervous when she approached a staff room (field notes, March 16, 1990). On the other hand, that same day I expressed the view of the center's faculty on why the sole aboriginal faculty member had left the year before—"for a better job." One of the more talkative students abruptly stopped participating in the class discussion.

My strategy for the course from the beginning had incorporated the principle of students as "co-directors of the curriculum" (Shor & Freire, 1987:91) on the premise that the practice of negotiating the contents and specific requirements of the course provided students with some power over the direction and content of their own learning. In our first meeting, for example, the students had chosen not to write a midterm exam. Students were given the right to establish the criteria for the evaluation of their major assignment and to distribute marks between the different assignments. However, codirection was as much a strategy for my own practical survival, providing a means of correcting for my own errors, as it was a statement of political principle. For example, in the original course outline that I presented to students, I had made reference to a sit-in in a public office as one of several alternative tactics students might wish to employ as a means of meeting the course requirement for a collective activity publicly directed against racism. The students' reaction to the notion was so vehement that I quickly moved to the recommendation for the production of a play, an activity utilizing the skills they had learned through working with the progressive drama educator on staff. The idea was well received by most. Contents of the course evaluations at the end of term revealed that the students had, indeed, valued the power that the negotiated curriculum gave them.

On "Shooting Yourself in the Foot"

In my experience, the problems with dialogical education at the postsecondary level outlined here are quite typical. I anticipated them and consciously acted to minimize their occurrence. However, I unconsciously committed two errors during the first third of the course that led to student resistance and limited our potential achievements. First, I inadvertently subjected the students to an abstract theoreticism and language that initially alienated all of them. Second, in a somewhat related error, I allowed an idealistic commitment to my aims for the course to override a sound interpretation of what was possible given the material and ideological context we were working in. It is conceivable that without the process of dialogue and negotiation that had simultaneously been established, I would have alienated myself from the students for the entire course.

Our first meeting was devoted to the distribution and discussion of the course outline and a lecture I had written delivering a Marxist interpretation of Canadian Indian educational history. Both the course outline and

the lecture used theoretical language that was too confusing for the students. To prepare the students for their written assessment of the local
multiculturalist educational policy, I also distributed as a reading assignment a copy of a paper I had written on multiculturalism. The paper was
written in academic language and was so incomprehensible that it was
necessary to jettison the planned work for our second meeting and endeavor to translate it into understandable English. At the end of term, one
student summarized her response to our first encounters: "I was ready to
give up. He lectured in words I did not understand, and I left not knowing
what had been said. His outline was beyond my comprehension" (course
evaluation, March 30, 1990:1).[6] Clearly, working to develop organic intellectuals does not allow for excessive intellectualism. It is quite possible for
academics committed to social change to at the same time unconsciously
be guilty of elitism (Freire, 1983; McLaren, 1989). Different social class
positions had presented different language systems and codes to the students and myself, a problem not uncommon in similar efforts (Shor &
Freire, 1987). I had not been prepared for the political problem my lecture
and writing produced. Consequently, I shifted strategically towards careful
attention to the integration of key theoretical concepts with the ongoing
student accounts from their personal lives and from discussions. Imbued
with an idealistic commitment to the struggle against racism as I defined it,
I was confused and suspicious of the students' initial resistance to the
general orientation of the course and to the anti-racist project I had assigned.
A more sensitive and materialist analysis of the context I was working in
might have alleviated my dismay. Their reactions to the proposed course
seemed initially to be motivated by three sentiments: first, "You might get
yourself in trouble" (field notes, Jan. 5, 1990); second, a sense of fatalism,
summarized by one student's persistent argument that "they control us
anyways" (field notes, Jan. 5, 1990), and therefore anti-racist education is
futile; third, the course was not a methods class, that is, the students were
not learning techniques and strategies for teaching social studies. By their
own account, some students had come to SUNTEP to escape from a degrad-
ing life, which many aboriginal women in the province must live out. This
motivation was often based on maternal concern for the future of their
children. Their immediate goal was to gain access to the "cultural capital"
(Bourdieu & Passeron, 1977) offered by a university education. To achieve
greater economic security required considerable sacrifice, as their sharing
of textbooks and living in cramped low-rental apartments testified. They
were not, therefore, enthused to invest in a political enterprise designed by
a white, financially secure, middle-class male.

It would soon become clear that opposition to the project also had roots
in the racism of the local school systems. Racism is a condition from which
aboriginal people do not escape. My initial lack of attention to this reality
made another student resist the project of the course. In response to my

early announcement that the course was being used, in part, for research purposes, she "felt at the beginning that this course was only taught for use as research. This kept me from listening to what Rick was teaching. [I] felt us Natives were being used again and if [the course] failed, it failed, no great loss, we won't try it on the Whites then. [This] made what he taught at the beginning go through one ear and out the other" (course evaluation, March 30, 1990).

The sense of exploitation expressed by this student was consistent with her experience in the program and the experience of many SUNTEP students. These preservice teachers are often or usually labelled as "SUNTEP students" during field placements in the public and separate schools, and it is commonplace for students to be asked or told to teach "the Native unit." Other curriculum interests they may have in music or language arts, and so on are treated as secondary. Furthermore, SUNTEP is viewed by many to be a "second-rate program" (field notes, February 15, 1990).[7] Therefore, in the words of one student, "TEP schools [i.e., aboriginal (T)eacher (E)ducation (P)rograms] involve a lot of pressure when attending them, because when one does something wrong, we all did it wrong" (field notes, Jan. 19, 1990). Doing "something wrong" can range from missing a day of field placement without sufficient notice or saying or doing something that is deemed as inappropriate by the cooperating teacher. Thus, the insecurity that most preservice teachers feel during the placement (Ginsburg, 1988) is reinforced and strengthened by this labelling process.

Our fifth meeting became the critical day on which my pedagogic ideology and my institutionalized authority as a university teacher met head-on with the students' racialized cultural experience. The day would be described by one student as "homework day" (field notes, February 15, 1990). The planned agenda for the day was held hostage while I was confronted with students' accumulated frustrations with the course. They were intimately familiar with the nature of racism, they insisted. What they did not have an understanding of was "how to teach social studies." The students argued that they had to be "excellent" to overcome the expectations (or lack of same) of cooperating teachers during field placement or internship.[8]

The students attacked the assignment for a public presentation. They argued that the inferior social status of the program required them to perform as model preservice teachers throughout their teacher training in order to have an equal opportunity for employment. One of the students, Barbara, cited the case of a SUNTEP student who "said something" during field placement at the local Indian Residential School, the ramifications of which were still being heard and felt within the SUNTEP center. "And they like us!" she stressed. "You've got a job!" she reminded me. It was resolved that the play, which was being produced because "you wanted us to do it," would not have to be presented publicly (field notes, Feb. 15, 1990).

Organic intellectuals live the experience of subordinate groups and share the everyday passion and resistance of that group. The women's social position as students is somewhat different from that of their working-class or unemployed kin. However, they continue to share the anger and resentment of other aboriginal people at being labelled and objectified, when they are designated as second-rate SUNTEP students or as research subjects for this study. They continue to be excluded from access to opportunity, such as teaching school subjects of their choice. Initially, my idealism blinded me to these connections. The strategy of dialogical education made it possible for the students to educate me and rescue the course.

"Just Getting Us Mad All Over Again"

Organic intellectuals not only share the pride, anger, insecurities, and sense of marginalization of their social group, but also possess a theoretical and collective consciousness of the nature of their oppression. As the course progressed, both qualities became increasingly evident. Student resistance to the imposed project of training for anti-racist education did not dissipate entirely after "homework day." One student approached the program coordinator later to grieve that I was failing to teach them anything useful, but was "just getting us mad all over again" (field notes, March 8, 1990). Indeed, anger and outrage were common during the first half of the term. At the same time, students were systematically reexamining their own life histories and social conditions, and beginning to develop a theoretical framework to explain what they remembered and still saw. Some were also broadening their perspective of the world. By late February I had lectured on the roots of multiculturalism in the political economy of crisis as well as on the opposition between the ideologies of multicultural and anti-racist education. The students had completed critiques of local multicultural education policies and had read articles on the portrayal of Indians in children's books (Lewis, 1987) and the reproduction of racism in schools (Ortiz, 1988). We had examined selected children's books available in Saskatchewan for their portrayal of Indians and identified the racist practices and attitudes in the schools they had attended or worked in. We had drawn from their experiences to illustrate the racial division of labor in the region, and we had begun to review the text.

Students' collective analyses and critiques of their own social conditions were beginning to emerge out of their work together. For example, in their written analyses of local multiculturalist education policies, which included a recommendation for the affirmative action hiring of aboriginal people, one student observed that "many times the Boards may hire Native people, but not for a position of teacher, but as an aide, janitor, cook, etc." (personal document, Jan. 19, 1990). Several of the students made reference to the unequal hiring practices of provincial school divisions they had observed. Lois, one of the two Cree women in the course, recognized the reification and continued marginalization of indigenous culture in her local community's school:

Multicultural education has had a positive effect on our reserve. It has made Indian people more aware and proud of their culture. . . . [B]ut it does have its drawbacks. The reproduction of cultural stereotypes. . . . The Cree Language program gives Indian people a feeling that they are contributing to the curriculum. But in reality I saw only one White student enrolled in Native Studies and not one [White] student was part of the language program. (Personal document, Jan. 19, 1990)

The program calls for involving indigenous parents in the school. Another student, Tracy, criticized the marginal role of indigenous parents in the school program:

The Catholic system feels that parental involvement will increase if the parents plan and prepare nutrition programs. It has been my experience that they bring in an Aboriginal parent to prepare and deliver the lunch. She rarely comes into the class, her name is "the apple lady" or "snack lady." She has no identity and does not effectively interact with the student population. (Personal document, Jan. 19, 1990)

One of the parents in the group, Mary, explained how "race" and class differences impede a school division's efforts to encourage nominal aboriginal involvement on parent committees: "Some parents like to get involved, but they feel intimidated by . . . professional people. They are unsure of themselves They are used to being scoffed at and don't want it to happen anymore" (personal document, Jan. 19, 1990). Mary also had teaching experience. She wrote from the standpoint of an indigenous teacher to describe her sense of alienation on a teaching staff and to warn of the possible outcome from multiculturalist "solutions":

I feel that a lot of pressure is placed on Aboriginal teachers to correct these "problems" that are being faced by Aboriginal students. . . . I feel that . . . Aboriginal teachers are looked at very critically. Watching them to "slip" in any area so that they can say that they are not really "qualified" to teach in this system. [Aboriginal teachers] have to be careful that they don't step on any toes. They are constantly being watched by their peers. . . . If [hiring aboriginal teachers] fails [to change conditions concerning aboriginal students' "success" in schools], the Aboriginal teachers will get the blame, and the cycle continues—blaming the Aboriginal people for the failure. (Personal document, Jan. 19, 1990)

The unskilled, marginalized, and/or low-status role that aboriginal people play in schools had been addressed by more than one of the policy analysts in our class and provided a springboard for classroom work on the racial division of labor. When we met in early February, the students provided other examples from their life experience. Tracy told of her brothers, who work for a local auto parts supplier owned by sons of the local Castle family. "They've really tried [to get better jobs in the company]," she recounted bitterly (field notes, February 2, 1990). But better jobs have not been made accessible to them. Yet "Castle Brothers" is the label used to give recognition to the work her brothers do, she said. Barbara provided the example of the local McDonald's fast-food outlets. White people work at the counters, and aboriginal people clean the floors. SUNTEP itself was cited as an example. "We don't have any Native people here," one of the women noted. I pointed out that SUNTEP did have an aboriginal person, Laverne, on staff. "She's the secretary," another student pointed out with more than a trace of resentment, "and she should be running this place!" I asked if these conditions were generally accepted by aboriginal people as the natural order of things. In some cases they are, it became clear. I used this as a means to illustrate and reinforce the concept of hegemony.

Issues under consideration during these first weeks did not ignore the lives of children in schools. For example, we reviewed research demonstrating the social reproduction of the racial division of labor through the everyday practices of teachers and school administrators in California (Ortiz, 1988). The students were openly angered by the California data. When I asked them to compare conditions in California with their own experience in schools, either as students or teachers, the evidence of social reproduction through Saskatchewan schooling accumulated quickly.[9] In an informal discussion after the class that day, one of the students, Kate, referred to the disclosure as a "great experience. . . . You don't really think about those things until we started to talk about them. They you say, 'Yeah, that does happen'" (field notes, Jan. 19, 1990).[10]

During these first weeks, the students were indeed becoming "mad all over again." The negative reaction of the students to the course at this stage points to the necessity for anti-racist educators to go beyond critique to constructing practical programs for change. However, the students' anger was also being legitimized, both as classroom discourse and as curriculum content, and in relation, as well, to the generalized phenomenon of racism. New theoretical concepts—ideology, hegemony, social reproduction—were being introduced, and more familiar concepts (for example, racism) were being reexamined and used to analyze and describe local and personal experiences at a systemic level. By collectively and vocally remembering their frustration and pain, the students were openly resisting the conditions that caused it.[11] Together, we were recognizing the pressing necessity to transform existing conditions in order to eliminate such suffering and oppression in the future.

Synthesis

It is the capacity of the intellectual to organize her class that makes her an organic intellectual. This subsection reviews the consolidation of the students' understanding of aboriginal experience and organic interest in change with a theoretical consciousness of how to begin doing it. Our first five meetings represented a process of students and teacher coming together on at least two levels. First, the abstract theoreticism of the teacher and the concrete knowledge of the students became increasingly integrated. Second, a broad analysis of the dimensions, scope, and problem of racism emerged at the same time as the somewhat desperate interest of the students in learning practical skills and understandings for teaching practice began to be met. For the balance of the term, a synthesis of these forces occurred as the students developed a theory for educational change based on anti-racist education and critical pedagogy.

The remainder of our meetings combined elements of theory with analytical discussion of a section of the text. The text consisted of a number of prepared models from which to teach anti-discrimination lessons. Students would arrive at class with up to two handwritten pages of notes from which to argue in small groups for the validity of a lesson from the text and make recommendations for adaptations to local conditions. The students' enthusiastic acceptance of the text may have been motivated by the concrete proposals for action it represented. However, some students were also finding the material of personal value, as one student noticed when she chose to convince her daughter that in fact some dentists are women. Her practical experience directly related to a textbook activity concerned with the gendered division of labor. Practical suggestions laid out in the text were supplemented with lecture and discussion around a selection of other quite instrumental and concrete matters, such as how to do role playing in a classroom, organizing field trips, or alternative evaluation strategies.

We also began to examine the ideology of social studies curricula for each school grade. My work as a teacher was made easier by the "good sense" of the students. For example, as we reviewed the assertions of the Grade 1 curriculum, concerned with the family, one student who had already worked in the classroom repeatedly uttered, "I never noticed that." Her education was aided by her peers, however. The assertion that the father is the head of the family and that "father plants the potatoes [while] mother makes the potato scallops" was greeted by two single mothers with "Bullshit!" and "That's a crock!" (field notes, Feb. 23, 1990). On another occasion, I asked the students how children in school were affected by curricular content that did not correspond to their own lived experience. The women responded emphatically. They had felt different, uncomfortable, and self-blaming because they were made to feel like exceptions and therefore "wrong." Dominant forms of social studies curricula also contribute to a kind of "ignorance," I was informed, because students are afraid to ask questions that are relevant to their lives since they are "abnormal" and do not want to expose this (field notes, March 16, 1990). The students were speaking from their own experience and histories.

In March we began to examine the nature of cultural (re)production in schools and, based on a preselected reading, the notion of resistance based on open dialogue. For example, in one meeting, students discussed Fordham's (1988) analysis of the tensions academically successful black students experience as they strive for high achievement. Fordham's analysis is based on a case study of six high-achieving black high school students. Mary said that she had identified herself with one of Fordham's students. Barbara turned to her and asked, "'Rita,' right"? Mary was "Rita" (Fordham, 1988: 67–69). Surprised, I asked Barbara how she had recognized Mary. Barbara claimed that she had also identified with the same person and turned to Fordham's description of "Rita" as "intelligent, creative, hostile, sarcastic, assertive, garrulous, comedic, and manipulative" (p. 67). The other students acknowledged that they were also "Rita," arguing that this is the way to "make it" through school. Kate claimed that "teachers do it to kids," remembering that her teachers would say, "Kate, I know you can work hard, you can do it." They would not do this to other Métis children (field notes, March 16, 1990). Dialogue was providing a space for students to develop a critique of schooling practices through reflection on the construction of their own identities.

Popular theater offers an opportunity to "act back" against forms of social oppression that have been experienced by its participants, who devise their own scripts and characters. The students found eminent pleasure in the completion of their major assignment, the play production. On the day of the production, I worked in an adjoining room while the students rehearsed. My work was continuously interrupted by their resounding and gleeful laughter on the other side of the wall. The students had reproduced their recollections of racialized schooling in the form of a one-act play.

Two classes at the end of the term seemed to solidify the students' commitment to critical pedagogy and resistance in education. In the first, we reviewed Michelle Fine's (1989) strategy for "naming." Fine analyzes the ways in which schools serve to "silence" student "voice," In opposition to "silencing," she recommends "naming," which refers to "those practices which facilitate critical conversations about social and economic arrangements, particularly about inequitable distribution of power and resources by which some students and their kin suffer disproportionately" (Fine, 1989: 157). Through an informal lecture, I moved through Fine's identification of ways of silencing, illustrating each with examples. Student response was rather casual until I identified "appropriating dissent" and made reference to the customary role of student governments in incorporating student grievances within a set of relations that pacify rather than mobilize students.

One of the younger women, Wendy, murmured, "Same as here." Suddenly, the classroom erupted in a flood of angry grievances as students expressed their sentiments about the center. They did not take their concerns to the nominally democratic student/staff meetings because they felt impotent, their voices drowned by the concerns and interests of other student groups. The SUNTEP center's student government was of little value because "everything revolves around two or three people" (field notes, March 15, 1990). They had made requests to the staff and administration that had either been ignored or responded to belatedly. To issue a complaint was like "getting an 'X' beside your name." The coordinator had called their concerns "crap." Again, referring to the staff, a student said, "They're supposed to be counselors, but if I tell one [of my personal problems to a staff person], they'll take it to the rest of the staff." Another student claimed that "it's not a safe place anymore." Their critique spread to the parent organization of the center, saying, "It's not just the staff, it's [the executive director], too," and described the effect of new rules that had been imposed without consultation to regulate student access to the new building. Thus, the students had identified not only several ways in which they were being silenced in the program at different levels of authority, but also some of the concrete effects of the silencing. As the explosion came under self-motivated control, a student concluded, "We're here because we're supposed to change [society]. We're Métis! We don't *want* to conform anymore" (emphasis in original). They had finished. Sudden silence.

"How do you feel about 'naming' as a form of educational endeavor?" I asked quietly, still awed by the force of the students' vocal resistance.

"Naming?" Kate queried.

"We just did it," Barbara answered (field notes, March 15, 1990). The students had collectively begun to describe the nature of their own powerlessness and oppression, within their own culture. Abstract notions were made concrete. By giving voice to their powerlessness and oppression, they had taken the first step towards developing a strategy and means for effective resistance and reform. Given that the naming had taken place within the local space of their classroom, they had experienced the school as a site of political struggle (Giroux & Simon, 1989) and had realized one possibility for critical pedagogy. At the same time, the fact that this experience was not generalized outside of the classroom and we took no action on these grievances identified a limitation of the center. If I had an opportunity to teach the course again, I would encourage students to analyze the institutional sources of their grievances and to develop a program for practical change. This was impossible in the course because the "explosion" took place in our second to the last class meeting, and the students would be permanently leaving the center after the last meeting.

The second solidifying event occurred on the evening students had been asked to attend a public meeting to commemorate the International Day for the Elimination of Racial Discrimination. Together, we were members of a crowd of less than one hundred in a motel meeting room listening to a panel of experts speak on the question of racial discrimination. Only one of the five panelists was aboriginal, and he was a professional from another city. Three of the panelists were whites: two from the local Catholic clergy, the other a local school division administrator. We sat for an hour listening to the speakers. The isolation of the panelists from the experiences of these aboriginal women was glaring. For example, one panelist observed that "I finally woke up. . . . I realized that there were poor people" (field notes, March 24, 1990). The panel presentations were followed by a talk-show format in which those in attendance were invited to ask questions of the panelists. I rose to challenge the composition of the panel. Immediately afterwards, I glanced across the room to where the students were sitting. Barbara thrust her fist upwards, grinning broadly and clapping loudly with the other students. The next morning she told me proudly before class, "I don't care who saw me do that" (field notes, March 24, 1990). When we met for class, the session began with a standing ovation from the students for my actions the previous evening. Much of the class was taken up with the students' expressions of anger towards "being subordinate again" (field notes, March 24, 1990).

In these final weeks, the students had consistently deepened their organic relations with their own personal histories with the experiences of their classmates specifically, and with other aboriginal people in general. They had remembered their sense of alienation from school curricula while at the same time developing a theoretical critique of school knowledge as ideological reproduction. Discussions of course readings had concretized the meaning of cultural reproduction. The production of the play had been simultaneously an act of critical remembering and an act of resistance as they constructed scenes and script that named the racist and abusive forms of schooling they had known in their earlier lives. In February, on "homework day," they had named forms of oppression from outside the SUNTEP center. In March, they collectively named their powerlessness within the center. The action in itself provided some ownership of the space they spoke within. The students had taken control of the classroom discourse for their own use. Teacher-student relations had been temporarily democratized, and the women had learned a method for teaching that will remain rooted in their experience. At the "Racial Discrimination" evening, the students had begun to resist their subordination publicly and collectively. During these final weeks, organic connections with other aboriginal people and their capacity for contributing to resistance and change had been strengthened.

RESULTS

Two sources of data are available for evaluating the accomplishments of the course: final exams and course evaluations. As an "objective" data source, final examinations suffer from the liability that they are produced for an audience, the instructor, who must assign a grade. Students cannot help but be aware that the instructor will tend to favor knowledge towards which she or he is subjectively biased. Final exams are also written under a strict time limitation and do not encourage reflective thought. Nevertheless, the level of critical analysis that students have achieved will be more or less represented through responses to appropriate questions.

The final exam for the course consisted of two questions. The first asked students to "develop an autobiographical essay in which you demonstrate the usefulness of a selection of [the concepts introduced during the course] for explaining your own educational careers." In the selections that follow, which represent the recollections of several students, parentheses were constructed by the students at the time, whereas square brackets set off my own insertions.

During my education as a young [girl, I] experienced many forms of racism. However, at that time I didn't know what racism was. I just figured the teachers hated me. I resisted education in the elementary grades because I knew I couldn't do or get better grades than Janet (White French girl) so instead I [would] "fool around" (talk and laugh during lessons). . . . We [got] to the point where I would bad mouth the teacher and she'd say, "You're all the same" (Métis). I had to give up or else I would get sent to the principal's office like every Métis person. . . . By the teachers making me and my Métis friends feel like we were not as good as the White kids and having a low expectation of us (ideology that Métis people are dumb), we fulfilled it by getting angry, resisting and rebelling. . . . I got to Junior High and was getting over all my hatred for the White girls, probably because I was now trying to fit in with them. I was not causing anymore trouble to the teachers, but just going along with the flow (hegemony). They had won. . . . (In high school) I was on the SRC committee, but only because I had quit rebelling. . . . When I heard teachers calling Métis students down I didn't do anything about it because I liked where I was and didn't want to go down. I accepted the idea (ideological hegemony).

Lois's autobiographical account is also worth quoting at length:

I knew by Grade 3 or 4 that I was never going to be asked any difficult questions. When I went home I never said anything about how I was treated in school. I figured that these are teachers and this is how I was supposed to [be] learning in school. I remember a couple of times trying to talk to my parents but they had gone to Residential schools and they were treated worse. . . . The concept (that) I feel is useful in describing and analyzing my experience is hegemony because . . . to (my parents), schools knew what was best for everyone. They thought that the school had power over them and as long as they sent us everyday to school, everything would be all right. The hidden curriculum concept describes how I was taught in school. The books we used never had any positive things to say about [N]ative people. We . . . read books and saw films that depicted [N]ative people as lazy, unreliable savages . . . with no ambition to do anything. The concept I feel that describes some of my school experience is . . . ideological hegemony and social reproduction.

Tracy remembered how she strived to be a good, acceptable student in school. She was very quiet, which in retrospect she felt "reinforced the label that Métis or Indians are 'dumb' and don't know anything. This kept me down and reinforced a racist label." Looking back, she viewed her behavior as a form of "cultural reproduction." Tracy referred to a high school teacher who "would always put women down" because they were perceived as "stupid when it comes to algebra and geo-trig" as a form of "silencing." She was self-critical about "[calling] Indians down because everyone else did" and referred to this as the realization of hegemony. She was also self-critical about accepting the "hidden curriculum" of competition.

Despite their critique of the SUNTEP program on the day they "named," most of the students referred to their experience in SUNTEP with pride and appreciation because they had developed their sense of identity and history. However, one of the students, Hazel, added that professors from the university

have classed us as poor little natives who have a hard time to understand concepts, (and) therefore they attempt to teach in simple language and terms. The University. . . views us as different and therefore demand(s) we do a residency at the university to prove we are capable of acquiring a teacher's certificate. The (program's parent organization) views us as untrustworthy, and therefore [has] strict rules we must abide by. By doing all of these things to us, the above are working towards reproducing what they view as a Métis society.

Barbara, who "was a cultural reproducer to the extent that I got married right out of high school because I was never shown or told that I could do anything else," was also concerned about the contradictory effect of the program. She argues that she was:

forming a new . . . cultural production because (SUNTEP students) are not the cloned or standard type of teacher the (university) turns out each year. We have different views, ideals, and values. (However), everything I am learning at SUNTEP and the education I am getting is forming a cultural production to such an extent that I am now almost always excluded from my family. . . . [A]s far as my brothers and father are concerned, I am no longer relevant. . . . Maybe that is why some people continue to culturally reproduce.

The statements six of eight of the students made on formal course evaluations at the beginning of our final meeting may have provided them with more freedom to express their assessments of our collective experience. The forms were collected by a student, then mailed to the Department of Curriculum Studies at the University of Saskatchewan. They were then transcribed into a single typewritten report and returned to me. Thus, the responses are anonymous. The students were made fully aware of this process, to minimize possible coercion or influence from me. The following data are presented from an analysis of the themes that emerged within the students' discourse.

Every one of the students referred to their negative reactions at the beginning of the term. While 50 percent (three students) of this small sample said their initial reaction was that the course content was irrelevant, two noted a relationship between "power" and my inaccessible and abstract theoreticism. As one said, "At the beginning of the class, I felt that the instructor had most of the power because he lectured to the point where we understood nothing." On the other hand, both students expressed experiencing a sense that "speaking out meant something" after the group's confrontation of me led to changes.

Four of the six students explicitly valued the process of negotiation, while others expressed their appreciation of the dialogical approach. Referring to negotiation, one of the students claimed that "there seemed to be an equal amount of power from both instructor and student because we were always consulted and asked for an opinion when assignments were given." Concerning dialogue, a student who felt that "his method of teaching was good because he made us think and allowed us to voice our own thought and opinion" was representative. The dominant valuations from the students (five of six) were that the course taught them something about themselves and that it would aid them in "influencing this much needed change." For example, one student found that "this course allowed me to look at my education and how I can change it when I'm out there so it doesn't happen to others like me." Another claimed that "I learned a lot about what the instructor wanted us to learn but I also learned a lot about myself. . . . [T]he lessons I learned were and are very valuable." A third commented, "I felt that this class was/is helping me understand why I was treated this way. I wanted to learn more about how to make the system better. . . . This class has provided me with positive ideas about what I would use when I go out teaching."

Appreciation for teaching strategies introduced in the class was also consistently expressed in students' final exams. Support was most strongly expressed for the strategies of dialogue and "naming." Wendy, for example, claimed that the course was "a primary example of student voice in the classroom. This had an effect on us because we were allowed to see what can occur in a classroom which focused on student voice. . . . I want my classroom to be a 'safe place' were student voice is most important."

Tracy agreed that the course had "given me a voice—my student voice." Barbara noted that "by allowing us to bring up our grievances . . . naming took place." Hazel supports "critical pedagogy" because it "allows for students' personal experience" (field notes, April 6, 1990). There are signs here of a commitment to a democratic classroom that incorporates dialogue, children's cultural experience, and the possibility of critique.

CONCLUSION

The results reflected in the final exams and the course evaluations show that the aboriginal women in this study are potentially organic intellectuals. They speak from the experience of aboriginal people schooled in a racist and class-divided province. The accounts that have been cited throughout this chapter, in the students' papers on multiculturalist education policies, in their account of the regional racial division of labor, in their discussion of schooling for indigenous children, in their reflections on alienation from school curricula, and in their reactions to their subordinate position at the "Racial Discrimination" evening provide corroborating evidence to the thesis that the students speak from the subject position of marginalized and racialized people. After the course, they could claim a theoretical consciousness from the fields of anti-racist education and critical pedagogy to articulate the systemic roots of racist and class-biased schooling. They also have the elements of a "language of possibility" to begin the process of change. Evidence from the "homework day" account and the "naming" experience, some evidence from the "Racial Discrimination" evening, and substantive evidence from the course evaluations also demonstrate that the women have an interest in active resistance and in effecting change.

There is no certainty that the SUNTEP students will fulfill the role of organic intellectuals, however. One of the women already speaks of her estrangement from her family because of her academic training. Furthermore, pressures will continue to be exerted on these future teachers to withdraw from the struggle for change. A commitment to actively resisting the power structure was less evident at the beginning of the course. At least two of the women managed to get through school by adopting a form of "racelessness" (Fordham, 1988), through identifying with nonaboriginal students and joining in discriminatory practices against aboriginal students. The response of the preservice teachers to the racism exercised against SUNTEP students within the local school systems was to adopt a defensive strategy of being "excellent" teachers, which meant, in part, not appearing to be troublesome. It takes unusual courage and stamina to maintain an active commitment to social and educational change, so the students should not be condemned if they begin to conform as hegemonic pressures on them persist.

The discussion shows, however, that they are not "cloned and standard-type" preservice teachers. Rather, they are "cultural producers" engaged in "the constitution of identity through the reaccentuation of speech genres" (Flores & Yudice, 1990:73). Specifically, as they appropriate elements of

critical educational discourse and integrate them with their own autobiographical histories and lived negotiation with racist school structures, they
will produce new forms of teaching attitudes and practice. Their practical
consciousness of the everyday world means that at one level they understand the nature and processes of racism better than the most theoretically
advanced college instructor. They have incorporated opportunities to learn
and develop strategies for change, the confidence that they can make a
difference without taking unrealistic risks, and a more theoretical and
systematic understanding of the general character of racism and racist
schooling.

What I was able to offer them, despite errors of theoreticism and idealism, was both the opportunity and the information to develop a more
objective, systematic, and critical analysis of racist education, the first stages
of a strategy to confront it, and some sense of their own power in the
classroom. A critical pedagogy based on democracy and critical analysis of
students' own biographies and lived cultural lives was a necessary condition for meeting these goals, as it provided the space and process for the
women's empowerment as students and subsequent confidence building,
as well as for the maturation of their critiques and self-criticisms. The errors
I initially made might have been avoided if my commitment to negotiation
had included a more collective and intellectually honest negotiation of
course requirements, if I had applied my materialist philosophy and theoretical celebration of "lived culture" to more fully respecting the capacity
of my students to determine their own cultural form in the context of the
actually existing political economy. In other words, the content of students'
responses to the course requirements should have been examined in the
context of their racialized position as preservice teachers at the outset of the
course. The cultural politics of the classroom would have been improved if
my commitment to dialogue had begun with the use of a language that was
intelligible to the students. As it was, I initially came very close to providing
a leftist reproduction of the classic contradiction between the ideology of
the school and teacher and the cultural form of the students.

Three abiding lessons remain from this experience. First, critical pedagogy creates an elasticity in the social relations of the classroom that is
forgiving. Without a dialogical strategy, conflicts between the students and
myself would probably have remained unresolved. Through dialogue, we
can support aboriginal preservice teachers' efforts to incorporate formal
educational discourse and critical theory on terms that may not produce
alienation from their communities at the same time as we "unlearn [our]
privileged discourse so that . . . [we] can be heard" (Spivak, 1990:57). We
can also continue to learn ways of working with rather than on our students'
cultural lives. Second, progressive teacher educators have to continue to
work towards a more satisfactory integration of concrete ideas for practice
in everyday classrooms, which we can share with preservice teachers, and

more abstract and general critiques of conventional schooling and visions of an educational future. To quote Paulo Freire, "It is not that methods and techniques are not important. But they must serve the objectives contained in a cultural plan" (1983:78). Third, we will also do well to remember Freire's advocacy of the practice of thinking about practice, through which practice is perfected" (1983:25). In other words, self-conscious practice provides an opportunity to resolve contradictions between teachers' "common sense," inherited from our own elementary and secondary schooling and colleges of education, and our theoretical consciousness as critical pedagogues.

NOTES

1. "Language of possibility" and "language of critique" as used in this chapter are shorthand phrases for referring to opposite sides of a contradiction manifested in contemporary capitalist schools in North America (Carnoy & Levin, 1985). "Language of possibility" refers to concepts, theories, and practices that offer the practical possibility of advancing the interests of subordinate populations within the school as a site of political struggle. "Language of critique" refers to the accumulation of insights and theoretical analyses that have been produced over the past twenty years to show the ways in which class, race, and gender inequalities are reproduced within everyday schooling practices and curricula. The two phrases are developed at length in Aronowitz and Giroux's (1985) *Education under Siege*.

2. In 1981, for example, 81.5 percent of the elementary school teachers in Canada were women (Marshall, 1987:8).

3. There are a number of reasons for this problem, not the least of which is the low base salary offered to employees through a program substantially dependent on government grants for its operating capital.

4. For a discussion of the problem of minority role models, see R. Austin's (1989) *Saphire bound!* pp. 539–78.

5. By "practical" here I mean the integration of theory building with the practical lives of the students. Freire observes that "it is not possible to divorce the process of learning from its own source within the lives of the learners themselves" (1983:42), and goes on to argue that

only at a distance can [students] get a perspective that permits them to emerge from that daily routine and begin their own independent development. The necessary precondition to taking a distance from "dailiness" is the analysis of past and present practice and the extension of this analysis into their possible future, remembering always that every practice is social in character. (1983:57)

6. We are reminded of Spivak's (1990) observation that "there is an impulse among literacy critics and other kinds of intellectuals to save the masses, speak for the masses, describe the masses. On the other hand, how about attempting to learn to speak in such a way that the masses will not regard as bullshit" (p. 56).

7. This is commonplace amongst schools and programs produced as affirmative action programs, and is a feature of "commonsense" racism (Marable, 1985).

8. I was later approached by a student and advised that students were not in opposition to contextualizing social studies material; they were objecting to what seemed like a relative absence of it. I was also advised that the students felt they could risk confronting me without suffering for it, whereas they would not have felt the same with other instructors they have had.

9. Among the experiences reported by the students concerning the schooling of aboriginal children in Saskatchewan were: (1) when aboriginal children move to the city, they are "automatically" placed one grade behind their incoming status; (2) when they move to a new school, immediate placement in the "resource room" is frequent; (3) conversations on the playground in the aboriginal language continue to be discouraged; (4) standardized tests continue to be administered; (5) there is outright rudeness towards aboriginal students from teachers.

10. The generalizations I make here are simplistic. In some ways, students had or were taking action on issues of importance to them before the class began. On the first day of class, for example, one student angrily shared a racist sheet circulating in the community that advertised "open [hunting] season on Indians." Another student, who had worked as a teacher, had been disciplined by her employer because she had taken action against a parent's physical abuse of one of her students.

11. The students were engaged in dialogue not only with their teacher, but with each other. This contributed to the deepening of a "group ethos, the very stuff of self-formation" (Flores & Yudice, 1990:74).

7

Teaching against the Grain: Contradictions and Possibilities

Roxana Ng

I began this chapter with the notion of writing about anti-racist and anti-sexist education from a critical pedagogy perspective. As my thinking developed, however, I found myself turning to my own and other minority teachers' teaching experiences in postsecondary educational settings and our trials and tribulations in implementing alternative classroom practices that are both contradictory and exciting. At first, this troubled me; I feared I was getting off topic, especially when the deadline for submitting the first draft of this chapter drew near. But the anguish and desire with which I have been grappling since I began teaching almost ten years ago would no longer be subordinated to professional discipline. So I found myself writing about the contradictions and possibilities of critical teaching in the academy from a rather personal perspective.

As my writing progressed, I turned increasingly to the writings on feminist pedagogy, to other women writers who have spoken of their own pains, trials, and tribulations as teachers attempting to subvert an enterprise that is both oppressive and liberating. It is their writings that have given me the inspiration and courage to write about my experience and to continue the search for alternative ways of thinking, writing, learning, and teaching that have transformative potentials.

Thus, I begin this chapter with a deep gratitude to all the writers whose work I have consulted, to the students and colleagues with whom I have shared my own thinking and earlier drafts of this chapter, and to members

An abbreviated version of this chapter entitled "Teaching against the Grain: Contradictions for Minority Teachers" is published in Jane Gaskell and Arlene McLaren (eds.), *Women and Education: A Canadian Perspective*, 2nd ed. (Calgary: Detselig Enterprises Ltd., 1991).

of this writing project who have offered encouragement and support for my tentative effort. In particular, I thank Bob Regnier, who was the project's discussant for an earlier version of this chapter, for reminding me that I am indeed on track in terms of the project we undertook. He wrote in his discussion of October 19, 1990, when the contributors of this book congregated to discuss the chapter manuscripts:

> You offer a way to grieve and lament the limitations and contradictions in our pedagogies without carrying them as guilt. Your example, of acknowledging "the pains, the trials and tribulations" of yourself as a critical pedagogue . . . centres consideration about the critical pedagogue as "subject." You expose the heart of commitments that critical pedagogues often write about in abstract terms even though they feel them deeply and personally. At the same time, you reveal the personal tentativeness, vulnerability, uncertainty and contradictions of searching and re-searching for a way of teaching that is truly emancipatory.

INTRODUCTION: CONCEPTS AND METHOD

This chapter unfolds, then, as an exploration into the contradictions and possibilities of critical teaching from the standpoint of the minority teacher. I am using the term "minority" in its standard sociological usage; it refers to people who are relatively powerless in the hierarchy of power and authority. Thus, although women as a group and blacks in South Africa are numerically the majority, in power terms they are minorities. As I am both a woman and an ethnic minority (i.e., nonwhite, non-British in Canada), I use the term "minority teacher" to refer to both minority statuses. The term "minority," then, is applied broadly to members of subordinate groups vis-à-vis the dominant group, and includes women and ethnic and racial minorities.

I am using the term "critical teaching" to include the discourses that question and challenge existing knowledge base and power relations. These discourses include critical pedagogy, anti-racist education, and feminist pedagogy. I make no claim here to provide a systematic review of these burgeoning bodies of work. Throughout this chapter, I draw on writings in the literature to throw light on and guide my own pedagogical beliefs and practices.

Although it is true that each of these discourses is substantively different and ridden with internal debates, one common feature is that they are all concerned with power and inequality. In the words of Peter McLaren, a major proponent of critical pedagogy, critical theorists "begin with the premise that men and women [and I would add people belonging to ethnic and racial minority groups] are essentially unfree and inhabit a world rife with contradictions and asymmetries of power and privilege" (McLaren, 1989:166).[1]

Barbara Thomas, in spelling out the differences between multicultural and anti-racist education,[2] also points out that the recognition of unequal power between groups is the salient feature of anti-racist education. She writes:

Anti-racist education posits that diversity *per se* is not the problem. . . . It is the significance that is attached to the differences, and more importantly, the way that differences are used to justify unequal treatment that is the problem—i.e. racism. It is unequal power that limits the dimensions of one's culture that can be legitimately expressed. More significantly, it is unequal power that limits one's ability to earn a living, meet basic needs, make one's voice heard. It is unequal power that makes the struggle for self-respect . . . a formidable task. (Thomas, 1987:105)

Certainly, feminist pedagogy, growing out of feminist theory and women's studies, begins with the premise that men and women are unequal and have differential access to power structures. This has led to a distortion in the construction of knowledge itself, so that what counts as knowledge and much of what we learn in the formal educational process are one-sided and biased.[3]

Thus, one of the major aims of these critical approaches to education, diverse though they are, is to develop critical consciousness among the students/learners and to empower them (for example by reducing the power differential between teachers and students, or by involving students in curriculum development). The long-term goal implicit in these pedagogical approaches is the belief that democratizing the classroom and empowering students will lead to changes in structures of inequality. Jargon such as "emancipatory teaching," "student empowerment," "pedagogy for radical democracy," and so on are the leading principles of critical teaching.[4]

The assumption is that critical teaching is by definition subversive. The role of the critical teacher is to bring into sharp relief the historical inequalities that have been entrenched in social structures and to facilitate the radicalization of students. With the exception of feminist pedagogy, the power differential between the teacher and students is rarely problematized. While the literature on feminist pedagogy is attentive to issues of power, there is a tendency to treat power differential as existing merely between teachers and students.[5] There is little examination of power as a dynamic relation that permeates classroom interactions. In exploring the contradictions of critical teaching, I wish to examine the way in which power, embodied in and enacted by all participants in educational settings, operates to sustain existing forms of inequality, in order to discover how to alter these relations. I will discuss how "power" is conceptualized next.

On Power and Authority

In sociology, power is viewed frequently in macro terms, as a property of social structures and institutions. For example, the police have the power and authority to charge and arrest people who are seen to be breaking the law; policemen are empowered by law to keep order and arrest those deemed to be disrupting the social order. Men have power over women by virtue of their control over major societal institutions and structures. This is a common way to understand power sociologically.

Here, I want to put forward the notion of power as a dynamic relation that is enacted in interactions. My understanding is derived from theorization and empirical investigations in interpretive sociology, beginning with the work of Weber and more recently in ethnomethodology.[6]

In particular, Pamela Fishman's analysis of conversations between intimate couples illustrates succinctly how unequal power between women and men is enacted, established, and maintained in interactional settings. In her study, Fishman analyzed the conversational patterns and strategies of five heterosexual couples by tape-recording their conversations in their homes. The couples had the right to turn off the tape recorder or edit out conversations as they liked. On the whole, Fishman felt that the tape recordings represented conversations that occurred in natural settings. In analyzing these mundane conversations, she found marked differences in women's and men's conversational strategies and patterns. Men tended to make more statements and control the topics of conversations. Women tended to support conversations by using minimal responses such as "hmm," whereas men used such responses to end conversations. In conclusion, Fishman argued that gender relations are not givens; they are negotiated on an ongoing basis (Fishman, 1978). Her analyses, as well as those of other researchers, demonstrate that power and hierarchical relations are not abstract forces operating on people. Power is a human accomplishment, situated in everyday interaction; thus, both structural forces and interactional activities are vital to the maintenance and construction of social reality.

It is this notion of power as a dynamic relation, which is negotiated continuously in interactional settings, that I want to draw attention to here. I am making a distinction between "authority" and "power." In the context of this chapter, "power," however derived, is a more individual property which is subject to negotiation interactionally. "Authority," on the other hand, is formal power granted to individuals through institutional structures and relations. Thus, the police have legal authority to take certain courses of action. Teachers have authority over students as a consequence of their ascribed role in the educational system. But in an interactional setting, this authority can be challenged by those without formal power.

On Commonsense Sexism and Racism

In addition, I want to explicate how sexism and racism, as relations of domination and subordination that have developed over time and saturate all interactional contexts, are operative in educational settings. I use the term "commonsense sexism and racism" to refer to those unintentional and unconscious acts that result in the silencing, exclusion, subordination, and exploitation of minority group members—that is, what people generally refer to as sexist and racist attitudes. In an earlier work, I argued and showed that gender, race, and class are relations, not just analytical categories that are sutured[7] into the development of Canada as a nation; activities such as the building of the railway for the nation's westward expansion, exploiting Chinese men through a system of indentured labor, and at the same time forbidding the immigration of Chinese women constitute an example of the conjunction of race, gender, and class in nation building (Ng, 1989).

It is through the process of colonization and nation building that we see how racism and sexism became crystallized as systems of domination and subordination. In this chapter, as in my earlier writings, I want to get away from the notion that sexism and racism are merely products of individuals' attitudes (of course they cannot be separated from people's attitudes) by emphasizing that they are systems of oppression giving rise to structural inequality over time. Indeed, certain norms and forms of action are so entrenched that they have become the "normal" and taken-for-granted ways of doing things. Pamela Fishman's study, quoted above, can be seen as an example of how commonsense sexism operates, when men unconsciously and automatically control and direct topics of conversations. The other side of the coin is that women, all too often, actively perpetuate their own subordination by not only deferring to men, but actually doing the work of supporting conversations in which their centrality is minimized.

Himani Bannerji (1987) was among the first Canadian writers to introduce the concept of "commonsense racism." The term "common sense," used in the everyday vernacular, denotes ordinary good sense. The present usage is derived from Gramsci's work, and refers to the incoherent and at times contradictory assumptions and beliefs held by the mass of population (see Sasson, 1982:13). Commonsense racism and sexism can refer to the norms and forms of action that have become ordinary ways of doing things of which people have little consciousness, so that certain things, to use Bannerji's term, "disappear from the social surface" (Bannerji, 1987:11). Sexism and racism *are* normal ways of seeing, thinking, and acting.[8]

I want to add that if we treat sexism and racism as commonsense features of the world (in the way in which I use the term, following Gramsci and others), then we can see that none of us are immune to or separated from these features of society. Educationally, it is the responsibility of critical teachers to begin to explicate them, so that we can confront our own racism and sexism, and to work towards eradicating them in all spheres of social life.

Methodological Issues

In addition to making use of secondary sources, this chapter includes my own teaching experience in a university setting over the past ten years, especially my experience in the last five years teaching in a graduate school of education. Putting my commitment to democratic pedagogy into practice, I have always experimented with unorthodox teaching techniques. Since 1989, when I asked students to keep a journal on their own progress in an advanced graduate seminar, Feminist Theory and Methodology, I began to record my own and the students' responses in this and other classes. These records enter in various ways into the writing of this chapter, as data, reflections, and analytical remarks.

As well, I am including as data anecdotal remarks I collected over the years. While the use of anecdotes is not normally accorded scientific status in scholarly writings, I am advocating their use in explicating the taken-for-granted features of everyday life—in explicating commonsense sexism and racism. These mundane, offhand remarks are used to illustrate how power is enacted interactionally and how commonsense sexism and racism operate as part of the relations that constitute our educational experience. That is, rather than dismissing them as anecdotal, they are treated as essential features of a larger social organization. My assumption is that analyzing them will tell us something about the social organization in which these remarks are embedded. This is similar to the way in which Dorothy Smith treats individual experience:

> If you've located an individual experience in the social relations which determine it, then although that individual experience might be idiosyncratic, the social relations are not idiosyncratic. [All experiences] are generated out of, and are aspects of the social relations of our time, of corporate capitalism. These social relations are discernible, although not fully present or explicable, in the experiences of people whose lives, by reason of their membership in a capitalist society, are organized by capitalism. (Campbell, n.d.)[9]

In this chapter, I write as a teacher—as a middle-class woman and a member of the intelligentsia with some authority and privileges; as a woman of color who is marginal in the overall system of authority and privilege; as a social scientist who is supposed to be rational, analytical, and detached; and as a sensuous, living individual (to borrow Marx's phrase) who has emotions and feelings. These positions and identities do not sit well together. They give rise to contradictions and dilemmas that I, and every human being in her or his multiple locations and subjectivities, experience and must deal with continuously. It is nevertheless in these contradictions that I exist, and therefore think, speak, and write.

In writing this chapter, therefore, I do away with the false notion that the knower/writer can be "objective," as is commonly assumed in social scientific writing, that she can occupy a position that transcends all viewpoints. I attempt to preserve the knower/writer as an active subject in the text, grappling with her own multiple locations and contradictions. I believe that it is in confronting these contradictions and dilemmas that all of us may come to grips with what haunts us and propels us to work towards a better world. As Cynthia Cockburn writes: "It is precisely out of the process of bringing such contradictions to consciousness and facing up to illogicality or inconsistency, that a person takes a grip on his or her own fate. Politically, it is of vital importance that we understand how we change" (Cockburn, 1983:13).

POWER AND AUTHORITY: CONTRADICTIONS FOR THE MINORITY TEACHER

Although there has been an increasing recognition among progressive academics, including critical teachers, to assert the importance of gender, race, and class in social analyses, in actual fact how relations of gender, race, and class operate in educational settings remains unexplicated. In this section, I will explore how commonsense sexism and racism penetrate the power dynamics between minority teachers and students.

In the discourses of critical teaching, feminists are among the first educators to describe and analyze problems encountered by female teachers in the classroom. Based on her own teaching experience, Friedman observes: "Any kind of authority is incompatible with the feminine" (Friedman, 1985:206). This sexist and patriarchal assumption denies the woman teacher her right to speak as a figure of authority. "To be 'woman,' she has no authority to think; to think, she has made herself 'masculine' at the cost of her womanhood" (ibid.:206). The fact that female professors are sometimes addressed as "Mrs.," rather than "Professor" or "Dr." like their male counterparts, is an example of the denial of female teachers' authority at a superficial but telling level.[10]

To be a woman and a university teacher, one's power and authority are undermined constantly by existing gender relations that operate in society at large. In examining ninety-four student evaluations she received from a sociology course, Susan Heald found that only three mentioned content on women and feminist issues as positive. Most students considered her approach problematic and the issues she raised digressing from the formal curriculum: "A slightly opinionated personality emerged on feminist issues which is all right but sometimes took the topic under discussion astray. Perhaps a less biased approach to certain issues. I feel her feminist attitudes, at times, interfered with the understanding of some course content" (Heald, 1989:23).

A feminist perspective, then, is seen to be biased knowledge, vis-à-vis pure knowledge. Teaching from this critical perspective further undermines the credibility of a female teacher. Interestingly, the positive qualities of Heald's classroom, such as students having space to voice their opinions, small group discussions, and cooperative learning, were not treated by the students as part of her pedagogical approach. Rather, they were seen to be features of her personality. If a teacher is female and/or a member of a racial minority and engages in critical teaching, she is in a position of double jeopardy.

Minimally, then, sexism manifests itself in the classroom in terms of students' challenge to the female teacher's authority and credibility. More endemically, women's presence in institutions of higher learning is met with overt hostility. This hostility manifests itself in minor incidents such as sexist jokes and graffiti, traumatic events (for women) such as campus rapes, and the shattering tragedy of the Montreal massacre in the fall of 1990.[11] The following illustration from the *Toronto Star* brings sexism as a systemic property in higher educational institutions into focus:

An outgoing woman attending a big-city university is unaware that a male classmate has an abnormal interest in her. During a class, she expresses views counter to his idea of how she should feel about the issue being discussed. After class, in front of witnesses, he slams her against a wall, calls her names and verbally abuses her. She complains to the administration, asking that he be charged with assault, but is persuaded that the matter should be handled internally. A conviction, she is told, would perhaps destroy the future of a good student. It is suggested that she tone down her contribution to discussions. The university is to make arrangements for the man to continue his education under individual tuition. (Quinn, 1990)

While this example concerns the experience of a female student, female professors' experiences are not drastically different. For example, Sheila McIntyre, a law professor at Queen's University, detailed in a memorandum to her faculty dated July 26, 1986, the hostile incidents directed at her by law students, especially male students. She received no support from her colleagues and the administration until she resigned and took her case to the press and the Canadian Association of University Teachers (CAUT). Even though CAUT took up her case, with the final result that she was offered a tenure-track position at Queen's (as opposed to the two-year term appointed into which she was originally hired), some of her male colleagues both at Queen's and at CAUT felt that she "had jumped the gun" and mishandled the whole situation.[12] The fact that these comments were made and received as being perfectly sensible pinpoints precisely the embeddedness of sexism in our collective consciousness. Her case is not unique, but is an example of what female faculty face as part of their lives on campus.[13]

For a racial minority female teacher, the devaluation of her authority and credibility is compounded by her race and ethnicity. Her presumed inferiority has its roots in the history of the colonization of Canada, which resulted in the vertical mosaic (Porter, 1967), and in the inequality between the developed countries and the Third World as a result of the imperialist expansion of the West. Speaking from my own experience as a Chinese woman, I have frequently been called "cute" by my students and occasionally by colleagues. (Yes, it is meant to be a compliment, but why do I think of Suzie Wong when people say that?)[14] Many comment on my accent, either as practically flawless or as needing improvement. In one university where I taught, a group of female students expressed the concern that my voice (with the accent) was too soft, and therefore the other students laughed at me after class. They wondered whether I could increase my volume or behave more authoritatively (or both). Ironically, I once overheard a comment between two male professors regarding a woman in a sessional appointment who had applied for the tenure-track job in the department. They were not in favor of this candidate because her voice was too strident: "You can hear her all the way down the hall when she is lecturing."

To be a minority teacher in a higher educational institution is to be continuously at risk. The risk increases when minority teachers attempt to instill critical consciousness among the students, as the experience of Susan Heald shows. Over the years of my teaching, I have had students complain both about the content of my courses and my teaching methods. On one occasion, when I taught a course called Cross-Cultural Education, a male student complained to the department chair about the content of my course halfway through the academic year. Although it was clear from the course outline that I had included gender relations as an integral part of cross-cultural education, he maintained that there was no reason why this should be part of the curriculum. He had come to the course wanting to learn about multicultural education and techniques of controlling a multiracial classroom. Instead, he argued that he only received materials on how schooling produced and maintained social inequality. He conducted an analysis of the course contents and concluded that 35 percent of the material dealt with gender (in addition to race) relations; if he added the number of times "women" were mentioned in the lectures, the percentage increased to 50 percent. He felt that he was being shortchanged and demanded that I change the course content or be fired. The department chair supported the student and requested that I change the course halfway through the year, in spite of the fact that this was the only complaint. He did not want the student complaining to the administration, and cautioned me about giving this student a bad grade, in case he appealed his grade. In this example, we see how men collude with each other intentionally or unwittingly to assert male dominance (Ng, 1993).

The kinds of experiences reported here are experiences that I and other minority professors encounter on a regular basis. Thus, even when they have been granted formal institutional power, other practices are at work in the university setting that strip minority teachers of their right to speak and act as figures of authority (see Hoodfar, 1992; Ng, 1993). The preceding examples illustrate how commonsense sexism and racism operate to disempower minority professors of the legitimate power they may have earned.

In describing the sexist encounters of female and feminist teachers, I do not mean to suggest that men are the only instigators of these practices. Women, both students and university staff, including secretaries and peers, collude and participate in the denigration of female authority. In other words, women's presumed inferiority and lack of authority are internalized by *both men and women*.

Because gender and racial lines are so clearly drawn in the hierarchy of the academy, in which the power holders and power brokers are primarily white men, minority professors are marginalized even when they have gained entry to the academy. It is no longer curious to me that in some universities where I have taught, female students interested in gender relations and women's studies asked white male professors to supervise their work, while calling upon me to give them references and feedback on a regular basis and to complain about their supervisors. Similarly, I am a member on several thesis committees of minority students who are working in race and ethnic relations (one of my specializations) chaired by my (white) male colleagues, who may be working in other fields altogether. As Friedman observes, women are called upon to play "the role of the all-forgiving, nurturing mother whose approval is unconditional" (Friedman, 1985:206), but they cannot be granted intellectual leadership. And when indeed female professors act in their professorial role, as a number of my senior colleagues do, they are the recipients of intense resentment and hostility from students, ironically including feminist students.

In exploring the experience of feminist academics and how feminist pedagogical discourse informed their practice, Ilona Miner discovered that feminist faculty were subject to excessive criticisms by female students. (She did not interview male students in her study.) For critical teachers, especially feminist teachers, attempts at critical teaching can be acutely painful experiences, as one informant revealed:

If you are a feminist you are very exposed, particularly because you have to have this moral commitment to the women's movement, and to what feminists share. Therefore the criticisms that students make, they're often made very harshly, and they're often made as though as a teacher you have no insides and they can hurt you as much as they want, and you're not seen as someone who feels pain. It would be nice to see another version of feminist pedagogy that called on students to see that teachers are also human, are also women. . . . I think of one or two people here . . . who went through absolute fucking hell from groups of feminists, who if you heard them talking you think, yes, . . .wonderful, open, free, etc. And then you'd hear the other side of it. You'd see this person in awful pain and in tears, and I don't know how to put those two things together. I think there is some real problem with feminist pedagogy as an orthodoxy. (Miner, 1990:16)

Ironically, Miner found that when male teachers incorporated feminist principles in their classrooms, they got more praise and a warmer reception from female students (Miner, 1990). This is another aspect of commonsense sexism that manifests itself in the classroom.

Thus, a major contradiction for minority teachers implementing critical teaching is that as they attempt to humanize the classroom, as figures of authority, their own humanity is taken away. There is a fundamental tension in the notion of empowerment: as they attempt to empower students, minority teachers are disempowered.

In the next section, I explore the power professors, including minority professors, do have over students, and the contradictions for critical teaching therein.

INSTITUTIONAL POWER AND STUDENT RESISTANCE

Minority status notwithstanding, professors do possess real authority over students conferred by the institutional structure(s) of which they are a part. One of the major criticisms by Elizabeth Ellsworth of theories of critical pedagogy is that they have left this fundamental power relation between teacher and student unproblematized (Ellsworth, 1989). While the literature on anti-racist education tells of the silencing of minority students, it does not address this power issue directly. Again, it is feminist teachers who have undertaken to explore this tension, perhaps because their own marginality in the power structure is such a poignant part of their work process. Thus, Barbara Roberts writes: "I personally think that such a relation [between professor and student] is inherently abusive, and that exercising this type of power over another person is by definition abusive, even if not *done* abusively (emphasis in the original) (Roberts, 1988:3). In exploring the paradox of the feminist professor as a "bearded mother" (Morgan, 1988), Kathryn Morgan writes, "If the feminist teacher actively assumes any of the forms of power available to her—expert, reward, legitimate, maternal/referent—she eliminates the possibility of educational democracy in the feminist classroom" (Morgan, 1988:50).[15]

Their views paint a pretty grim picture of the possibility of critical teaching; indeed, they suggest the impossibility of education as an empowering tool in a patriarchal and hierarchical society. Furthermore, in implying that the adoption of any form of power by women professors is oppressive and potentially abusive to students, they unwittingly deny women the right to be experts and intellectual leaders, in much the same way that students deny minority teachers these rights (see Friedman, 1985). However, I do think that they point out an important issue for the critical teacher to explore, and that is that institutional authority *is* an embodied and oppressive feature in a pedagogical setting *regardless of the intention of the teacher*. These analysts point the way for examining how commonsense sexism and racism enter our consciousness and practice in insidious ways. Here, I wish to explore two ways in which commonsense sexism and racism operate in the classroom.

First, professors do have control over the forms and content of knowledge, a control they take completely for granted, irrespective of their own race and gender. This authority is conferred by their formal position in the class structure and the hierarchy of the academy. It is part of the institutional relation into which we enter and over which we have some, but never total, control. We can be more or less open about student input, but we cannot go into the class without a course outline and have the students design it. This is especially true for those of us in marginal positions (e.g., part-time, sessional, untenured positions) in the university hierarchy.[16]

More fundamentally, the learning environment in postsecondary institutions is organized in such a way that the student must learn whatever the course offers and *"display* what she has learned, *that* she has learned" (emphasis in the original) (Roberts, 1988:5) to the teacher. Roberts points out correctly that this is the basic contradiction of feminist, and I would add other, forms of critical teaching. I want to underscore that this is an institutional feature of the work process of teaching, and not an attribute of individuals. The crucial point is not to deny the existence of such constraint(s) and assume that somehow, with good intentions and skills, the critical teacher can reverse this process and turn the classroom into a democratic place (as theorists of various forms of critical pedagogies, including Kathryn Morgan, imply). The university classroom is *not*, by definition, a democratic place. To pretend it can be is to deny that hierarchy and institutional power exist. It is to delude ourselves that democracy and empowerment can be achieved by goodwill alone. I will explore the possibility of working within the constraints of institutional power later.

Second, and more insidious, what we know how to do well, that is, teach students how to construct rational arguments and conduct objective analyses, is also shot through with gender, racial, and class subtexts. In her critique of critical pedagogy, Elizabeth Ellsworth insightfully points out that forms of rational thinking and arguing, which we develop and refine through the educational process, are already racist and sexist because they set up as opposite an irrational "Other" (Ellsworth, 1989:301; see also de Beauvoir, 1952).

Another realm in which people's taken-for-granted assumptions operate at a completely spontaneous level is through the routine accomplishment of classroom interactions. Similar to the way in which minority teachers' authority is routinely challenged in the classroom, teachers also enforce their authority by controlling topics and forms of discussion. It is in analyzing interactional, including conversational, strategies that we begin to unpack the depth of commonsense sexism and racism.

Examining interactions between professors and students in a feminist classroom by means of conversational analysis, Stockwood (1990), writing from the position of a student, describes how feminist professors exercise their authority to control topics of discussion. In the documented case, the professor used interruptions and questioning, among other strategies, to curtail disagreements and redirect the topic(s) of discussion. But this is not a game played by the professor alone. Students reinforce their own subordinate position by *allowing* themselves to be interrupted or by using comments such as "I don't know" to soften potential confrontation and disagreement between themselves and the professor. Analyzing a segment of the dialogue between herself and the professor, Stockwood writes:

What is interesting is that I was, in my mind, very clear about my position, a position that I would not have retreated from under different circumstances where I felt an equal in the discussion. I was, in effect, structuring talk in order to elicit agreement from the professor. What is also interesting is that I chose not to, or was unable to[,] articulate my position. Somehow the location of the professor as judge, tutor, critic, and evaluator of the students' scholastic abilities set up a relationship between us that was not only locally produced through talk, but also extra-locally managed through the normative requirements regulating teacher-student interaction. . . . While the professor was speaking, I chose not to self-select a turn to talk to rectify this understanding [between herself and the professor] even though I could have theoretically regained the floor by . . . an interruption, or by introducing a repair at the next available transition-relevancy place. . . . I felt it was inappropriate to interrupt the professor. Given the public nature of the dialogue and my own preconceived notions that the professor's right to the floor ultimately takes precedence over mine, I did not attempt to interject at the next available transition-relevancy place, rather I waited until the professor clearly signalled turn completion. My waiting, based on my interpretation of appropriate student-teacher interaction, serves to illustrate how I effectively contributed to reinforcing dominant-subordinate relations. (Stockwood, 1990:11, 12–13)

Stockwood's analysis shows clearly that power is a relation that has to be negotiated continuously in the classroom between teacher and students. Professors, including feminist teachers, use a number of dialogic strategies to assert the authority conferred on them by the institution. Students participate by either cooperating with the professor, as the above example shows, or refusing to grant her such authority by confrontational and other strategies.

For those of us who have taught undergraduate classes, especially first-year classes, we are well aware of the tactics used to disrupt the classroom dynamic and challenge teacher authority. These tactics include

chattering among classmates, passing notes, and creating other distur-
bances that disrupt the flow of the lesson, not to mention direct confrontation by questioning and forcefully disagreeing with the professor in charge.
Ultimately, in most situations, the professor's authority prevails due to the
position she occupies in the educational hierarchy vis-à-vis the student.
While she has formal authority in the classroom, her *power* is subject to
challenge. In the case of the minority teacher, her power is challenged more,
due to the marginal position occupied by minority groups in the society at
large.[17]

In addition to interactional strategies that professors employ consciously
to assert their authority in the classroom, sexism and racism operate at a
more subliminal level. Since I know of no study of classroom interactions
in the university setting with regard to the professor and students based on
racial differences, I make use of the work by Sara Michaels on a Grade 1
classroom as an illustration (Michaels, 1986).

Michaels's study focuses on discursive patterns of a racially mixed Grade
1 classroom with half white and half black students. By tape-recording an
activity called "sharing time" and conducting classroom ethnography,
Michaels discerned two distinct intonation patterns and discourse styles
among the black and white students. She noticed that the white students'
discourse style tended to be topic centered. That is, the discourse was tightly
organized, centering on a single topic or series of closely related topics,"
with thematic development accomplished through lexical cohesion, and a
linear ordering of events, leading quickly to a punch line resolution"
(Michaels, 1986:102). By contrast, black students tended to use a topic-as-
sociating style. That is, their narrative pattern consisted of a series of
segments or episodes that were implicitly linked in highlighting some
person or theme (Michaels, 126:103). Michaels further noted that Mrs. Jones,
the teacher, who was presumably white, was much more successful at
picking up on the white students' topics, interjecting at the right moment
with questions to help the student develop the theme of his or her narrative.
She was less successful at picking up on the black students' stories. In fact,
she often mistimed her question and interrupted the child in midclause.

Moreover, the teacher appeared to have difficulty discerning the topic of discourse
and anticipating the direction of thematic development. As a result, her questions
were often thematically inappropriate and seemed to throw the child off balance,
interrupting his or her train of thought. In cases where the child continued to talk,
undaunted, these turns were often cut short by the teacher, who jokingly referred
to them as "filibusters" on occasion. (Michaels, 1986:108)[18]

From a liberal perspective, this kind of situation can be interpreted as a
problem in cross-cultural communication. More seriously, from the vantage
point of critical teaching, we must recognize and acknowledge that this is
how students are silenced in the classroom. This example shows how the

teacher acts unconsciously to reinforce the subordination of black children, and as such constitutes an instance of how commonsense racism operates interactionally.

In their reflective paper on their respective experiences as student and professor in a graduate seminar, Magda Lewis and Roger Simon unpacked how the silencing of female students occurred in spite of the intention of the male professor (Lewis & Simon, 1986). With regard to my own teaching experiences, the following incident is telling:

This story concerns a course called Gender Stereotyping that I offered to a group of student teachers around 1985. In an attempt to show how gender hierarchy was routinely established, I used the study by Pamela Fishman of intimate heterosexual couples described previously.

The Fishman study is one of my favorite teaching pieces because it is both illuminating and provocative. Students' standard reaction is to discredit the study by saying, "It's not true." Women, they maintain, are the dominant ones because they talk more. I would then ask them to do some empirical research to determine whether indeed Fishman's observation could be corroborated or rejected.

Similar reactions occurred on this occasion among the eight female and two male students in the class. As the discussion and debate ensued, I noticed another dynamic going on in the classroom. The women started to make faces to each other and giggle. When I asked what was going on, they just giggled more, and started to write and pass each other notes. As the class progressed, I became increasingly frustrated and mystified. Finally, when the class concluded, one student, a young woman who was assertive and maintained that she was definitely the more dominant one in her marriage, came and talked to me.

She told me that the female students noticed, as the class proceeded, that I was giving the men more air space. Indeed, I was interrupting the women more than the men, and they felt I was sexist! I was completely stunned by this revelation, and took the next two classes to discuss, in more depth, the embeddedness of gender hierarchy and sexism in our own consciousness. The group also made a pact that they would take responsibility to remind each other and me when such patterns occurred in the future so that we could change not only our ideas, but our practice.

This example pinpoints precisely the insidiousness of racism and sexism, not only in institutional structures but in our individual and collective consciousness as well. It throws light on the contradictions faced by critical teachers. In spite of our theoretical commitment to a pedagogy of empowerment, as human beings we, too, have internalized the power relations that predominate in society. In our everyday activities, the people to whom we defer and over whom we exercise our power and authority are all constitutive and reflective of the patriarchal and racist ordering of the society of which we are a part. We show, not so much through theory, but more significantly through practice, what critical teaching is all about. We, too, participate in the systems of oppression of the very members of society whom we want to empower.

POWER RELATIONS AMONG STUDENTS AND THE ROLE OF THE CRITICAL TEACHER

There is an additional dimension of power dynamics operative in the classroom that goes beyond the realm of critical teaching, and that is the power relations that exist among students. Again, these relations are in place outside the classroom, and are brought into the classroom by all members who are its constituents. Commonsense sexism and racism, as well as other features that permeate institutions of higher learning, frequently find their liveliest manifestations in the classroom.

In "A discourse Not Intended for Her: Learning and Teaching within Patriarchy," Magda Lewis wrote eloquently of the silencing that she and other female students experienced in a graduate seminar that explored the relation between language and power (Lewis & Simon, 1986). Roger Simon, as a critical teacher in this seminar setting, attempted to open up space for female students to participate actively and equally in discussion. He used Janice Radway's *Reading the Romance* (1984) as a major text to organize discussions around the relationship between subjectivity and forms of social practice (Lewis & Simon, 1986:463). As the seminar progressed, what emerged was a distinction between the ways that male and female students read the text, and who defined how the text should be treated in the classroom. Increasingly, the women felt unable to participate because the forms of discussion were controlled by the men and their notion of female inferiority. Speaking to each other during class breaks, the women

> uncovered the perspective from which the men in the class discussed Radway's work, . . . the subtleties of how they twisted the analysis until the subjects of Radway's study fit the image that was required to sustain the notion of male superiority. We came to understand the oppressive relation within which women become the subjects of male discourse. it became clear that the only difference between us and the women in Radway's study was that as graduate students we lived out and contested the partriarchic social relations under different circumstances. The oppression was no less felt, and the struggle no less difficult. We were the women in Radway's study. The women in Radway's study were us. In a moment of collective insight we understood that we are our history, and our history is laid within patriarchy. (Lewis & Simon, 1986:466)

The classroom, being part of a white male–dominated hierarchy, always confers privilege to those members who are the dominant group. This is true in a "standard" classroom (versus a "critical" classroom in which the teacher is committed to an alternate pedagogy), in the use of mainstream curricular materials and the assumption of traditional power relations. Even in a critical classroom, the interactions among students are frequently organized by forms of discourse that marginalize members of minority groups. In the preceding example, we see that male students take for granted their right to speak and control the contents of classroom discussions. Minority members both defer to and feel silenced by their dominance.

In the years of my teaching, I had observed that it is not uncommon for minority students to interrupt each other more, thereby granting students from the dominant group (usually white males with the "proper" accent and so forth), and occasionally white women, more time and space to make their views known. White male students, especially, face less challenge among their peers, regardless of how unsound their views and opinions may be. (As we saw earlier in this chapter, the threat of male violence, both actual and symbolic, is always present as a check on female insubordination.)

It is worthwhile describing in some detail the interactional dynamics in a course I offered called Sociology of Minority Groups. Unlike other courses in the institution in which I teach, this course had about equal numbers of white students and minority students (as opposed to having predominantly white students). Among them were two extremely vocal young black students, a man and a woman, who took on the role of policing "correct" positions on anti-racism in classroom discussions. Apart from dominating the discussions, they also disrupted discussions, especially when other minority students, notably women from non-European backgrounds, attempted to put their views forward. On one particularly memorable occasion, an older black woman was severely chastised when making a presentation on the lack of representation of black women in educational administration. She was told in no uncertain terms that she had adopted the dominant perspective by suggesting that black women should attempt to seek upward mobility in mainstream power structures. By contrast, the white male students were able to contribute to discussions with few interruptions, and their opinions, no matter how unsound, would be treated jokingly at worst. When I interceded and mediated in these discussions, my authority was challenged and I was accused of attempting to silence the two vocal students because of the minority position they represented.

This example is interesting on several dimensions. Regardless of whether the older black woman's analysis or position was correct, a classroom that adopts the principles of critical teaching should enable the airing of multiple voices. In this classroom, principles of anti-racist education were used by some students as a control mechanism to suppress other voices that deviated from their own. It is interesting to observe that in this class, the relatively large number of minority students interrupted or were interrupted by each other more often than they interrupted students from the dominant group. This phenomenon suggests a form of internalized colonialism whereby members of minority groups treat as less credible and authoritative the opinions of their own members, while deferring to members of the dominant group.

In adopting theories of critical pedagogy to teach a course entitled Media and Anti-racist Pedagogies, Elizabeth Ellsworth came to the conclusion that "students' and my own narratives about experiences of racism, ableism, elitism, fat oppression, sexism, anti-Semitism, heterosexism, and so on are partial—partial in the sense that they are unfinished, imperfect, limited; and partial in the sense that they project the interests of 'one side' over others" (Ellsworth, 1989:305). Based on this experience, she challenged the principle of critical pedagogy that assumes the unity of "the student voice." She observed that this voice is itself fragmented, that people speak from their "multiple and contradictory social positionings" (ibid.:312).

In a standard classroom, the mode of discourse characterized by debate and winning arguments is highly valued and therefore unproblematic. It became problematic in my, and other critical teachers', classrooms, which employ a different set of pedagogical principles and assumptions. Students, including minority students, have learned ways of displaying to the professor what counts as learning and as being a good student (see Roberts, 1988), which in part involves conforming to the standard mode of discourse, such as winning an argument. My approach, on the other hand, negates this mode of exchange and renders it invalid. In so doing, I, as the figure of authority, devalue what the students know how to do. In the eyes of the students, my minority status in the larger society makes my authority questionable, especially when my teaching methods deviate from the normal ways of doing things.

It is also interesting that by utilizing these alternate principles, I implicitly give students permission to interrupt each other and challenge me in the name of critical teaching, however interpreted. This occurred in the preceding example that I gave, and also in an advanced seminar, Feminist Theory, Methodology and Education, which I offer yearly. The first year I taught this graduate seminar I asked students to use the class as a forum to share research of theirs that they wished to improve. I had used this method in senior undergraduate seminars before and found it highly effective in encouraging cooperative learning among the students. Usually, even an academically marginal student would improve her or his presentation and writing skills over time and by the end of the course.

In this particular seminar, we developed a format where the student who wished to have her research worked on by the class would circulate her written work at least one week prior to the class; she also gave us some idea of what she found problematic so far and how she wanted her work to be discussed. The next seminar would be organized as a working session on this particular piece of research. To my horror, some of these discussions became not only heated but downright nasty, as class members held onto their respective brands of politically (and therefore theoretically) correct positions and criticized the presenter and each other in frequently destructive ways. In one poignant case, a lesbian student who was exploring the relationship between obesity and lesbianism became completely devastated. My own intervention was met with hostility from some members of the seminar. As I later discovered when I read the journals students submitted, they felt that I was silencing them contrary to my promise to implement feminist pedagogical principles in the classroom (see also Miner, 1990).

Leaving aside the real authority a teacher can and indeed does command, I want to draw attention here to how the rhetorics and ideology of feminism, anti-racism, and critical pedagogy are used as ideals against which members of the class are measured—and frequently found lacking. In this way, these critical approaches can and do become new forms of orthodoxy that are themselves oppressive (Miner, 1990). Meanwhile, students to whom the interventions are directed do feel rejection and pain, and their feelings must not be minimized. It is in this kind of situation that we confront fully the contradiction of classroom democracy, which is so much part of the rhetoric, if not the practice, of alternative pedagogies. At the same time, I would maintain that it is also through facing up to these contradictions that we come to grips with the limits and boundaries of critical teaching within a hierarchical structure and begin to explore the possibilities therein.

To begin, then, critical teaching must recognize that the university, as do other institutions of learning under contemporary forms of capitalism, operates with a meritocratic system (see Bowles & Gintis, 1976). Rewards in this structure are given to those who can demonstrate that they are more meritorious than others. There is a hierarchy of merits according to which faulty, as well as students, are rewarded differentially by getting grants, scholarships, or good references to enable them to compete successfully both within the university and outside it. Students survive, therefore, by excelling and competing with one another for the few positions at the pinnacle of this system. Indeed, competition is the very basis of university education.

This system does not present itself as a problem in the standard classroom because it is set up in conformity to the same system of merit and reward. However, it presents a dilemma for the critical teacher because critical teaching explicitly or implicitly challenges the system and attempts to transform what we have come to identify as oppressive features of the educational process. But ultimately, the critical classroom, too, is located within this award system. To survive, students have to get good grades by competing with one another. The systemic nature of this dynamic penetrates a critical classroom. Among other oppressive forms of social life, sexism, and racism, themselves systems of domination and oppression, are the ingredients that constitute the cornerstone of our meritocratic educational system.

But the curriculum, testing instruments, and rules for competition and excellence are not neutral. Feminist scholars have shown that what is treated as natural and objective knowledge is in fact one-sided and biased. Knowledge in ideological structures, including universities, is developed by men—I would add white, ruling-class men—for men based on the experiences of men (see Smith, 1975). Examining educational materials on aboriginal people and multiculturalism in Canada, Lewis (1987) and Manicom (1987) found that they are written from a white supremacist standpoint even when information on other (than British and French) cultures is incorporated into the school curriculum. In her exploration and analysis of skills-oriented versus process-oriented teaching and their differential effects on black and white children, Lisa Delpit has identified "a culture of power" at work in the classroom that operates to disadvantage black students who live outside that culture (Delpit, 1988). Thus, this system of competition for excellence tends to be more advantageous to the individuals who share the same premise, perspective, and code of exchange as those in power. These individuals tend to be white men from particular class backgrounds.[19] If minority students wish to compete and excel in this system, they must learn to internalize the standpoint and code of the "culture of power" and operate within it. This is one way that internalized colonialism expresses itself in the classroom. Furthermore, as we move up and through the educational hierarchy, the competition becomes keener. As competition intensifies, the possibilities of promoting critical and cooperative teaching become increasingly curtailed.[20]

In sum, a number of oppressive social forms are constitutive of and operative in the academy. I have tried to explicate how commonsense sexism and racism are manifested in the classroom through the silencing and devaluation of minority students, both by male students and by each other, because of the cycle of competition and excellence in which they and we are caught. Sexism and racism are among the multifaceted ways in which power relations organize classroom dynamics.[21] As critical teachers, unless we seriously analyze and confront the changing contours of these relations, critical teaching will remain a purely theoretical exercise.

POSSIBILITIES OF CRITICAL TEACHING

The literature on critical teaching has addressed variously curricular and pedagogical issues. For example, theorists of both critical pedagogy and anti-racist education are concerned with a critique of existing forms and content of the curriculum, which negate the experiences of minority groups (racial minority and working class students). Together with feminist pedagogy, they are also concerned with classroom process: the airing of multiple voices and experiences. The contradictions I examined above in part arise out of the insistence of allowing previously oppressed members to speak out (frequently at the expense of suppressing other voices), and attempts by critical teachers to democratize the classroom (I myself have taken this for granted).

In an article in the *Harvard Educational Review*, Lisa Delpit examines the implications of a skills-oriented approach versus a process-oriented approach for black students. She makes clear that she is not favoring one approach over another (although there is a tendency for critical teachers to indeed do this). Rather, based on her and others' experiences as black teachers, she suggests that a process-oriented approach works well for students who already know the code and rules of the subject matter. Such code and rules are established by the dominant group, and what operates in the classroom is "the culture of power" (Delpit, 1988:282). Since black students are outside the culture of power, they are ignorant of the code that operates in the classroom, and thus a process-oriented approach in fact disadvantages them from competing within the educational hierarchy. To empower students who are not already participating in the culture of power, teachers can explicitly state the rules of that culture, making acquiring power easier for these students (ibid.:282). Thus, with regard to teaching writing, she is calling for a skills-oriented approach for black students, who have not learned the code of the culture of power, so that they can survive in that culture.

One of the messages in Delpit's discussion is that the critical teacher must assume his or her authority explicitly and teach students the skills necessary for surviving and competing effectively in the "culture of power." This is an issue about which I have frequent debates with some of my white colleagues. They maintain that students must be free to develop their thinking and writing without being told by the professors the rules of certain scholarly conventions. I am often described as the tough teacher who insists on receiving written materials according to certain scholarly and stylistic formats. As a woman of color who has spent years of my life figuring out what is required of me in order to do acceptable academic work, I realize how important it is to teach these skills explicitly. Reading Delpit's article makes me realize that for members of the dominant group, this is something that is taken for granted, and thus invisible. What needs to be pointed out is that teachers have different experiences, and therefore different teaching styles, based on our gender, race, and other identities that are developed over time. This informs the way we teach, which falls outside of the process versus skills debate. In every classroom encounter, the strategies we use must be worked out in situ rather than as abstract principles that are used regardless of contexts.

Furthermore, as critical teachers, we must recognize that a classroom is not isolated from the society at large. In our enthusiasm, I think we want to believe that our teaching can change our students, and by extension the world. Indeed, as Linda Briskin has pointed out, no single classroom can "overcome the realities of a racist, heterosexist patriarchal capitalist society. It can only engage with them" (Briskin, 1990:14). Ultimately, we need to link the theoretical understanding derived from the classroom context to the real-life struggles of minority people occurring outside the classroom. In reflecting on the limits of critical pedagogy, Ellsworth (1989) describes how students decided to launch a series of activities on campus to raise awareness of racism and demands for change. In the institute in which I teach, we have formed an anti-racist network of faculty, staff, and students outside of any particular classroom context. In the four years since its formation, it evolved from an informal support group to a pressure group that is pressing for the hiring of more minority faculty and staff, for expanding the existing curriculum to include minority perspectives, and for developing an anti-racism policy. Many members have formed alliances with anti-racist groups and participated in anti-racist activities in the city. It is by encouraging students, not to mention ourselves, to participate in struggles outside of the classroom that we indeed empower students to take control over their lives and change the world, not by eloquent rhetorics that do not stand the test of practice.

Thus, while classroom process is important, it is equally important for the critical teacher to assume the responsibility of directing students to an examination of how systems of inequality have emerged and developed historically and to point out the ways in which different forms of inequality have become part of our collective consciousness. By explicating some of the routine unconscious processes in which we engage, we can begin to confront our own contradictions and work towards change. In the final analysis, critical teaching is not only for the oppressed (i.e., for the students who are deemed to be recipients of our great theories and wisdom). It is for us as human beings, to help us liberate ourselves from the shackles of our own learning, which has been mediated by sexism, racism, and other forms of oppression. It is when we, too, engage in critical learning that we can hope to achieve the possibility of critical teaching.

NOTES

1. Critical pedagogy is not a coherent or monolithic body of work with a single theory or viewpoint. It is derived from various critical theoretical perspectives notably the critical theory of Habamas and the pedagogical theory of Paulo Freire. The major contemporary proponents of critical pedagogy include Henry Giroux, Roger Simon, Michael Apple, and Peter McLaren, among others. For a good introductory overview of critical pedagogy, see McLaren, *Life in Schools* (1989).

2. While multicultural education has been in vogue since the promulgation of the multiculturalism policy in 1971, anti-racist education is an emerging and relatively untheorized field of study in Canada. For various attempts to describe and analyze multicultural education, see Masemann (1978/79) and Young (1979).

For an excellent comparison of multicultural and anti-racist education, see Thomas (1987).

3. For a critique of knowledge making from a feminist perspective, see Dorothy E. Smith (1975). For one of the earliest collections of feminist pedagogy, see Culley and Portuges (1985).

4. Elizabeth Ellsworth provides a convincing self-critique of the pitfalls of critical pedagogy in her article "Why Doesn't This Feel Empowering? Working through the Repressive Myths of Critical Pedagogy" (Ellsworth, 1989).

5. Issues of power are posed in various ways by feminist teachers. Writing about their own experiences in the classroom, Sheila McIntyre (1986) and Susan Heald (1989) speak poignantly of the sexism directed towards them as teachers from students, especially male students. Barbara Roberts (1988) and Kathryn Morgan (1988), on the other hand, write of the power teachers, including feminist teachers, have over students in the classroom.

6. Max Weber (1969) defines power as the ability and chances of an actor to impose his or her will on another in a social relationship. Berger and Luckman (1967) take this notion further to suggest that particular people have the power to construct and impose their definition of reality on others. More recently, researchers in ethnomethodology and social linguistics have begun to analyze how power is enacted microsociologically. For example, Thorne and Henley's work (1975) mapped how men dominate women through the use of language. Fishman's (1978) conversational analysis, quoted in this chapter, shows precisely how conversational patterns between intimate heterosexual couples maintain existing power relations between the sexes.

7. I am indebted to Cameron McCarthy for the use of this word. He came up with it when members of this writing project helped me to clarify my conceptualization of gender, race, class, sexism, and racism in the aforementioned symposium.

8. Elsewhere, I have asserted that gender, race, and class are equally important relations to understand and explicate in social analysis (see Ng, 1989). While I have focused on racism and sexism in this chapter, I want to emphasize that class inequality and oppression are equally pervasive and important for us to explicate and eradicate.

9. This is recorded in a report entitled "An Experimental Research Practicum Based on the Wollstonecraft Research Group," by Marie Campbell. See also Smith (1987).

10. While this is not a universal phenomenon, I have observed this in more than one university where I have taught.

11. The Montreal massacre involved the shooting death of fourteen female engineering students by a frustrated young man who felt that his denial of entry into engineering school was due to the admission of female students. While his act could be interpreted as that of a madman, analyses of the event make it clear that his action, no matter how irrational, had targetted women whom he considered "feminist." This indicates the pervasiveness of sexism, including misogyny, in our culture. Here, I did not distinguish between the experiences of female students and female teachers. Although female students, due to their relatively powerless position in the university hierarchy, experience special problems such as sexual harassment, women as a minority group are marginal to the academy in general. More to

the point, their very presence upsets the status quo; it threatens male power and engenders hostility in the way I describe.

12. Even though I know this statement is in some sense scandalous and verges on gossip, I decided to include it because it is precisely the way in which sexism operates effectively as a silencing and disempowering instrument. I was party to some of these comments in a CAUT conference I attended to Toronto in March 1990.

13. See, for example, Nielsen (1979).

14. For the uninformed reader, Suzie Wong was a movie and television character in the fifties and sixties: a high-class prostitute of mixed Chinese and English parentage. As the protagonist of the film, she mesmerized the men, mostly Caucasian, she met by her grace and demure seductiveness, and they fought for the honor to protect and cherish her. At least in Hong Kong—a British colony—and Britain, the film and its sequels captured the hearts of Western and Chinese audiences alike, and led to the stereotype of Chinese women as lovely creatures who are in need of protection and love but who cannot be taken seriously.

15. Whereas I make a clear distinction between the terms "power" and "authority," Morgan (1988) does not make such a distinction. I find her discussion problematic because it fails to examine power as a dynamic process in the way that I try to capture in this chapter.

16. Various theorists have reflected on changing the form and content of education. See bell hooks (1988) and Russell (1981), for example, In her paper entitled "Interactive Phases of Curricular Re-vision: A Feminist Perspective, Peggy McIntosh (1983) describes a four-phase process of change. In the final phase, she envisions that the dichotomy between teacher and student would disappear and everyone would participate in developing and shaping the curriculum. While this kind of vision is important, it is not entirely possible under the existing structural constraints of universities.

17. See, for example, some of the school ethnographies in the symbolic interactionist tradition (Delamont, 1976; Hargreaves & Woods, 1984).

18. I am indebted to Sandra Ingram, who drew my attention to Michaels's work by sharing her own writing with me.

19. For an excellent study on class differences in students' differential educational experiences, see Connell et al. (1982).

20. For an interesting exploration of competition among women in the academy, see Keller and Moglen (1987).

21. Sexism and racism are by no means the only forms of subordination in the academy. Age, ability/disability, sexual orientation, body size, and so forth so constitute ways in which individuals are differentiated and silenced (see also Ellsworth, 1989). In the institution in which I teach, student statuses (part-time, full-time, Canadian and immigrant versus foreign students) are ways that students differentiate and discriminate among themselves. Part-time students, especially, feel marginalized and silenced because they have less access to the decision-making processes open to students who are available to attend meetings or classes during the day. This spills over to class dialogues that are geared towards the development and refinement of certain discourses with which they are less familiar (e.g., the discourse on critical pedagogy).

References

Adams, H. (1989). *Prison of grass*. Saskatoon: Fifth House Publishers.

Ahmed, L. (1992). *Women and gender in Islam*. New Haven: Yale University Press.

Alkali Lake Indian Band. (1985). *In Honour of All* (video). Alkali Lake, British Columbia, 78 minutes.

Allison, D. (1983). Fourth world education in Canada and the faltering promise of Native teacher education programs. *Journal of Canadian Studies, 18,* 102–18.

Althusser, L. (1971). Ideology and ideological apparatuses. In L. Althusser, *Lenin and philosophy and other essays*. New York: Monthly Review Publishers.

Ambrose, I. (1981). An HMI Perspective. In M. Craft (Ed.), *Teacher training in a multi-cultural society*. Lewes: Falmer Press.

American Association of Colleges for Teacher Education (AACTE). (1974). No one American model. *Journal of Teacher Education, 24,* 264–65.

Amin, S. (1989). *Eurocentrism*. New York: Monthly Review Press.

Anti-Defamation League of B'nai B'rith. (1986). *The wonderful world of difference: A human relations program for grades K–8*. New York: Anti-Defamation League of B'Nai B'rith.

Anti-Racist Teacher Education Network (ARTEN). (1986). *Occasional Papers #1–5.* Glasgow: Jordanhill College of Education.

Anti-Racist Teacher Education Network (ARTEN). (1988). *Occasional Paper #6.* Glasgow: Jordanhill College of Education.

Apple, M. W. (1979). *Ideology and curriculum*. London: Routledge and Kegan Paul.

_____. (1982). *Education and power*. Boston: Routledge and Kegan Paul.

_____. (1985). *Education and power*. Boston: Ark Paperbacks.

_____. (1986). *Teachers and texts*. New York: Routledge and Kegan Paul.

_____. (1987). Gendered teaching, gendered labor. In T. S. Popkewitz (Ed.), *Critical studies in teacher education: Its folklore, theory, and practice* (pp. 57–84). Philadelphia: Falmer Press.

Apple, M., and Weis, L. (1986). Seeking education relationally: The stratification of culture and people in the sociology of school knowledge. *Journal of Education* (Boston edition), 168(1), 7–34.

Arnold, M. (1971). *Culture and anarchy*. Indianapolis: Bobbs-Merrill.

Arnold, M. (1888). *Civilization in the United States: First and last impressions of America*. Boston: Cupples and Hurd.

Aronowitz, S., and Giroux, H. (1985). *Education under siege: The conservative, liberal and radical debate over schooling*. South Hadley, Mass.: Bergin and Garvey.

Assembly of First Nations. (1988). *Traditions and education: Towards a vision of the future*. Ottawa: Assembly of First Nations.

Austin, R. (1989). *Saphire bound!* 539–78.

Bagley, C. (1986). Multiculturalism, class and ideology: A European-Canadian comparison. In S. Modgil et al. (Eds.), *Multicultural education: The interminable debate*. Lewes: Falmer Press.

Baker, F. (1977). Development of the multicultural program: School of Education, University of Michigan. In F. Klassen and D. Gollnick (Eds.), *Pluralism and the American teacher: Issues and case studies* (pp. 163–69). Washington, D.C.: Ethnic Heritage Center for Teacher Education.

Baker, G. (1973, Winter). Multicultural training for student teachers. *The Journal of Teacher Education*, 24, 306–307.

Banks, J. (1972, January). Imperatives in ethnic minority education. *Phi Delta Kappan*, 53, 266–69.

———— (Ed.). (1973). *Teaching ethnic studies: Concepts and strategies*. Washington, D.C.: National Council for the Social Studies.

————. (1981). *Multiethnic education: Theory and practice*, 1st ed. Boston: Allyn and Bacon.

————. (1987). *Teaching strategies for ethnic studies*. Boston: Allyn and Bacon.

————. (1988). *Multiethnic education: Theory and practice*, 2nd ed. Boston: Allyn and Bacon.

Bannerji, H. (1987, March). Introducing racism: Notes towards an anti-racist feminism. *Resources for Feminist Research*, 16(1), 10–13.

Barron, L., and J. B. Waldran. (1986). *In 1885 and after: Native society in transition*. Regina: Canadian Plains Research Center.

Bastian, A., Fruchter, N., Gittell, M., Greer, C., and Haskins, K. (1986). *Choosing equality*. Philadelphia: Temple University Press.

Berger, P., and Luckmann, T. (1967). *The social construction of reality*. New York: Anchor Books.

Berlowitz, M. (1984). Multicultural education: Fallacies and alternatives. In M. Berlowitz and R. Edar (Eds.), *Racism and the denial of human rights: Beyond ethnicity* (pp. 129–36). Minneapolis: Marxism Educational Press.

Bernal, M. (1987). *Black Athena: The Afro-Asiatic roots of classical civilization*, (Vol. 1). London: Free Association Books.

Beyer, L. E. (1988). *Knowing & action: Inquiry, ideology and educational studies*. Philadelphia, Pa: Falmer Press.

Beyer, L., and Zeichner, K. (1982). Teacher training and educational foundations: A plea for discontent. *Journal of Teacher Education*, 33(3), 18–23.

Blackburn, R., and Mann, M. (1979). *The working class in the labour market*. London: MacMillan.

Blanchard, D. (1980). *Seven generations: A History of Kahnawake.* Kahnawake: Kahnawake Survival School.

Bloom, A. (1987). *The closing of the American mind.* New York: Simon and Schuster.

Bourdieu, P., and Passeron, J-C. (1977). *Reproduction in education, society, and culture.* London: Sage Publications.

Bowles, S., and Gintis, H. (1976). *Schooling in capitalist America: Educational reform and the contradictions of economic life.* New York: Basic Books.

Brah, A. (1992). Women of South Asian origin in Britain: Issues and concerns. In P. Braham et al. (Eds.), *Racism and anti-racism: Inequalities, opportunities and policies.* London: Open University.

Braham, P., Rattansi, A., and Skellington, R. (Eds.). (1992). *Racism and anti-racism: Inequalities, opportunities and policies.* London: Sage Publications.

Brandt, G. (1986). *The realization of anti-racist teaching.* Lewes: Falmer Press.

Briskin, L. (1990). *Feminist pedagogy: Teaching and learning liberation.* Ottawa: Canadian Research Institute for the Advancement of Women.

Brookes, A.L. (1990). Teaching, marginality and voice: A critical pedagogy not critical enough? In D. Henley and J. Young (Eds.), *Canadian perspectives of critical pedagogy.* Winnipeg: Canadian Critical Pedagogy Network.

Buchignani, N. (1980). Culture or identity? Addressing ethnicity in Canadian education. *McGill Journal of Education,* 5(1), 79–123.

Buckingham, D. (1987). The whites of their eyes: A case study of responses to educational television. In M. Strakaer-Welds (Ed.), *Education for a multicultural society* (pp. 137–43).

Bullivant, B. M. (1981a). Multiculturalism—pluralist orthodoxy or ethnic hegemony? *Canadian Ethnic Studies* 13(2), 1–22.

———. (1981b). *The pluralist dilemma in education: Six case studies.* Sydney: Allen and Unwin.

———. (1984). *Pluralism: Cultural maintenance and evolution.* Clevedon, England: Multilingual Matters Limited.

Burawoy, M. (1981). The capitalist state in South Africa: Marxist and sociological perspectives on race and class. In M. Zeitlin (Ed.), *Political power and social theory* (Vol. 2, pp. 279–335). Greenwich, Conn.: JAI Press.

Campbell, M. (n.d.). An Experimental research practicum based on the Wollstonecraft Research Group. Unpublished report, Department of Sociology, Ontario Institute for Studies in Education.

Canadian Society for the Study of Education. (1981). *Education and Canadian Multiculturalism: Some problems and some solutions.* Saskatoon: Canadian Society for the Study of Education.

Carby, H. V. (1982). Schooling in Babylon. In Centre for Contemporary Cultural Studies (Eds.), *The empire strikes back* (pp. 183–211). London: Hutchinson.

Carmichael, S., and Hamilton, C. (1967). *Black power.* New York: Vintage Books.

Carnoy, M. (1989). Education, state, and culture in American society. In H. A. Giroux and P. McLaren (Eds.), *Critical pedagogy, the state, and cultural struggle.* Albany: State University of New York Press.

Carnoy, M., and Levin, H. M. (1985). *Schooling and work in the democratic state.* Stanford, Calif.: Stanford University Press.

Carter, B., and Williams, J. (1987). Attacking racism in education. In B. Troyna (Ed.), *Racial inequality in education* (pp. 170–83). London: Tavistock.

Carter, S. (1990). *Lost harvests*. Toronto: University of Toronto Press.

Cherrington, D., and Giles, R. (1981). Present provision in initial training. In M. Craft (Ed.), *Teaching in a multicultural society*. Lewes: Falmer Press.

Cockburn, C. (1983). *Brothers: Male dominance and technological change*. London: Pluto Press.

Cole, M. (1989). Monocultural, multicultural, and anti-racist education. In M. Cole (Ed.), *The social context of schooling*. Lewes: Falmer Press.

Connell, R. W. (1987). Curriculum, politics, hegemony, and strategies of change. Unpublished paper, Department of Sociology, Macquarie University.

————. (1989). Curriculum politics, hegemony, and strategies for social change. In H. A. Giroux and R. I. Simon (Eds.), *Popular culture, schooling and everyday life*. Granby, Mass.: Bergin and Garvey.

Connell, R. W., Ashenden, D. J., Kessler, S., and Dowsett, G. W. (1982). *Making the difference: Schools, families and social division*. Sydney: George Allen and Unwin.

Cornforth, M. (1977). *The theory of knowledge*. New York: International Publishers.

Cortes, C. (1973). Teaching the Chicano experience. In J. Banks (Ed.), *Teaching ethnic studies: Concepts and strategies*. Washington, D.C.: National Council for Social Studies.

Counts, G. (1932). *Dare the school to build a new social order?* New York: John Day.

Craft, M. (Ed.). (1981). *Teaching in a multicultural society: The task for teacher education*. Lewes: Falmer Press.

Crichlow, W. (1985). Urban crisis, schooling, and black youth unemployment: A case study. Unpublished paper, Department of Education, University of Rochester.

————. (1990). "A social analysis of black youth commitment and disaffection in an urban high school," unpublished Ed.D. diss., Department of Education, University of Rochester.

Cubberley, E. P. (1909). *Changing conceptions of education*. Boston: Houghton Mifflin.

Culley, M., and Portuges, C. (Eds.). (1985). *Gendered subjects: The dynamics of feminist teaching*. Boston, London: Routledge and Kegan Paul.

Cummins, J. (1986). Empowering minority students: A framework for intervention. *Harvard Educational Review*, 56(1):50–68.

Czitrom, D. (1983). *Media and the American mind: From Morse to McLuhan*. Chapel Hill: University of North Carolina Press.

de Beauvoir, S. (1952). *The second sex*. New York: Knopf. Vintage Books Edition, 1974.

Delamont, S. (1976). *Interaction in the classroom* (2d ed.). London and New York: Methuen.

Delpit, L. (1988, August). The silenced dialogue: Power and pedagogy in educating other people's children. *Harvard Educational Review*, 58(3), 280–98.

Department of Education. (1992). *Initial Teacher Training (Secondary Phase)*. London: Department of Education.

Department of Education and Science (DES). (1981). *West Indian children in our schools: Report of the Committee of Enquiry into the Education of Children from Ethnic Minority Groups* (Rampton Report). London: HMSO.

_____. (1985). *Education for all: Report of the Committee of Enquiry into the Education of Children from Ethnic Minority Groups* (Swann Report). London: HMSO.

_____. (1987). *Quality in schools: The initial training of teachers.* London: HMSO.

Edgerton, S. (1989). Love in the margins: An epistemology of marginality in Ellison's *Invisible Man* and Morrison's *Beloved.* Unpublished paper, Department of Curriculum and Instruction, Louisiana State University.

Education Week Staff. (1986, May 14). Here they come ready or not: An *Education Week* special report on the ways in which America's population in motion is changing the outlook for schools and society, *Education Week,* pp. 14–28.

Elijah factor apparent. (1990, August 25). *The Star Phoenix* (Saskatoon).

Ellsworth, E. (1989, August). Why doesn't this feel empowering? Working through the repressive myths of critical pedagogy. *Harvard Educational Review,* 59(3), 287–324.

Fine, M. (1989). Silencing and nurturing student voice in an improbable context: Urbana adolescents in public school. In H. A. Giroux and P. McLaren (Eds.), *Critical pedagogy, the state, and cultural struggle.* Albany: State University of New York Press.

Fish, J. (1981). The psychological impact of field work experience and cognitive dissonance upon attitude change in an human relations program. Ph.D. diss., University of Wisconsin–Madison.

Fishman, P. (1978, April). Interaction: The work women do. *Social Problems,* 25(4), 397–406.

Fiske, J., and Hartley, J. (1978). *Reading television.* London: Methuen.

Flores, J., and Yudice, G. (1990). Living borders/buscando America: Languages of Latino self-formation. *Social Text* 24, 57–84.

Fordham, S. (1988, Feb.). Racelessness as a factor in Black students' school success: Pragmatic strategy or pyrrhic victory? *Harvard Educational Review,* 58(1), 54–84.

Frank, A. G. (1981). *Reflections on the world economic crisis.* New York: Monthly Review Press.

Fraser, G. (1990, Sept. 26). PM unveils Indian agenda. *Globe and Mail* (Toronto).

Freire, P. (1970). *Pedagogy of the oppressed.* New York: Herder and Herder.

_____. (1973). *Education for critical consciousness.* New York: Seabury Press.

_____. (1978a). *Pedagogy in process: The letters to Guinea Binneau* (C. St. John Hunter, Trans.). New York: Seabury Press.

_____. (1978b). In *Starting from Nina: The Politics of Learning* (film). Toronto: Development Education Center.

_____. (1985). *The politics of education: Culture, power and liberation.* South Hadley, Mass.: Bergin and Garvey.

Friedman, S. S. (1985). Authority in the feminist classroom: A contradiction in terms? In M. Culley and C. Portuges (Eds.), *Gendered subjects: The dynamics of feminist teaching.* Boston, London: Routledge and Kegan Paul.

Gamoran, A., and Berends, M. (1986). *The effects of stratification in secondary schools: Synthesis of survey and ethnographic research.* Madison: National Center on Effective Secondary Education, University of Wisconsin–Madison.

Garcia, E. (1974). Chicano cultural diversity: Implications for competency-based teacher education. In W. Hunter (Ed.), *Multicultural education through competency-based teacher education*. Washington, D.C.: American Association of Colleges for Teacher Education.

Gibson, M. (1984). Approaches to multicultural education in the United States: Some concepts and assumptions. *Anthropology and Education Quarterly*, 15, 94–119.

Gill, D., Mayor B., and Blair, M. (Eds.). (1992). *Racism and education: Structures and strategies*. London: Sage Publications in association with the Open University.

Ginsburg, M. (1988). *Contradictions in teacher education and society: A critical analysis*. London: Falmer Press.

Giroux, H. A. (1983). *Theory and resistance in education: A pedagogy for the oppression*. South Hadley, Mass.: Bergin and Garvey.

———. (1985). Introduction to P. Freire's *The politics of education*. South Hadley, Mass.: Bergin and Garvey.

———. (1988). *Teachers as intellectuals*. South Hadley, Mass.: Bergin and Garvey.

———. (1991). Modernism, postmodernism, and feminism: Rethinking the boundaries of educational discourse. In Henry Giroux (Ed.), *Postmodernism, feminism, and cultural politics: Redrawing educational boundaries* (pp. 1–59). Albany: State University of New York Press.

———. (1992). Curriculum, multiculturalism, and the politics of identity, *NASSP Bulletin* (December 1992).

———. (1993). *Living dangerously: Multiculturalism and the politics of difference*. New York: Peter Lang.

Giroux, H., and McLaren, P. (1986). Teacher education and the politics of engagement: The case for democratic schooling. *Harvard Educational Review*, 56(3), 213–38.

Giroux, H. A., and Simon, R. (1989). Popular culture and critical pedagogy: Everyday life as a basis for curriculum knowledge. In H. A. Giroux and P. McLaren (Eds.), *Critical pedagogy, the state, and cultural struggle* (pp. 236–52). Albany: State University of New York Press.

Giroux, H. A., et al. (1989). Curriculum study and cultural politics. In H. A. Giroux and R. Simon (Eds.), *Popular culture: Schooling and everyday life*. South Hadley, Mass.: Bergin and Garvey.

Glazer, N., and Moynihan, D. P. (1963). *Ethnicity: Theory and experience*. Cambridge, Mass.: Harvard University Press.

Gollnick, D. (1980). Multicultural education. *Viewpoints in Teaching and Learning*. 56, 1–17.

Goodwill, J., and Sluman, N. (1984). *John Tootoosis*. Winnipeg: Pemmican Publications.

Gramsci, A. (1971). *Selections from prison notebooks* (Q. Hoare and G. Smith, Trans.). New York: International Publishers.

Grant, C., and Sleeter, C. (1985). The literature on multicultural education: Review and analysis. *Educational Review*, 37(2), 97–118.

———. (1989). *Turning on learning: Five approaches for multicultural teaching plans for race, class, gender and disability*. Columbus: Merrill.

Grant, L. (1984). Black females' "place" in desegregated classrooms. *Sociology of Education*, 57, 98–111.

———. (1985). Uneasy alliances: Black males, teachers, and peers in desegregated classrooms. Unpublished paper, Department of Sociology, Southern Illinois University.

Grundy, S. (1987). *Curriculum: Product or praxis*. London: Falmer Press.

Haig-Brown, C. (1988). *Resistance and renewal*. Vancouver, Tillacum.

Hall, S. (1988). The toad in the garden: Thatcherism among the theorists. In C. Nelson and L. Grossberg (Eds.), *Marxism and the interpretation of culture*. Urbana: University of Illinois Press.

Hargreaves, A., and Woods, P. (Eds.). (1984). *Classroom and staffrooms: The sociology of teachers and teaching*. Milton Keynes, UK: Open University Press.

H. Elijah. (1990, Sept. 17). Speech sponsored by the Law Society and the Native Law Society, University of Saskatchewan.

Harper. V. (1976). *Following the red path*. Vancouver: New Star Books.

Heald, S. (1989, Dec.). The madwoman out of the attic: Feminist teaching in the margins. *Resources for Feminist Research (RFR)*, 18 (4), 22–26.

Henley, R., and Young, J. (1986–87). Multicultural teacher education: Part 1, faculties of education and state policies of multiculturalism. *Multiculturalism*, 11(1), 17–19.

———. (1987a). A clouded vision: Faculties of education and issues of ethnicity in English-speaking Canada. *Journal of Educational Administration and Foundations*, 2(1), 37–51.

———. (1987b). Multicultural teacher education: Part 2, ethnic minority representation in faculties of education. *Multiculturalism*, 11(2), 3–8.

———. (1989a). Multicultural teacher education: Part 3, curriculum content and curriculum structure. *Multiculturalism*, 12(1), 24–27.

———. (1989b). Multicultural teacher education: Part 4, revitalizing faculties of education. *Multiculturalism*, 12(3), 40–41.

———. (1990). Indian education in Canada: Contemporary issues. In Y. Lam (Ed.), *The Canadian public education system*. Calgary: Detselig.

———. (Eds.). (1991). Canadian Perspectives on Critical Pedagogy. Winnipeg: Canadian Critical Pedagogy Network.

Hesch, R. (1989a). Education equity in Saskatchewan: A time(ly) review. Unpublished manuscript.

———. (1989b). The political origins of the Saskatchewan Urban Native Teacher Education Program. Unpublished manuscript.

Heschel, J. (1962). *The prophets* (2 vols.). New York: Harper and Row.

Hirsch, E. D. (1987). *Cultural literacy: What every American needs to know*. Boston: Houghton Mifflin.

History of the international position of the Haudesaunee. (1991). In *Chronology of Events, Historical Background*. Kahnawake, Quebec: Haudenosaunee Mohawk Nation Kahnewake Branch Kanien'kehaka.

Hommen, L. (1986). On the "organic intellectualism" of Antonio Gramsci: A study of the concept as a contribution to the politics of adult education. Unpublished master's thesis, University of Saskatchewan, Saskatoon.

Hoodfar, H. (1992). Feminist anthropology and critical pedagogy: The anthropology of classrooms' excluded voices. *Canadian Journal of Education*, 17(3), 303–20.

hooks, b. (1988). *Talking back: Think feminist; thinking black.* Toronto: Between the Lines.

———. (1989). *Talking back.* Boston: South End Press.

———. (1990). *Yearning: Race, gender and cultural politics.* Toronto: Between the Lines.

Hopkins, T., and Wallerstein, I. (Eds.). (1980). *Processes of the world system.* Beverly Hills, Calif.: Sage.

James, C.L.R. (1963). *The black Jacobins.* New York: Vintage.

JanMohamed, A., and Lloyd, D. (1987). Introduction, Minority discourse—what is to be done? *Cultural Critique, 6,* 5–17.

Jaschik, S. (1980). Scholarships set up for minority students are called illegal. *The Chronicle of Higher Education,* 37(15), A-1.

Jones, D. C., Stamp, R. M., and Sheehan, N. M. (Eds.). (1979). *Shaping the schools of the Canadian West.* Calgary: Detslig.

Jordan, J. (1985). *On call: Political essays.* Boston: South End Press.

———. (1988). Nobody mean more to me than you and the future life of Willie Jordan. *Harvard Educational Review* 58(2), 363–74.

Kaestle, C. (1983). *Pillars of the republic: Common schools and American society, 1780–1860.* New York: Hill and Wang.

Keller, E. F., and Moglen, H. (1987). Competition and feminism: Conflicts for academic women. *Signs: Journal of Women in Culture and Society.* 12(3), 493–511.

Kelly, U. (1990). "On the edge of the eastern ocean": Teaching marginality and voice. In H. A. Giroux and R. Simon (Eds.), *Canadian Perspective on Critical Pedagogy.* Winnipeg: Canadian Critical Pedagogy Network.

Khanum, S. (1992). Education and the Muslin girls. In G. Sahgal and N. Yuval-Davis (Eds.), *Refusing holy orders.* London: Virgo Press.

King. E. (1980). *Teaching ethnic awareness.* Santa Monica: Good Year.

Kirk, D. (1986). Beyond the limits of theoretical discourse in teacher education: Towards a critical pedagogy. *Teaching and Teacher Education,* 2(2), 155–67.

Kleinfeld, J. (1975). Positive stereotyping: The cultural relativist in the classroom. *Human Organization,* 34, 269–74.

Kliebard, H. (1986). *The struggle for the American curriculum 1893–1958.* Boston: Routledge and Kegan Paul.

Kolakowski, L. (1985). *Main currents of Marxism* (Vol. 3), (P. S. Falla, Trans.). Oxford: Oxford University Press. (Original work published 1978.)

Lake, R. A. (1983). Enacting red power: The consummatory function in Native American protest. *Quarterly Journal of Speech,* 69, 127–42.

Lalonde, M. (1990, August 25). Shippers blame PM for railway chaos. *Globe and Mail* (Toronto).

Lawrence, E. (1983). In the abundance of water the fool is thirsty: Sociology and black "pathology". In Centre for Contemporary Studies (Eds.), *The empire strikes back* (pp. 95–142). London: Hutchinson.

Lazreg, M. (1988, Spring). Feminism and difference: The perils of writing as a woman on women in Algeria. *Feminist Studies,* 14(1), 88–107.

Lewis, D. (1976). The multicultural education model and minorities: Some reservations. *Anthropology and Education Quarterly,* 7, 32–37.

Lewis, M. (1987). Native images in children's books. In J. Young (Ed.), *Breaking the mosaic* (pp. 108–144). Toronto: Garamond Press.

Lewis, M., and Simon, R. (1986). A discourse not intended for her: Learning and teaching within patriarchy. *Harvard Educational Review*, 56(4), 457–72.

Liston, D., and Zeichner, K. (1991). *Teacher education and the social conditions of schooling*. New York: Routledge.

———. (1987). Critical pedagogy and teacher education. *Journal of Teacher Education* (Boston edition), 169(3), 117–37.

Lortie, D. (1975). *Schoolteacher: A sociological study*. Chicago: University of Chicago Press.

Louisiana State University. (1988). *1988–1989 General catalog*. Baton Rouge: Louisiana Publications.

Luke, C., and Gore, J. (Eds.). (1992). *Feminism and critical pedagogy*. New York: Routledge.

Lynch, J. (1986). An initial typology of perspectives of staff development for multicultural teacher education. In S. Modgil, G. Verma, K. Mallick, and C. Modgil (Eds.), *Multicultural education: The interminable debate*. London: Falmer Press.

Mackie James, B. (1989). *Something to live for, something to reach for: Students of a Native survival school*. Saskatoon: Fifth House Publishers.

Magsino, R. (1985). The right to multicultural education: A descriptive and normative analysis. *Multiculturalism*, 9(1), 4–9.

Mallea, J. (1989). *Schooling in a plural Canada*. Clevedon, Philadelphia: Multilingual Matters.

Manicom, A. (1987). Ideology and multicultural curriculum: Deconstructing elementary school texts. In Jon Young (Ed.), *Breaking the mosaic: Ethnic identities in Canadian schooling*. Toronto: Garamond Press.

Marable, M. (1983). *How capitalism underdeveloped black America: Problems in race, political economy, and society*. Boston: South End Press.

———. (1984). *Race, reform, and rebellion: The second reconstruction in black America, 1945–1982*. London: Macmillan.

———. (1985). *Black American politics: From the Washington marches to Jesse Jackson*. London: Verso.

Marshall, K. (1987, Winter). Women in male-dominated professions. *Canadian Social Trends*, 7–11.

Masemann, V. (1978/79). Multicultural programs in Toronto schools. *Interchange*, 9(3), 29–44.

———. (1981). Comparative perspectives on multicultural education. *Education and Canadian multiculturalism* (Canadian Society for the Study in Education Yearbook). Saskatoon.

Masemann, V., and Mock, K. (June, 1986). Multicultural teacher education. Paper presented at the annual CSSE Conference, Winnipeg.

McCarthy, C. (1988). Rethinking liberal and radical perspectives on racial inequality in schooling: Making the case for nonsynchrony. *Harvard Educational Review*, 58(3), 265–79.

———. (1990). *Race and curriculum*. London: Falmer Press.

McCarthy, C., and Apple, M. W. (1988). Race, class and gender in American educational research: Towards a nonsynchronous parallelist position. In

L. Weis (Ed.), *Class, race, and gender in American education* (pp. 9–39). Albany: State University of New York Press.

McCarthy, C., and Crichlow, W. (1993). *Race, identity and representation in education*. New York, London: Routledge.

McCaskell, T. (1989). *Multicultural/multiracial residential camps for secondary school students*. Toronto: Toronto Board of Education.

McIntosh, P. (1983). Interactive phases of curricular re-vision: A feminist perspective. Unpublished paper, Center for Research on Women, Wellesley College.

McIntyre, S. (1986, July 28). Gender bias within the law school. Memorandum to all members of Faculty Board, Faculty of Law, Queen's University.

McLaren, P. (1980). *Cries from the corridor*. Toronto: Methuen.

———. (1989). *Life in schools*. Toronto: Irwin.

McLaren, P., and Dantley, M. (1990). Leadership and a critical pedagogy of race: Cornel West, Stuart Hall, and the prophetic tradition. *Journal of Negro Education*, 59(1), 29–44.

McLellan, D. (1979). *Marxism after Marx* (2d ed.). London: Papermac.

McLeod, K. (1990). Multiculturalism and multicultural education in Canada: Human rights and human rights' education. Paper presented in Multiculturalism, Teaching and Learning: A Colloquium, May 27–June 2, Vancouver.

McNeil, L. M. (1988). *Contradictions of control*. New York: Routledge.

Metro Youth Task Force 1990, September. *Issues Arising from Consultations*. Municipality of Metropolitan Toronto, Policy and Planning Division, p. 3.

Michaels, S. (1986). Narrative presentations: An oral preparation for literacy with first graders. In J. Cook-Gumperz (Ed.), *The social construction of literacy*. Cambridge: Cambridge University Press.

Miles, R. (1989). *Racism*. London, New York: Routledge.

Miner, I. L. (1990). Women teaching women: A contradiction in terms. Unpublished paper, Department of Sociology, Ontario Institute for Studies in Education.

Ministry of Education of Ontario. (1987). *The development of a policy on race and ethnocultural equity*. Toronto: Ministry of Education.

———. (1988). *A synopsis of public responses to the report of the provincial Advisory Committee on Race Relations: The development of a policy on race and ethno-cultural equity*. Toronto: Ministry of Education of Ontario.

———. (1993). *Anti-racism and ethnocultural equity in school boards: Guideline for policy development and implementation*. Toronto: Ministry of Education of Ontario.

Modgil, S., Verma, G., Mallick, K., and Modgil, C. (1986). *Multicultural education: The interminable debate*. Lewes: Falmer Press.

Mohanty, C. (1988). Under Western eyes: Feminist scholarship and colonial discourses. *Feminist Review*, (30), 61–88.

———. (1993). On Race and voice: Challenges for liberal education in the 1990s. In B. Thompson and S. Tyagi (Eds.), *Beyond a dream deferred*. Minneapolis: University of Minnesota Press.

Montalto, N. (1981). Multicultural education in the New York City public schools, 1919–1941. In D. Ravitch and R. Goodenow (Eds.), *Educating an urban people: The New York City experience*. New York: Teachers College Press.

Moodley, Kogila A. (Ed.). (1992). *Beyond multicultural education: International perspectives*. Calgary, Alberta: Detselig Enterprises Ltd.

More, A. (1980). Native Indian teacher education in Canada. *Education Canada*, 20, 32–41.

Morgan, K. P. (1988). The paradox of the bearded mother: The role of authority in feminist pedagogy. Unpublished paper, University of Toronto.

Morrison, T. (1989). Unspeakable things unspoken: The Afro-American presence in American literature. *Michigan Quarterly Review*, 38(1), 1–34.

Mukherjee, A. (1988). From racist to anti-racist education: A synoptic view. Unpublished paper, Toronto Board of Education.

Mullard, C. (1985). Racism in society and school: History, policy and practice. In F. Rizvi (Ed.), *Multiculturalism and educational policy* (pp. 64–81). Geelong, Victoria, Australia: Deakin University Press.

Mullings, L. (1984). Ethnicity and stratification in the urban United States. In M. Berlowitz and R. Edari (Eds.), *Racism and the denial of human rights: Beyond ethnicity* (pp. 21–38). Minnesota: Marxist Educational Press.

Murphy, K., and Smillie, R. (1986). *Story circles*. Saskatoon: Saskatchewan Teachers Federation.

Native self rule on the agenda. (1990, Sept. 4). *Globe and Mail* (Toronto).

National Indian Brotherhood. (1973). *Indian control of Indian education*. Ottawa: The Brotherhood.

New Democrats. (1990). Education Discussion Paper #2. One of a series of discussion papers on education issues prepared by the office of NDP Education critic Richard Johnston for the members of the Ontario New Democrat party.

Nielsen, L. (1979, November). Sexism and self-healing in the university. *Harvard Educational Review*, 49(4), 467–76.

Ng, R. (1981). Constituting ethnic phenomenon: An account from the perspective of immigrant women. *Canadian Ethnic Studies* 13(1), 97–108.

———. (1987). Ethnicity, schooling and the social division of labour: A response to Jackson. In J. Young (Ed.), *Breaking the mosaic* (pp. 183–89). Toronto: Garamond Press.

———. (1989). Sexism, racism, and Canadian nationalism. In J. Vorst (Ed.), *Race, class, gender: Bonds and barriers*. Toronto: Between the Lines and Society for Socialist Studies.

———. (1991). Sexism, racism, and Canadian nationalism. In D. Henley and J. Young (Eds.), *Canadian Perspectives on Critical Pedagogy*. Winnipeg: Canadian Critical Pedagogy Network.

———. (1993). "A woman out of control": Deconstructing sexism and racism in the university. *Canadian Journal of Education*, 18(3), 189–205.

Nkomo, M. (1984). *Student culture and activism in black South African universities*. Westport, Conn: Greenwood Press.

O'Connor, T. (1989). Cultural voice and strategies for multicultural education. *Journal of Education*, 17(2), 57–74.

Ogbu, J. (1978). *Minority education and caste*. New York: Academic Press.

———. (1988). Class stratification, racial stratification, and schooling. In L. Weis (Ed.), *Class, race, and gender in American education* (pp. 163–82). Albany: State University of New York Press.

Ogbu, J., and Matute-Bianchi, M. (1986). Understanding socio-cultural factors in education: Knowledge, identity, and school adjustment. In California State Department of Education (Ed.), *Beyond language: Social and cultural factors in schooling language minority students* (pp. 73–142). Los Angeles: Evaluation, Dissemination and Assessment Center, California State University.

Olneck, M. (1990). The recurring dream: Symbolism and ideology in intercultural and multicultural education. *American Journal of Education,* 98(2), 147–74.

Olneck, M., and Lazerson, M. (1980). Education. In S. Thernstrom, A. Orlov, and O. Hanlin (Eds.), *Harvard encyclopedia of American ethnic groups* (pp. 303–19). Cambridge, Mass.: Harvard University Press.

Omi, M., and Winant, H. (1986). *Racial formation in the United States.* New York: Routledge and Kegan Paul.

Ortiz, F. I. (1988). Hispanic-American children's experiences in classrooms: A comparison between Hispanic and non-Hispanic children. In L. Weis (Ed.), *Class, race and gender in American education* (pp. 63–86). Albany: State University of New York Press.

Osborne, K. (1987). Ideology, class and culture: A response to Mallea. In J. Young (Ed.), *Breaking the mosaic* (pp. 57–62). Toronto: Garamond Press.

Ottawa must change approach to native land claims. (1990, August 22). *The Star Phoenix* (Saskatoon).

Perlman, J. (1989). *Ethnic differences.* New York: Cambridge University Press.

Pettigrew, L. (1974). Competency-based teacher education: Teacher training for multicultural education. In W. Hunter (Ed.), *Multicultural education through competency-based teacher education.* Washington, D.C.: American Association of Colleges for Teacher Education.

Picard, A. (1990). Mohawks demand amnesty for bingo. *Globe and Mail* (Toronto).

Poelzer, I. (1989). Métis women and the economy of Northern Saskatchewan. In J. Vorst et al. (Eds.), *Race, class and gender: Bonds and barriers.* Toronto & Winnipeg: Between the Lines and Society for Socialist Studies.

Popkewitz, T. (1987). Ideology and social formation in teacher education. In T. S. Popkewitz (Ed.), *Critical studies in teacher education: Its folklore, theory and practice* (pp. 2–34). Philadelphia: The Falmer Press.

Porter, J. (1967). *The vertical mosaic: An analysis of social class and power in Canada.* Toronto: University of Toronto Press.

Purpel, D. (1989). *The moral and spiritual crisis in education: A curriculum for justice and compassion in education.* South Hadley, Mass.: Bergin and Garvey.

Purrich, D. (1987). *Our land: Native rights in Canada.* Toronto: James Lorimer.

Quinn, P. (1990, Sept. 8). Is life on campus really safe? *The Toronto Star,* p. G1.

Rabinow, P. (1986). Representations are social facts: Modernity and post-modernity in anthropology. In J. Clifford and G. E. Marcus (Eds.), *Writing culture.* Berkeley: University of California Press.

Radway, J. (1984). *Reading the romance: Women, patriarchy, and popular literature.* Chapel Hill: University of North Carolina Press.

Raggett, M., and Clarkson, M. (1976). *Changing patterns of teacher education.* Lewes: Falmer Press.

Ramirez, M., and Castenada, A. (1974). *Cultural democracy, bicognitive development, and education.* New York: Academic Press.

Ravitch, D. (1990). Diversity and democracy: Multicultural education in America. *American Educator*, 14(1), 16–48.

Regnier, R. (1988, October). Acting and taking care of people at the Saskatoon Native Survival School. *Our Schools Our Selves*, 1(1), 22–44.

_____. (1990), Sept. 20). Interview with Emil Bell.

Riesman, D., Glazaer, N., and Denney, R. (1969). *The lonely crowd*. New Haven: Yale University Press.

Rizvi, F. (1986). *Ethnicity, class and multicultural education*. Geelong, Victoria, Australia: Deakin University.

Roberts, B. (1988, June). Canadian women's studies classrooms as learning sites: Dis-abling double messages. Paper presented at the Canadian Women's Studies Association annual meeting, Windsor.

Rugg, H. (1932). Social reconstruction through education, *Progressive Education*, 9, 11–18.

Rushton, J. (1981). Careers and the multicultural curriculum. In J. Lynch (Ed.), *Teaching in the multicultural school* (pp. 163–70). London: Ward Lock.

Russell, M. (1981). An open letter to the academy. In *Building feminist theory: Essays from Quest*. New York: Longmans.

Sahgal, G., and Yuval-Davis, N. (Eds.). (1992). *Refusing holy orders: Women and fundamentalism in Britain*. London: Virgo Press.

Said, E. (1979). *Orientalism*. New York: Vintage Books.

_____. (1988). Representing the colonized: Anthropology's interlocutors. *Critical Inquiry*, 15(2), 205–25.

_____. (1993). *Culture and imperialism*. Toronto: Alfred Knopf.

Sarupt, M. (1984). *The politics of multiracial education*. London: Routledge Kegan Paul.

Saskatchewan Human Rights Commission. (1985). *Education equity*. Regina, Saskatchewan: The Commission.

Sasson, A. S. (Ed.). (1982). *Approaches to Gramsci*. London: Writers and Readers.

Schiro, M. (1978). *Curriculum for better schools*. Englewood Cliffs, N.J.: Educational Technology Publications.

Schmidt, P. (1989, October 18). Educators foresee "renaissance" in African studies. *Education Week*, p. 8.

Schniedewind, N., and Davidson, E. (1983). *Open minds to equality*. Englewood Cliffs, N.J.: Prentice-Hall, Inc.

Sharp, R. (1980). *Knowledge, ideology and the politics of schooling*. London: Routledge & Kegan Paul.

Shor, I., and Freire, P. (1987). *A pedagogy for liberation*. South Hadley, Mass.: Bergin and Garvey.

Simon, R. (1983). Critical pedagogy. In T. Husen and N. Postlethwaite (Eds.), *International encyclopedia of education*. Oxford: Pergamon Press.

_____. (1987). Being ethnic/doing ethnicity: A response to Corrigan. In J. Young (Ed.), *Breaking the mosaic*, (pp. 31–43). Toronto: Garamond Press.

_____. (in press). *Teaching against the grain: Essays for a pedagogy of possibility*. Westport, Conn.: Bergin and Garvey.

Sleeter, C. (1990). Staff development for desegregated schooling. *Phi Delta Kappan*, 72(1), 33–40.

Sleeter, C., and Grant, C. (1986, April). The literature on multicultural education in the U.S.A. Paper presented at the American Educational Research Association Conference, San Francisco.

Smith, D. E. (1975). An analysis of ideological structures and how women are excluded: Considerations for academic women. *Canadian Review of Sociology and Anthropology*, 12(4), Part 1, 353–69.

———. (1987). *The everyday world as problematic: A feminist sociology*. Toronto: University of Toronto Press.

Spivak, G. C. (1990). *The post-colonial critic*. New York: Routledge.

Stockwood, P. (1990, March). Out of the fat and into the fire: Confronting patriarchy in a graduate feminist seminar. Paper presented at the Atlantic Association of Sociologists and Anthropologists Annual Meeting, St. John, New Brunswick.

Sudarkasa, N. (1988). Black enrollment in higher education: The unfulfilled promise of equality. In national Urban League (Eds.), *The state of black America 1988*. New York: National Urban League.

Stevenson, W. and Lanceley, D. (1991, October). The student protest: Really a women's issue. *Aboriginal Women's Council of Saskatchewan Newsletter*, pp. 16–19.

Suzuki, B. (1984). Curriculum transformation for multicultural education. *Education and Urban Society*, 16, 294–322.

Swartz, E. (1988). *Multicultural curriculum development*. Rochester, N.Y.: Rochester City School District.

Tator, C., and Henry, F. (1991). *Multicultural education: Translating policy into practice*. Ottawa: Multiculturalism and Citizenship.

Tator, C. (1987/88, Winter). Towards anti-racist education. *Current*, 4(4), 8–11.

Terman, L. (1916). *The measurement of intelligence*. Boston: Houghton Mifflin.

Thomas, B. (1984, Fall). Principles of anti-racist education. *Currents*, 2(3), 20–24.

———. (1987a). Anti-racist education: A response to Manicom. In J. Young (Ed.), *Breaking the mosaic: Ethnic identities in Canadian schooling*. Toronto: Garamond Press.

Thorne, B., and Henley, N. (1975). *Language and sex: Difference and dominance*. Rowley, Mass.: Newbury House.

Tiedt, I., and Tiedt, P. (1986). *Multicultural teaching: A handbook of activities, information, and resources*. Boston: Allyn and Bacon.

Times Higher Education Supplement Staff. (1992, June 12). U day dawns for the former polytechnics, *Times Higher Education Supplement*, p. 8.

Titley, B. (1986). *A narrow vision*. Vancouver: University of British Columbia Press.

Tobias, J. (1983). Subjugation of the plains Cree 1879–1885. *Canadian Historical Review*, 64(4), 519–48.

Toronto Board of Education. (1976). *Final report of the work group on multicultural programs*. Toronto: Board of Education.

Troyna, B. (1984). Multicultural education: Emancipation or containment? In L. Barton and S. Walker (Eds.), *Social crisis and educational research* (pp. 75–97). London: Croom Helm.

———. (1987). Beyond multiculturalism: Towards the enactment of anti-racist education in policy, provision and pedagogy. *Oxford Review of Education*, 13(3), 307–20.

Troyna, B., and Carrington, B. (1987). Antisexist/antiracist education—A false dilemma: A reply to Walking and Brannigan. *Journal of Moral Education*, 16(1), 60–65.

Troyna, B., and Williams, J. (1986). *Racism, education and the state*. London: Croom Helm.

Trudeau, P. (1971). *Federal government response to Book IV of the Royal Commission on Bilingualism*. Ottawa: House of Commons.

University of Wisconsin–Madison Steering Committee on Minority Affairs. (1987). *Final Report*.

Verma, G. (1989). *Education for all: A landmark in pluralism*. Lewes: Falmer Press.

Vosko, L. (1989). *Student think: An anecdotal report on pop culture, racism and sexism in Toronto high schools*. Toronto: Toronto Board of Education.

Walking, P., and Brannigan, C. (1986). Anti-sexist/anti-racist education: A possible dilemma. *Journal of Moral Education*, 15(1), 16–25.

Watson, K. (1984). Training Teachers in the United Kingdom for a multicultural society. *Journal of Multilingual and Multicultural Development*, 5(5), 385–400.

Watson, K., and Roberts, R. (1988). Multicultural education and teacher training—the picture after Swann. *Journal of Multilingual and Multicultural Development*, 9(4), 339–52.

Weber, M. (1930). *The Protestant ethic and the spirit of capitalism*. London: Unwin University Books.

———. (1969). *The theory of social and economic organization*. New York: Free Press.

Weiler, K. (1988). *Women teaching for change*. South Hadley, Mass.: Bergin & Garvey.

Weis, L. (1985). *Between two worlds*. Boston: Routledge and Kegan Paul.

Will, G. (1989, December 19). Eurocentricity and the school curriculum. *Morning Advocate*, p. 3.

Williams, M. (1982). Multicultural/pluralistic education: Public education in America "the way it's 'spoze to be." *Clearing House*, 3, 131–35.

Willis, P. (1977). *Learning to labour*. Lexington, Mass.: D. C. Heath.

Wilson-Smith, A., and Allen, G. (1990, Sept. 10). Legacies of mistrust. *McLeans*, p. 26.

Winnipeg School Division. (1989). *Report of the task force on race relations*. Winnipeg: School Division.

Wisconsin Department of Public Instruction. (1986). *A guide to curriculum planning in social studies*. Madison: Wisconsin Department of Public Instruction.

Witt, S. H. (1984). Native women today: Sexism and the Indian women. In A. M. Jaggar and P. S. Rothenberg (Eds.), *Feminist frameworks: Alternative theoretical accounts of the relations between women and men*. (2d ed). New York: McGraw-Hill.

Wood, G. (1985). Schooling in a democracy: Transformation or reproduction. In F. Rizvi (Ed.), *Multiculturalism as an educational policy*. Geelong, Victoria, Australia: Deakin University.

Wright, E. O. (1978). *Class crisis and the state*. London: New Left Books.

Wyatt, J. (1978). Native involvement in curriculum development. *Interchange*, 9(1), 17–28.

York, G. (1990). *The dispossessed*. London: Vintage.

Young, J. (1979). Education in a multicultural society: What sort of education? What sort of society? *Canadian Journal of Education*, 4(3), 5–21.

_____ . (Ed.). (1987). *Breaking the mosaic: Ethnic identities in Canadian schooling.* Toronto: Garamond Press.

_____ . (1991). Re-assigning the maintenance crew: A review essay based upon *The politics of Multiracial education* (M. Sarup, London: Routledge, Kegan Paul 1984). *Curriculum Inquiry*, 21(3), 363–75.

Index

About the Editors and Contributors

RICK HESCH teaches in the Faculty of Education at Lethbridge University, Lethbridge, Alberta.

CAMERON McCARTHY teaches in the Department of Curriculum and Instruction, University of Illinois at Urbana-Champaign.

ROXANA NG is Associate Professor of Sociology at the Ontario Institute for Educational Studies in Toronto.

ROBERT REGNIER teaches in the College of Education at the University of Saskatchewan, Saskatoon. He has been active in aboriginal education since the 1970s.

GOLI REZAI-RASHTI is a consultant on equity education for the Etobicoke Board of Education. She also teaches anti-racist education and women's studies at the University of Toronto and York University in Toronto.

JOYCE SCANE is research associate at Ontario Institute for Studies in Education.

PAT STATON is a research associate at Ontario Institute for Studies in Education.

JON YOUNG teaches in the Department of Educational Administration and Foundations, Faculty of Education, University of Manitoba, Winnipeg.